The Spirit of the

A 'factional' account of the
Parish of Caverswall and its people

Revised Edition 2000

by

M. J. W. Rogers

Three Counties Publishing Limited

'The Musical Spirit Of The Place'

This local tune may have served as the marching song of the Caverswall Local Volunteers, a local militia formed during the Napoleonic Wars.

Published by

Three Counties Publishing Limited

P.O. Box 435
Leek, Staffordshire
England, ST13 5TB

ISBN 0 9535239 - 3 - 4

Typeset by Clermont Ferrand Int.
and Printed in England by J. H. Brookes Printers Limited

The Spirit of the Place

Revised edition

Dedication

to Kathleen, Jane
and James

(My inspiration)

Preface

The second edition of this 'factional' account of the parish of Caverswall contains much new material relating principally to the families who at one time or another lived in or held the castle. Some individuals are included, like Richard Plunkett whose service record only came to light well after the first edition was published, like Mary Howitt the poetess and Robert Williams Buchanan, the writer with a self destructive streak. They are included because the richness of their lives adds a fascinating, human dimension to what is already an intriguing story. A copy of the will of Sir John Wyldeblod came to hand through the generosity of a descendant. Several family trees have been included as have a number of additional illustrations most of which were not available when the first book was published. Brief histories of the two village schools have been added for their work has played an important part in the life of the village for almost two hundred years.

In this 'factional' account historical fact has been used to provide the framework upon which material woven from folklore, myth, legend and the trivia of the daily round of ordinary folk has, occasionally, been draped. The purpose of this approach is to try to impart a sense of what life in Caverswall might have been like at various stages in its history. Nothing which is known to be historically inaccurate has been knowingly included.

The starting point for the story is the physical geography of the parish since an understanding of place is fundamental to an appreciation of the lives and work of the people. Traces of those lives and that work are still visible and in one sense it is hoped that this book will serve as a guide to a tour of the parish. In part it was written in the hope that it might bring a new sense of awareness and excitement to familiar objects and places. It seeks to present the shy and fleeting shades of a rural scene in a manner that brings both enjoyment and understanding. Shakespeare observed that 'the isle is full of noises' : for me Caverswall is full of shadows. It is my hope that this book will enable others to feel and understand the shadows of a unique past which surround this ordinary and yet very special village.

If there is any merit in what follows let it be seen as a public thank-you to those people of Caverswall who some forty years ago welcomed me as a stranger and by receiving me as a friend taught me the true meaning of the spirit of the place.

M J W Rogers
2000

ACKNOWLEDGEMENTS

Insight, understanding and awareness grow but slowly. They are the product and consequence of direct teaching, actual learning and casual experience. To that vast array of teachers who have struggled with the indifferent clay of my intellect, to individuals like Mr. Fred. Stitt who was County Archivist and William Salt, Librarian for much of the time that the book was being researched, to my wife whose pragmatic response when the computer 'crashed' kept me sane, to those individuals like Mrs. Ina Butler nee Greensmith, Mr. and Mrs. J. K. Slinn, Mr. Roger Wildblood and Mr. S. Brindley who have loaned me material or pictures or who have drawn my attention to features which I might otherwise have missed, to Lord Barnard for permission to reproduce the pictures of the Vanes and to organisations like the Courtauld Institute for permission to reproduce the pictures of William Jolliffe, William Holles Vane and Lady Frances Hamilton: the Staffordshire Record Society: Keele University for granting me access to the Warrillow Collection and to the War Museum, I owe a substantial debt of gratitude. Standing on the shoulders of such giants makes the mere task of writing relatively easy.

M J W R
2000

CONTENTS

Table of Capsules

These capsules contain brief outlines of families or individuals associated with the castle, the parish or the village. They are written in note form to convey the available evidence in the most appropriate manner. They are not complete family histories but relate almost exclusively to those persons who could claim some direct contact with the village or parish and whose lives, achievements or social status contain something of interest. They can be read as part of the main text or in a stand alone sequence.

THE STORY OF CAVERSWALL CASTLE

A CHRONOLOGY

The information contained in the following table represents the best available. In many instances there is no precise evidence to show exactly when the castle changed hands or the extent to which the owners actually lived in it. The transition from a simple wooden tower built by Ernulf for safety, into a wooden tower on an earth mound, into a stone keep possibly with a wooden stockade, into a fortified manor house with battlements and a moat and finally into a gentleman's residence was a prolonged and gradual process. The table simply attempts to give some shape to that evolution. It seems probable, given the situation of the castle, it stands on what is essentially a flat site protruding from a sandstone ridge, that it was never more than a strongly built mansion. The need for protection against unhappy Saxons would have made the rapid construction of a secure wooden tower a priority. The siting of such a tower on an artificial mound, about 150 feet square, itself built on a tongue of sandstone, would have created an encircling ditch which natural drainage would have turned into a moat. *The mound rises from all sides of the moat built up with a great buttressed wall of splendid masonry'* (Country Life 1911). Water for the moat would have been drawn naturally from local springs caused by the fact that the bulk of the sandstone ridge, below which the village lies, rests on top of a layer of marl creating a spring line. One such spring still exists outside Yard Farm, evidence suggests another near or just beyond The Hollows and a third further along towards the church. Once the area had been pacified the move to create a status symbol in the form of a strong, stone built tower lying behind a stockade encircled by a moat followed. When the substantial house with a tower which could act as a last line of defence if the dwelling were attacked had been completed, the request to fortify it was necessary, to avoid the accusation that an illegal stronghold had been established.

The certain date for permission to crenellate (to furnish with battlements or loopholes) is 1275 suggesting that the main building was complete by that date.

There is no hard evidence to support the local myth that an escape route using a tunnel linking the castle to Catchems Corner ever existed. It is just possible that this story may have its roots in the problems experienced by the Catholic gentry during Tudor and later times and the use of a priest's hole to shelter itinerant priests before helping them on their way. Was it fugitive priests or unwary travellers who were caught at Catchems Corner? Similarly stories of a ghost in the castle, a lady from Aberdeen was allegedly slain for her money, could only hold water if the lady and the link with Aberdeen could be verified. The only apparent Scottish link is through Lady Frances Hamilton whose first husband was brother to the dishonourable James Duke of Hamilton and Brandon Knight of the most Ancient Order of the Thistle. If ever the castle held an unquiet female spirit it must surely be that of Lady Frances. It is, of course, just possible that the ghost is the spirit of a long dead nun, one who died, perhaps, in childbirth, if the 19th. century whispers about babies drowned in the moat during the occupation of the castle by nuns are anything more than part of the local gossip put about to drive them out. Nor is there any substance in the story that Cromwell's cannons were set up on Swan Bank to fire at the castle. Who was Kitty and why did she walk the lanes? Who was 'Gypsy Pete'? Where were 'tater barn', Burton's house. Porter's field, Ravage Lane and the slang? Where was the haunted well? Such myths, names and stories are an important part of a rich village tradition and should not be allowed to die for they are part of a popular mythology and contribute fleeting shadows to the story of the past. Even without such stories the history of the castle is a fascinating one.

Date	Building	Personality
800 AD	Saxon Hall	Cafhere
1060 AD	Saxon Hall	Ulviet, a free man
1068 AD	Norman Tower (of wood)	Ernulf de Hesdin, liege man of Robert de Stadford
1100 AD	Norman Tower (of wood)	Henry de Caureswelle
1150 AD	Motte and Bailey Castle	Walter de Kaverswelle
1180 AD	Motte and Bailey Castle	Thomas de Kaverswelle
1200 AD	Motte and Bailey Castle	Robert de Kaverswelle
1223 AD	Stone Mansion, moated stockade	Philomena, daughter of Robert
1240 AD	Stone Mansion, moated stockade	Henry de Kaveriswelle (by marriage)
1275 AD	Fortified Mansion	William de Kaveriswelle
1292 AD	Stone Keep with walls	Joan de Kaveriswelle
1310 AD	Stone Keep/ Castle	Richard de Kaveriswelle
1347 AD	Stone Keep/Castle	William de Kaveriswelle
1360 AD	Stone Keep/Castle	Peter de Kaveriswelle
1410 AD	Stone Keep/Castle	Petronilla, cousin to Peter
1411 AD	Stone Keep/Castle	Thomas de Marchyngton (by marriage)
1426 AD	Stone Keep/Castle	William Venables (by marriage)
1480 AD	Stone Keep/Castle	Nicholas Montgomery
1480 AD	Stone Keep/Castle	John Montgomery
1515 AD	Stone Keep/Castle	Dorothy Montgomery m. Sir Thomas Giffard
1540 AD	Stone Keep/Castle	Elizabeth Giffard m. Sir John Port

1560 AD	Stone Keep/Castle	George Hastings 4th Earl of Huntingdon m daughter of Sir John Port and Elizabeth Giffard
1582 AD	Stone Keep/Castle	Ralph Browne (Lessee)
1606 AD	Stone Keep/Castle	George Cradock
1628/30	New castle as home.	Mathew Cradock
1636 AD	Castle as home	George Cradock
1642 AD	Castle as home	Lady Dorothea Cradock
1643-45 AD	Castle as strongpoint	Lady Dorothea Cradock but held by a Parliamentary garrison.
1655 AD	Castle as home	William Jolliffe of Leek
1689 AD	Castle as home	William Jolliffe (Junior)
1703 AD	Castle as home	Lucy Jolliffe m William Vane, First Lord Vane
1734 AD	Castle as home	Lucy, Viscountess Vane (widow)
1735 AD	Castle as home	James, Duke of Hamilton (Lessee)
1742 AD	Castle as home	William Holles Vane ('The Imbecile') m Frances Hamilton
1759 AD	Castle as home	Lady May, Countess of Stamford.
1780 AD	Castle as home	Members of the Parker family
1795 AD	Castle as home	Mr. Brett a banker from Stone
1800 AD	Castle as home	Inherited by Booth Grey son of Lady May
1806 AD	Castle as home	Sir Thomas Lowten (Lessee)
1809 AD	Castle as home	Isaac Worthington (Lessee)
1810 AD	Castle as home	The Tidesmore Family
1811 AD	Castle as convent and school	Community of Benedictine Nuns
1853 AD	Castle as home	Mr. Holmes of Liverpool
1854 AD	Castle as home	Sir Percival Radcliffe, Bart.
1878 -1890 AD	Castle as home	Godfrey Wedgwood
1890 AD	Castle much modified	Mr. William Eli Bowers
1911- 32 AD	Present castle	Mrs. Alice Bowers (widow)
1933 AD	Religious House/convent	Servants of the Holy Ghost
1960 AD	Religious House/convent	Daughters of the Heart of Mary

1978 AD	Private accommodation	Sold in separate units to:

<table>
<tr><td>Mr. R Bellamy</td><td>Mr. A Ham</td></tr>
<tr><td>Mr. P Bunn</td><td>Mr. A Lucas</td></tr>
<tr><td>Mr B. Milner</td><td>Mr. C Mallett</td></tr>
<tr><td>Mr. T. Sherlock</td><td></td></tr>
</table>

1993 AD	Private accommodation	Separate units, one of which is in the ownership of Mr. Sargent and offers exclusive Bed and Breakfast accommodation. Other elements occupied by Mr. Bellamy, Mr. Bunn, Mr. Forbes and Mrs. Sherlock.

Caverswall Castle and Moat - from St. Peter's Churchyard

Drawing by Kevin Salt

EXPLANATORY NOTE

The region covered by this work lies within an area delineated by lines joining Cellarhead and Forsbrook in the east, Blythe Bridge and Normacot in the south, Adderley Green and Bucknall to the west and Eaves and Cellarhead to the north. Within that general region the greatest emphasis is laid upon that area which originally constituted the greater parish of Caverswall.

Where possible the spelling employed for each location is that current at the time to which the text refers, thus Caverswall which began life as 'Cafhere's Walle' becomes successively 'Caureswelle', 'Kaveswelle', 'Kaveriswelle', 'Careswelle', 'Careswall' and 'Caveswell' before achieving its contemporary form.

When visible features of the landscape are mentioned they are identified in such a way that the reader may readily identify the lingering traces of a modest past.

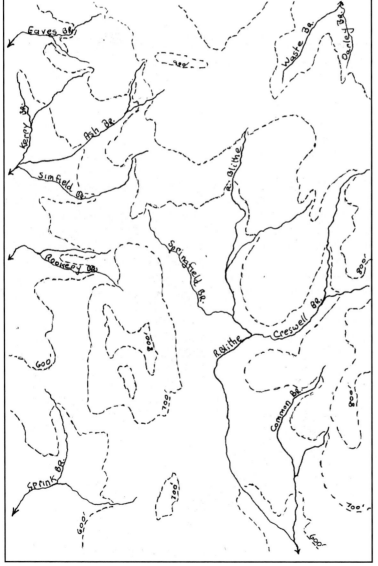

*Caverswall
Relief
and Drainage*

THE PHYSICAL BASIS OF THE PARISH

The two highest points in the parish lie to the east and north where the land rises to over 275m O.D. From north-east to southwest across the parish the land falls in a series of terraces broken by the broad valley of the misfit River Blithe. West of the Blithe the sequence is briefly reversed with the 250m high bulk of Park Hall Hills matching the 250m terrace above Caverswall Common. Beyond the impressive bulk of Park Hall Hills the land drops with extruding tongues of higher land to below 200m and the south-eastern edge of the Potteries Basin.

One clearly defined watershed runs from north-west to somewhat east of north joining Wetley Moor to Overmoor along the line of the A52. A second runs from slightly east of north southwards from Wetley Moor through Park Hall Hills and Pinewood towards the sandstone ridge at Meir Heath.

The valley of the Upper Blithe as thus delineated forms an elongated, broad and flattened V shape with its mouth opening southwards. It is within this valley and upon the higher ground which surrounds it that the people of Caverswall have sought to work out their destinies over the past seven or eight thousand years.

A Glacial Erratic - This relic of the ice age lies in the High Street

50,000 B.C.

SEEDED, ROOTED, FRUITED IN SOME LAND

In the face of steadily increasing warmth, the great ice sheets retreated northwards leaving behind a landscape of desolation. Their combination of irresistible movement and great weight had constituted a relentless erosive force which had shaped into smoothness the higher, rugged rocks of Park Hall, Cellarhead, Wetley Moor and Hardiwick whilst simultaneously gouging out the broad, shallow valley which today lies at the heart of the geographical parish.

From the fast retreating snout flowed a swelling torrent of meltwater which poured in a powerful yellow-green flood southwards from the ridge at Cellarhead, filling the valley between the higher land with a muddy morass drained by a broad river. Gradually the flow diminished and dwindled to an unpretentious stream before drying into a series of stagnant pools. Dropped by the retreating ice-sheet on the face of the land lay detritus ranging in size from great, shiny, ice-smoothed, water-polished erratics to a fine tawny silt which gradually dried into a yellowish clay. Some of those erratics are still visible, notably in The Square, the High Street and at the corner of the barn in the yard of Dove House Farm, there is another in Winterfield Lane and yet another at Richmoor Hill.

Following the ice northward, creeping across the brown, stony waste came the soft, powerful greens of the Arctic mosses and lichens over which waved the slender stalks of rank, coarse grass. In the sheltered, south-facing hollows, dwarf birches, willows and alder trees appeared. They sprang from seeds blown by the wind, carried by birds or passed in animal droppings. The seeds germinated, took root and flourished, pushing their way above the tossing carpet of sour grasses. On the slopes of the valley sides from Meir, through Park Hall, Hulme, Ash Bank, Cellarhead, Sheepwash, Roughcote, Caverswall and Black Birch Hollow there appeared a vast carpet of colours. Enlivened by the intense warmth of the brief summer sun an expansive carpet of campion, rock-rose, monks-hood, purple saxifrage, Iceland poppy, forget-me-not, thrift, yarrow, willow-herb and countless other flowering plants spread and blossomed bringing strident colours and heavily scented airs to a valley untrodden by man. Across that colourful carpet passed a succession of creatures, beasts like the hairy reindeer, musk ox, woolly rhinoceros, hare, lemming, cave lion, cave hyena and straight tusked elephant. Overhead skeins of wild geese wove migratory patterns across the sky whilst vicious, feathered death in the shape of the huge snowy owl, powerful eagle, deadly hawk and swift falcon stalked the careless leveret and the skulking lemming. In the marshy pools, over the flower heads and around the stunted bushes twisted and moved a vast and incredibly varied cloud of insect life. On the millstone rocks of Wetley Moor, plant and animal waste slowly decayed into a peat-like mass which steadily choked the upward and northward advance of all save the most hardy of the stunted bushes and trees. Gradually, shrubs gave way to trees which in turn became a blanket of tangled, impenetrable forest. Only along the hill tops and ridges was the land not totally choked by a waste of fallen trees, bushes, thorny undergrowth, swamp and rank grass. These open stretches or ridgeways became the highways of early man.

CAVERSWALL ABOUT 40,000 B.C.

An artist's impression of the area now known as High Street as it may have looked sometime about 40,000 B.C. after the retreat of the ice and before the growth of the forest cover which existed when the first men arrived in the area.

Some of the glacial erratics are still visible in the Square, at the corners of buildings and in the adjoining streets where they have been used to protect the corners of walls and buildings from the wheels of farm carts.

6,000 B.C.

HE HUNTED MY DEER

It was along such a ridgeway that the first visitors to the parish came. They were the farthest ripples of a tide of humanity stirred into motion by a drought in Central Eurasia 6,000 years before Christ. They followed the lines of that higher ground which made it possible for small hunting and exploring parties to travel outwards from the limestone uplands of the Peak District along the moor edge or Morridge and into the lower hills around Caverswall. There they found themselves above the vast, tree choked swamp which was to become Stoke-on-Trent. The arrowheads and ashes they left at Southlow and the axe head they dropped suggest only a fleeting occupation or perhaps nothing more than a brief moment of rest in the course of a quick reconnaissance of the lands they could see below their upland strongholds. There is, of course, always the possibility that the arrow head was not dropped by accident but was carried there in the body of a wounded animal. Those skin-clad hunters, armed with flint-tipped arrows and simple stone tools, were dwellers of the open skied uplands. They were men who felt ill at ease in the confines of the forest and who were poorly equipped to tackle the bears, wolves, boars, wild cats and most fearsome of all, the great wild ox or wisent, which roamed the forests of Caverswall at that time. Even more frightening must have been the unknown evils hidden in such a place, the ghosts, forest sprites and malevolent spirits whose intangibility in no way diminished their capacity for acts of malice. To such men the Caverswall valley was a place to shun.

(Adapted from R. J. Unstead)

'He hunted my deer'

100A.D.

THE AXES BEGIN TO BITE

In the years following the birth of Christ the climate entered upon a prolonged period of dry warmth. The marshy surrounds of the river began to dry out and tree growth flourished. A rich cover of oak forest with a carpet of ferns beneath the canopy spread wherever the soil was deep enough and dry enough to sustain it.

The unnamed River Blithe wove an uncertain course through the broad valley left behind by the long departed ice-sheets. Rank grasses and rushes struggled to live under the shade of the alder trees whose roots choked and tangled the margins of the sluggish stream. Just as the alders overshadowed the lesser riverside plants so the oaks towered over the alders spreading a vast green canopy across the whole landscape. The forest stretched in all directions as far as the eye of the hovering kestrel could see. Within the greater forest there were subtle variations. In the damper locations there were alder, birch and oak, on the dry, sandstone slopes oak trees and massive ferns brought a richer green to the eye. On the highest levels the trees were fewer, the land more open, until the peaty damp, tussocky grasses and sparse, stunted bushes of Wetley Moor brought a sense of openness to the whole before the land once again sloped away beneath the lofty canopy of oaks towards what is now Wetley Rocks and Cheddleton.

The earliest axe wielding settlers in the parish were the Iron Age people who possessed not just strong arms and iron axes but also the confident belief that somewhere within the forest could be found a friendly spirit to protect the village from the fell and foul fiends which still lurked beyond the stockade. The first axeblows had hardly begun to echo through the forest when the Romans drove one of their military roads through the southern part of the parish along the line of what is now the Uttoxeter Road and the sound of war-horns floated, wind borne, across the forested waste.

It is just possible that the mound which lies to the north of Cookshill on the eastern side of the road to Roughcote dates from this period. The mound is perfectly round its sides have a 45 degree slope and the top is truncated in a manner which cannot be attributed to normal weathering. There is a ditch all round the mound and no evidence of a causeway by which the mound could have been approached and no obvious approach road. It might just possibly be an Iron Age burial mound. It could be of Roman origin with a similar purpose. It may be of later date, perhaps medieval, it may have provided a base for a windmill. A local explanation that it is a 'pond turned upside down' in other words the material discarded when a pond for the watering of stock was created, fails on three counts. Firstly the shape is far too regular to have such a casual origin; secondly normal weathering would have affected such a casual deposit more extensively than has happened here; and thirdly there is no comparable pond which would surely have been where the mound is, on lower ground between two ridges. Other possibilities exist but are equally speculative, for instance it may have served as a marker for land given to the nuns by William of Caverswall in 1291 or again it may have served as a base or look-out point for a shepherd tending his flock near the 'rough cote'. When all speculative options have been considered, late Iron Age or early Roman seem reasonable possible dates for this strange feature.

200 A.D.

THE REIGN OF THE EAGLES

That road constituted the first major impact of Man upon the parish. Running from east to north-west it linked the garrison at Chester with the settlement at Holditch and both with Uttoxeter and the towns of the East Midlands so offering a route to London and ultimately, to Rome. Along it flowed the current of Roman provincial life clinging closely to the security offered by a main road through a forest wilderness.

Among the travellers passing through the region were those conveying salt from the salt fields of Cheshire to the settlements at Rocester and beyond. Evidence of their passage and that of their mediaeval successors lingers in the name of Salter's Lane whilst the unswerving line of Green Lane above Sheepwash is locally held to be evidence of a Roman origin.

The area had its share of villains. If most of the local artisans were truly 'worth their salt', a number were not. Among those must be reckoned the forgers who produced the bad money tokens unearthed in a garden at Lightwood in 1960. Buried to escape the military police sent by Probus to stamp out the practice of forgery around Caverswall and Trent Vale, the hoard was never retrieved. The fate of the coiner is unknown but the thrill of a detachment of legionaries hastening through the parish in his pursuit lingers on.

The cluster of hovels hidden in the forest north of the road saw little of Roman provincial civilisation consequently the hammer blows which shattered the walls of Rome were little more than whispers on the wind in Caverswall. Movement through the area, along the road, climbed to a peak of fervour and then gradually died as the military presence withdrew. Trade, travel and commerce slowly ossified, communities drew in upon themselves, languished and shrank. Bushes reached out into the cleared verges of the road, trees began to hide the sky. Fingers of grass rose skyward from seeds which had lodged by chance in the surface of the road. Silence returned with only a ribbon of vanishing road and a network of fast disappearing forest trails to speak of the transitory nature of man's first occupancy.

Green Lane - An extension of the old Salt Way which may, just possibly, be of Roman origin

400 A.D.

WHEN ROME WAS ROTTEN-RIPE

Another convulsion in Central Eurasia sent a further sequence of ripples through the peoples scattered over the face of Europe. Southwards the Huns, Goths and Vandals poured over the Alps and into Italy. In the west war bands of Angles, Saxons and Jutes made brief but vicious hit and run raids upon the Channel coast. Finding the rich Roman island soft, lax and unprotected the raids became more protracted until it became apparent that, shorn of the armed might of the legions, the Romano-British natives had no real power to oppose their assailants. Here and there small groups rallied to the support of leaders like Ambrosius Aurelianus and that shadowy, mystical and mysterious bear symbol Urt-hor or Arthur. Such men sought to weld the local levies into a fighting force but to no avail. No forces of such limited scale and quality could stem the increasing flood of family groups voyaging across the North Sea and the Straits of Dover: these groups cruised the coast and nosed into estuaries following the line of the river until river travel became impossible. They then abandoned their vessels and pushed forward, on foot, into the very heart of the soft, lush land. The Trent offered just such a highway and absorbed a vast number of these fierce immigrants. Each succeeding wave lapping over the most recent arrivals to settle in the next convenient spot.

The process of settlement can be deduced from an analysis of the place-names employed by these settlers. Such names are unlikely to have been used by the residents of a particular location but rather by their neighbours to describe adjacent settlements. From the forms of place-name used it seems probable that the 'ham on the Trent' (Trentham) and the 'village with a stockade on the Trent' (Stoke-on-Trent) were among the first locations settled. Then a tribe, the Werringa, led by a chief called Werra settled upon a site for their 'tun' or 'ingatun'. The chosen site lay near the crest of a long hill climbing away eastwards from the great valley of the Trent. There, at the head of a lesser streamlet between two small hills and below the towering bulk of the moorland to the north grew up 'Werringastun'. To the south a broad, forested valley covered with oak trees and watered by a marshy stream rich in fish, fowl and game, fell away, leaving the chosen site with a warm sun-trap location enhanced by the bulk of 'wet lea' or moorland which sheltered the site from cold north-easterly winds.

Further to the south a second group settled in a very similar location choosing a broad gap between a massive bulk of sandstone and a lesser hill of similar material. Again the site was blessed with a fresh water stream, offered a sunny, southerly exposure and stood above the forested river valley lying to the east. The site became known to its neighbours at Werringastun as 'West-ton', the 'ton' on the west bank of the river.

The massive sandstone rocks of Park Hall Hills are known to the geologist as Bunter Sandstone. To the hydrologist they resemble a great underground sponge full of water which can be tapped through bore holes and pumping stations like that at Sheepwash. To the earliest settlers they were important because it was the joint between the Bunter Sandstone and the neighbouring Keuper Sandstones and Marls that formed the spring line. A spring line is the line of locations at which springs issue forth, offering a constant and plentiful supply of fresh water for man and beast alike.

The earliest settlers in the region chose locations lying roughly two and a half miles apart although distance varied with the number of settlers entering the area and the quality of the land available. The first village units each controlled, or needed for survival,

Three simple sketch maps to illustrate the main features of the sites of the original settlements at Werrington, Weston Coyney and Hulme.

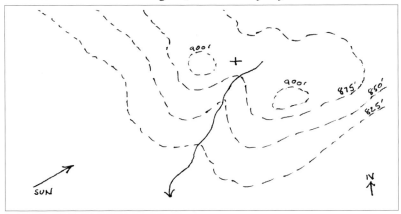

The site chosen by the people of Werringastun

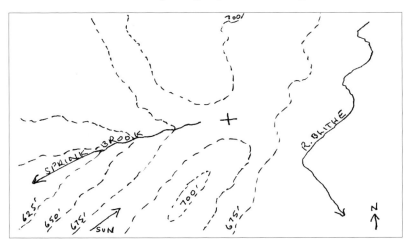

The site chosen by the people of West-ton

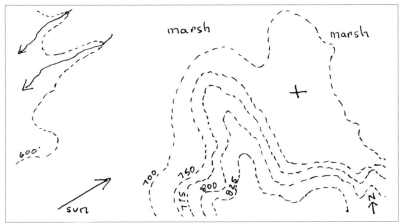

The site chosen by the people of Holm

something like 22,000 acres (or between 8,000 and 9,000 hectares) of land. As the communities grew and became strong enough to sub-divide they tended to split up with part of each family moving to a new location. Sometimes such relocations happened because a site better than that originally selected was discovered close at hand.

An exposure of Bunter Sandstone on Park Hall Hills

Sometimes, perhaps, the choice was made by an enforced decision to stop travelling. Historians may theorise about the processes which shaped the settlement pattern of Saxon England but like a mocking echo from the past coming as a reminder of the unchanging humanity of man can be heard the voice of the tired and heavily pregnant Saxon wife, 'I don't care about your theories husband, the baby is due and I want a decent roof over my head when it happens, we are stopping here!'

Such a decision may well have influenced the choice of the first site at Weston Coyney for there can be no doubt that it was the later settlement at Caverswall that was to flourish.

When the process of relocation or secondary settlement began the pattern of the place-names changed. From names which meant 'the settlement of ...' or 'the settlement on ..' the process of naming moved to the use of personal names, or as they just might have been at this date, Christian names. Thus Cafhere who found a spring at a joint between a tongue of Keuper Sandstone and the Keuper Marls of the valley floor gave Caverswall its name when his neighbours called his settlement 'Cafhere's Walle' or 'Cafhere's Spring'. Washerwall (Waesse-walle) belongs to the same second stage of settlement.

Gradually, throughout the area and roughly halfway between the earliest settlements there sprang up a pattern of secondary villages identifiable first by the use of personal names to describe them and then by the use of geographically descriptive names to help locate them. The locations chosen and settled in this way established the fundamental village pattern for the area which has survived to this day.

Local people came to know and to use such names as:

    Cafhere's Walle - Cafhere's spring - Caverswall
    Bucca's Halh - Bucca's secret place - Bucknall
    Werringastun - the village of Werra or of Werringa - Werrington
    Waesse Walle - Waesse's spring - Washerwall
    Ticca's Hyll - Ticca's Hill - Tickhill
    Cuccu's Hyll - Cuccu's Hill - Cookshill
    Fotes Broc - Fote's Brook - Forsbrook
    Dulverne - the place of delving or digging - Dilhorne
    Hean Lea - high meadow - Handley Banks
    Rough Cote - the shepherd's hut - Roughcote
    Wet Lea - the damp open space - Wetley

Sketch map
to show the
postulated
pattern of
the Saxon
Settlements

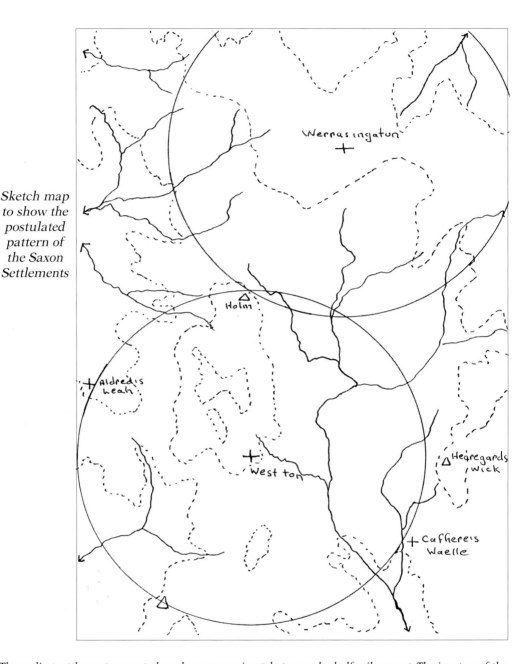

Werras ingatun
+

Holm

Aldred's
Leah
+

West ton
+

Heqregards
wick

Cafhere's
Waelle
+

The earliest settlements seem to have been approximately two and a half miles apart. The ingatun of the Werras and the settlement at West-ton (marked thus +) came first, the circles suggest their spheres of influence. Secondary settlements (was Aldred another son of the West-ton family?) were Aldred's Leah and Cafhere's Waelle. The third phase of settlements was Danish and is marked thus Δ
There is some doubt about the derivation of Werrington it may be either
'Werra's ingatun' - the village of Werra or 'Werringastun' - the village of the Werringas.

Efes - the border of the moor (moorside) - Eaves
Asche - the place where ash trees grow - Ash
Kerr - the overgrown marsh - Kerry Hill
Aldred's Leah - Ealdred's clearing in the wood - Adderley
West-ton - the village in the west - Weston (Later called by the Normans,
Westone sub Kevremont , the village to the west under the hill where goats
are found, Kevremont was later corrupted to Coyne and so, Coyney)

As population pressure increased and the process of settlement continued the size of each village area had to decrease. When the process was finally completed each village seems to have been able to lay claim to about 11,000 acres of land (or about 4,500 hectares) in the centre of which lay the houses and fields. Around each such nucleus spread the village's holding of forest and stream from which all of its necessities, with the possible exception of the weapons for defence or war, had to be won. In this way the foundations of the 'parish' were laid.

CAVERSWALL ABOUT 700 A.D.'

*The High Street as it might have looked about 700 A.D. when Cafhere moved
from his father's home at West-ton and built himself a hall near Cafhere's Walle*

Drawing by Francis Clare

CAFHERE- FOUNDER OF THE VILLAGE

One can only speculate about the Saxon/Anglian farmer who gave his name to the village. Using place-name analysis it is possible to argue that the earliest settlers identified locations by their physical features e.g. Trentham, the ham on the Trent or Werrington, the ingatun of Werra. It is unlikely that individual chiefs named their own settlements but rather that neighbours referred to other locations in terms which gradually became accepted through such use as place names.

A second technique asks questions about the size of the area needed to sustain a Saxon village. This varies with the locality and the quality of the land. In Caverswall it seems that an area of about 22,000 acres was required, initially, to sustain a community. Equally of course it may be that one settler did not wish to see or smell another man's smoke. Whatever the reason , if indeed there was only one reason, settlements within the Caverswall area seem initially to have been about two and a half miles apart. As settlements grew an oldest son would have moved out to set up on his own. To minimise the risk of conflict such sites were often chosen on the boundary of the paternal area and were referred to in descriptive terms e.g. Cafhere's waelle (Cafhere's spring) or Hecregard's wick (Hecregard's dairy farm.)

Cafhere would have lived by a calendar whose main components remain recognisable.

CAFHERE'S CALENDAR

Giuli	*(Yule)*	*December/January*
Solmonath	*(Month of Cakes)*	*February*
Hretha	*(Derivation uncertain)*	*March*
Eostre	*(Pagan ceremony, became Easter)*	*April*
Thrimilci	*(Cows milked thrice daily)*	*May*
Litha	*(Moon month)*	*June*
Flegamonath	*(Fly month)*	*July*
Weodmonath	*(Weed month)*	*August*
Halegmonath	*(Holy month · sacrifices)*	*September*
Wintirfyllith	*(First moon of winter)*	*October*
Blotmonath	*(Blood month)*	*November*
New Year's Day		*25th. December*
Modra Nech	*(Mothers' night)*	*26th. December*

Sketch map to show the suggested site of the first settlement at Cafhere's Waelle. The two small streams flowing to the River Blithe represent streams flowing from springs near the modern Yard Farm and near the future castle. The area between the two was to become the centre of the modern village.

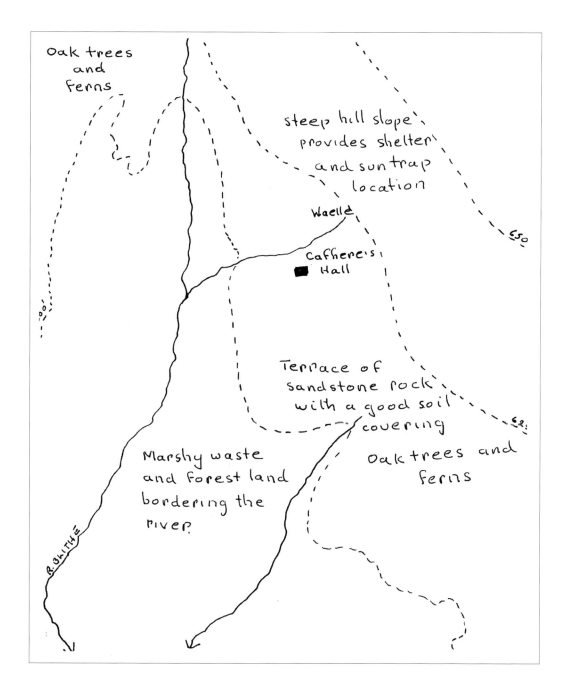

Oak trees
and
ferns

steep hill slope
provides shelter
and sun trap
location

Waelle

Cafhere's
Hall

Terrace of
sandstone rock
with a good soil
covering

Oak trees and
ferns

Marshy waste
and forest land
bordering the
river.

R. BLITHE

660 A.D.

THE CROSS CONQUERS

When the evil and ruthless King Penda of Mercia was slain in battle and his pagan host destroyed by the Christian King Oswy in 655 A.D. his son Wulfhere succeeded to the throne in his stead. After a brief flirtation with Christianity during which he married the Christian Ermenilda of Kent, Wulfhere reverted to paganism, making his camp near Stone the rallying point for unbelievers. It was there amid pagan practices and closed minds that Wulfhere's two sons Wulfad and Rufin were born.

The lads grew into fine huntsmen. One day Wulfad, chasing a fine white stag, found himself lost in a broad, forested, valley beyond the sandstone ridge north of his home. Searching through the forest, following the stag's trail he traced it to a sheltered spot where he found the stag drinking at a spring beside which a hermit had built his cell. Wulfad spent the night with Chad, for so the holy man was named and left on the morrow vowing to return with Rufin to hear more of the Christ of whom their mother spoke in her private moments. So potent was the teaching of Chad that Wulfad and Rufin became Christians. But, at home their visits to Chad had been noted. Their changing attitudes and an increasing readiness to challenge the pagan practices which surrounded them were observed and reported by evil tongues to Wulfhere.

When the truth was known Wulfhere's anger exploded into bloody action. Wulfad was caught and slain at the hermit's cell, Rufin was murdered in the forest and Chad returned to find his cell desecrated. When the blood lust ebbed from his brain Wulfhere was smitten with remorse, his conversion by Chad and the effective establishment of Christianity in North Staffordshire followed. It is not, perhaps, wholly unreasonable to nurture the belief that this incident might well have happened in or around Cafhere's Walle during the period of Chad's ministry among the pagans of the upper reaches of the Trent.

The building of the first tiny, church in the village followed soon after the completion of Chad's ministry. The new and unusual building was important to the village. Not only did it indicate the existence of a notionally Christian community with some pretensions to a cultured and caring life but it also served as a positive statement of the Christian faith at a time when mystery and black superstition were dominant elements in the human mind.

900 A.D.

THE FURY OF THE NORSEMEN

Some two hundred years after the church appeared at Cafhere's Walle smoke from cooking fires appeared over Hulme, Hardiwick and Normacot. Curious villagers left Cafhere's Walle, Aldred's Leah and West-ton and after creeping stealthily through the forest, found small family groups of Danes preparing to settle on carefully selected locations lying midway between the existing villages. Far enough away from each adjacent site to avoid charges of trespass the little Danish groups settled and waited. The residents watched until the newcomers had settled into a normal farming routine and then absorbed the new arrivals and their villages into the area and its way of life. The settlers at Normacot were generally identified as the people from 'the north-man's cote' whilst Hecregard who settled above and north of Cafhere's Walle at a location now called Hardiwick, soon earned such a reputation as a dairy farmer that his dwelling became known as Hecregard's wick or Hecregard's dairy farm. The settlers at Hulme named their own location for they selected a small tongue of land a semi-island or 'holm' - jutting out towards the marshy valley floor and referred to the place as 'the holm'.

Another ripple had passed through the tide of humanity, this time the source of the ripple lay in Ireland. When the first angry flush of their raiding excursions was over many of the Norsemen had found ready employ as mercenaries. A large group had settled in Ireland until reasons were found for their expulsion. Landing somewhere near Chester and led by Sihtric they travelled inland, settling at suitable locations and leaving evidence of their passage in a string of place-names Hough, Hulme, Thursfield, Knutton and Normacot. However, history is a little uncertain here and it is just possible that these new arrivals might have had a different origin. During 893 A.D. Alfred and the Danes were locked in bitter combat in a series of raids and battles covering the whole of Wessex and Mercia. In the late autumn of 893 the Danish war lord, Hasting, made one last desperate throw for victory striking north-west across Mercia before reaching the old Roman fortress of Deva on the Dee. There the Mercian fyrd trapped him and for two days held the Danes under siege. The onset of winter weather sent the fyrd home and left the Danes to winter in peace. In 894 A.D. the Danes left Deva in search of less hostile neighbours but it is not inconceivable that they left behind, both there and on their line of march, tiny elements of the war band who, for whatever personal reasons, age, wounds, marriage, greed, war sickness, chose to settle rather than follow their kindred.

It may well have been this incursion of Hasting into Mercia which brought King Alfred north from Wessex to Caureswelle where, legend tells us, he encountered and wed the White Lady of Caureswelle.

THE WHITE LADY OF CAVERSWALL

Every good village has, somewhere in its history, the stuff of legend and Caverswall is no exception. The legend of the White Lady seems to be part of the extensive oral tradition which evolved around the life and work of King Alfred; a tradition which includes the well known fiction of the burnt cakes.

The story of the White Lady of Caverswall has its roots in the time of King Alfred when Hasting, a Danish war lord, was ravaging the North Midlands. Legend has it that Alfred came north from Wessex and in Caureswelle met and married the White Lady around whose waist, and only hers, did the leaves of chastity flourish.

It could be that the White Lady was of Danish stock and that, in some way, the marriage represented some form of peace treaty or truce, pursued and realised; for Caverswall stands very close to the postulated line of the frontier fashioned through the agreement which led to the creation of the Danelaw.

Perhaps the story is true as it stands and there was but one virtuous woman in the area. Perhaps the girdle of chastity was a fact. Certainly there are similar stories about the mystic power of leaves from other parts of the world, stories which have some basis in fact. The legend may have something to do with the carving of a unicorn on the principal staircase in the tower of the castle. This fabulous beast could be captured and controlled only by a maiden of unblemished virtue.

It was not entirely coincidental that four of the seven scholars who were supporting Alfred in his attempts to raise the standard of scholarship throughout the land came from Mercia. It is possible that the White Lady was a symbol of the learning and scholarship of the area. If so the marriage could represent the willingness of Wessex to embrace Mercian scholarship.

However, another and more sinister explanation should be considered. In the mythology and folklore of building human sacrifice has an important part. The tradition of burying a human sacrifice in the foundations or of confining a victim within a wall space and leaving them, usually her, to suffocate or starve to death has a long pedigree. It was widely held that buildings could not be completely secure against disaster unless such a sacrifice were offered. It is possible that the legend of the White Lady refers to such a sacrifice made at the time when the stone castle was being built and the builders deemed it necessary to secure its future. Such a sacrifice could well have been carried out without the knowledge of the de Caureswelle family. It is not inconceivable that later stories of a ghostly female presence in the castle may be rooted in this ancient superstition.

The story could be of more recent origin and may stem from the period 1811 - 1853 when the castle was occupied by a group of nuns and their confessor. The villagers became hostile towards the nuns and put about a range of scurrilous stories designed to build resentment and drive them out. Among those stories were rumours of witchcraft, dark deeds behind locked doors, illegitimate babies drowned in the moat and nuns dead in childbirth. Could the White Lady be the spirit of one such?

With the final flurry of invasions over, life settled into a characteristic pattern. The Saxon village had one main building, the Hall and sometimes a church. Around the Hall but at an appropriate distance straggled the timber framed, thatched hovels of the villagers. In this area Caureswelle alone boasted a church. Even so Caureswelle was of no great size and it seems unlikely that the village in, say 900 A.D., exceeded more than 20 or 30 souls in size. The village year revolved around a pattern of winter cultivation of the stubble followed by a spring sowing, cultivation and a late summer harvest which was followed in turn by an autumn ploughing and sowing of the fallow land. This rhythmical, seasonal activity was centred upon one vast field, subdivided into three lesser fields each of which in turn was subdivided into individual holdings.- Wheat, barley (both for bread and brewing), rye, beans, peas, vegetables and herbs were the main crops. Bees provided honey, whilst cattle, pigs, sheep and an occasional horse completed the farmer's bestiary.

Food in Caureswelle was monotonous, scanty at best and not infrequently lacking. Death was no stranger to the straggle of huts which sprawled between Hall and church. Death from sickness, particularly among the youngest, was commonplace whilst death from starvation was not unknown. The starving peasants of Caureswelle would have found scant comfort in the words of Abbot Aelfric:

'The Almighty Ruler sometimes withdraws sustenance from men on account of their sins but nevertheless we believe that he whom hunger kills goes to God unless he was particularly sinful.'

The ploughman in Aelfric's colloquy records the general tenor of life as the people of Caureswelle knew it:

'I go out at dawn driving the oxen to the field and yoke them to the plough. It is never so harsh a winter that I dare lurk at home for fear of my master but when the oxen have been yoked and the ploughs have a coulter fastened to the plough, I must plough each day a full acre or more . . . I must fill the oxen's manger with hay and water them and clear out the dung.'

Yet there was also some division of labour and some degree of specialisation for Aelfric's ox-herd says:

'I labour much: when the ploughman unyokes the oxen I lead them to the pasture and all night long I stay by them to watch against thieves and again first thing in the morning I commit them to the ploughman well fed and watered.'

During the bitter winter weather the ox-herd probably spent the night beside them in the stall, one of the warmer places in the village.

Whilst the ploughman toiled away tilling the flat areas of land beyond the present church the shepherd drove his flock out to pasture on the high meadows at Hean Leah (now Handley Banks) wandering so far afield that it was necessary for him to build a 'rough cote' in which he could pass nights away from the village with his charges safely penned beside him:

'First thing in the morning I drive my sheep to pasture and stand over them in heat and cold with dogs lest wolves should devour them and I lead them back to their sheds and milk them twice a day and move their folds beside and I make cheese and butter and am faithful to my lord.'

Such must have been the way of life followed by the first villagers of Caureswelle in their tiny, self-sufficient village. Such people saw few strangers and seldom moved beyond the next village unless to seek a wife or barter away some surplus. Only the village leaders and perhaps, the priest, moved much beyond the confines of the village holding.

Around each cluster of hovels lurked the forest. No longer wholly feared with an unreasoning dread but certainly not understood and still regarded as the home of things evil. The tree edge of the clearing was pushed steadily backward as the villagers sought building timber, kindling and additional farmland. Tangible foes in the shape of bear, fox, wolf, badger and wildcat could be fought and conquered but the threat of the trackless waste and the hidden spirits of forest darkness were less easily countered. Only the church stood out against these dark corners of man's mind.

Imperceptibly Caureswelle extended its influence, increased its wealth and grew neater as it prospered. Under the leadership of Ulviet the Free Man it began to outstrip its neighbours, Westone led by Ulvric, Dulverne ruled by Godwin and Fotesbroc which languished under the idle Swain. As the most impressive display of wealth possible a small stone church was built to replace an earlier, more simple structure. Large enough to take the 50 or 60 souls of the immediate locality it was built of the soft red sandstone of the region.

So influential were the church and priest of Caureswelle becoming that half of the income of a daughter church at Stoke was passed to Caureswelle to assist with its work.

Sketch map to show how the village might have grown. Caureswelle at about 1,000 AD

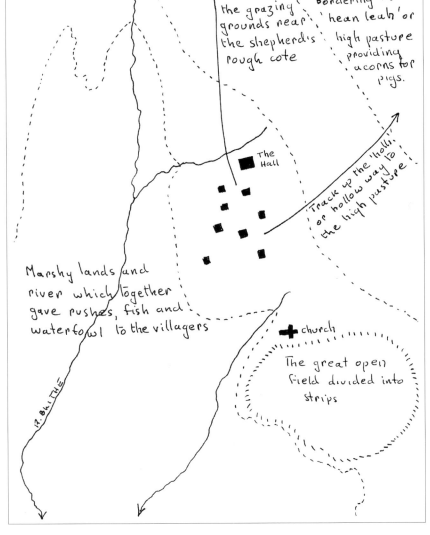

Track to the grazing grounds near the shepherd's rough cote

Oak Forest bordering the 'hean leah' or high pasture providing acorns for pigs.

The Hall

Track up the 'holh' or hollow way to the high pasture

Marshy lands and river which together gave rushes, fish and waterfowl to the villagers

R. Blithe

church

The great open field divided into strips

1066 A.D.

ENGLAND ON THE ANVIL

Those rumours of wars which actually reached the village did little to disturb its peace. The garbled news of mighty battles at Stamford Bridge and Senlac Hill and stories of the deaths of two powerful kings meant little to Ulviet's folk. The coronation of William of Normandy, whom history was to call 'The Conqueror' meant nothing to the people of Caureswelle. The subsequent insurrections and William's punitive devastation of the north added a new dimension to the rumours which wove threads of fear into the daily discourse of the villagers. Rumour became stark reality when a powerful, battle-scarred Norman built a tower at Stadford and calling himself Robert de Stadford, laid claim to the lands round about. In a short space of time Ulviet lost his lands, his liberty and, perhaps, his life. Ulviet was replaced as Lord of the Manor by a Norman, Ernulf de Hesdin by name!

It was in the bleakness of the winter of 1085 that the new king spoke deeply with his wise men at the Gloucester Gemot. In consequence, when the spring of 1086 gladdened the land, the King's men entered every shire in England to carry out a survey so thorough

'that there was not a single hide nor a rood of land, nor - it is shameful to relate that which he thought no shame to do was there an ox, or a cow, or a pig, passed by that was not set down in the accounts and then all these writings were brought to him.'

The grim-faced warriors in their chain mail coats and acorn shaped helmets stood stark and potent with menace as the supercilious, cruel faced clerks led by their obsequious Saxon guide questioned the villagers and recorded the wealth of Caureswelle as owned by its new Lord, Robert de Stadford.

'The same Robert holds one virgate of land in Caureswelle and Ernulf holds of him. Ulviet held it and he was a free man. There is land for four ploughs. In demesne is one plough and there are ten villeins and two bordars with three ploughs. There are six acres of meadow; and woodland one league in length and half a league in breadth; and there is half the church of Stoke with half a caracute of land. It is worth 30s.'

From such information it was not difficult to reconstruct the village of Caureswelle as it may have been in 1086.

Beyond the church and Dove House Farm sprawled a vast open field which required four plough teams to keep it in good heart. Held by Ernulf as part of his demesne or 'home farm' was a further area of arable land equivalent to a year's work for one plough team. Areas of neglect and under-cultivation were apparent for only three plough teams survived in a four-plough unit. Possibly a consequence of the death of some of the villagers during the savage hammering of the North which preceded the Domesday Survey.

In the area between the present school and the present castle, stretching away westward and south-westward to the rush-lined banks of the river, lay some six acres of meadows and grazing land. Along the line of 'High Street', up onto Handley Banks and out towards Roughcote lay an area of oak woodland a league in length and half a league in breadth. This special area contained those oak trees whose acorns served as fodder for the lean, runtish swine of the village and the rabbit warrens whose denizens served as a constant and ready source of fresh meat. Around the southern fringes of the forest during spring and summer the villagers placed their beehives so that the bees might have easy access to the greatest variety of pollen sources. Honey was the only sweetening agent the villagers knew and an important ingredient in many recipes. Beyond the immediate village, stretching away in all directions lay the forest proper into whose ferny fringes the more ambitious and industrious villagers were beginning to cut, seeking to capture for themselves an additional patch of cultivable land.

The general village plan must have been very much as it now is. To the west at the limit of the village on the terrace where Bank House now stands stood Ernulf's tower and its wooden stockade. Below it stood Ulviet's hall now a barrack room for Ernulf's retainers. Beyond the hall, straggling untidily towards the tiny stone church sprawled the dwellings of the villagers. Close to the church, using a tongue of sandstone as a base, were the beginnings of the huge mound upon which the permanent replacement for Ernulf's temporary strongpoint would be erected. At the point where the terrace of sandstone rock widened out the hovels drew apart to form a crude village square punctuated on its eastern side by the dominating bulk of the church. Opposite the church on the further side of the square stood one building slightly larger than its neighbours, the tavern. This was really little more than a large private dwelling where the skill of the housewife at brewing had earned her the title of 'ale-wife' to such effect that her beverages were served to paying customers in the overlarge living room of the hovel.

Each two-roomed hut had a small vegetable plot attached to it. In close proximity to each dwelling was a sprawling midden on which unwanted matter was dumped and which served as an open air toilet. Given the absence of toilet paper it is easy to appreciate the unsubtle humour of village folk who regarded the holly and the nettle as the two cleanest plants in the forest. Here and there the burgeoning buildings used as animal shelters bespoke a man whose beasts were thriving. The clear legacy of these farmsteads is apparent to this day in the number of farms whose yards and major accesses open directly onto one of the main village roadways.

Beyond the Square and below the general line of the village along what is now the High Street lay a marshy, reed-rich swamp, bounded on three sides by high land and drained by a stream which flowed between the present School and the Red House. More than one villager had given thought to the possibility of damming that stream to create a body of water which would attract waterfowl, provide fish and ensure a more certain supply of water power for the village's tiny corn mill. However, such projects took time and time was a scarce commodity in 1086.

Of the villagers Ernulf, the Lord of the Manor, was a warrior of sufficient calibre to have earned Caureswelle as his reward for supporting Robert and King William at Senlac and after. He actually owned only the land recorded as being 'in demesne'. This land was cultivated at his own cost and by his own labour. Ernulf was no mere battle hardened swordsman but a capable and practical farmer who could supervise work all day in the field and then mend tools and tend beasts until the light failed. He was directly responsible to Robert for the shrewd and skilled management of the village lands. Upon the success of his practices, the quality of his leadership and the prosperity of the village Ernulf's future depended.

The number of serfs or men who were not free is not recorded. Certainly a number must have been present but as the lowest of the lowly they were regarded as chattels not persons each with a dead value of exactly 40 Saxon pence.

Above the serf stood the villein or ordinary 'townsman' of which class Caureswelle boasted ten. These men were free. They owned land and could move up the social scale by their own efforts if they could acquire five hides of land. The hide was an uncertain measurement of land. It ranged from 120 acres in Kent to 40 acres in Wiltshire and seems to have some link with the amount of ground needed to support a family. Whilst villeins owned and could add to their land, they needed the support of the Lord and paid for that support in cash, kind and service. A dead villein was worth 200 Saxon shillings to his Lord by way of wergild or compensation.

The bordar, also a 200 shilling man, of which class Caureswelle possessed two, was a free but dependent tenant who owned his own house and land but received from his Lord two oxen, one cow, six sheep, seed for seven acres of land and all of his household goods and furnishings. In return for this support he paid his Lord through service for two days a week and three at harvest time. He paid a tribute in cash, barley, sheep, and poultry, owed both week-work and ploughing service, paid the hearth penny or Peter's penny and was required to feed one of his Lord's dogs.

By assuming that each villein and bordar was married it is possible to suggest that the population of Caureswelle in 1086 comprised 12 families each

A group of pupils from St. Peter's recreate the arrival in the village of the domesday assessors as part of the 1980 Festival

of between two and four souls, Ernulf's household, say 20 persons, a bachelor priest and an uncertain number of serfs or bond slaves. A lower figure of 45 persons and an upper figure of 90 seems not unreasonable. Overall the village community was strong and relatively prosperous.

Elsewhere the people were less well blessed. Bucenhole was an isolated and impoverished settlement whose one third of a hide and land for three ploughs had been held by one Chetel who could well have been a descendant of a Norseman, Ketil. Ketil may well have been a member of the group whose members settled Hulme, Normacot and Knutton. The change of name and ownership from the Saxon, Bucca, to the Norseman, Ketil suggests either marriage or a brief and bloody dispute.

At Westone the level of prosperity more closely paralleled that of Caureswelle, there the scribe recorded that:

'The same Robert holds one virgate of land in Westone and Ernulf de Hesdin holds of him. Ulvric held it. There is land for three ploughs. Woodland one league in length and half a league in breadth. It is worth 10s.'[3]

Ancient chronicles indicate that there must have been much opposition to the survey. Errors, omissions and oversights must have been inevitable. Some records may have been lost, for whatever reason. Local intransigence may have been partly responsible for the absence of Holm and Werynton from the record. The emnity between Saxon and Norman

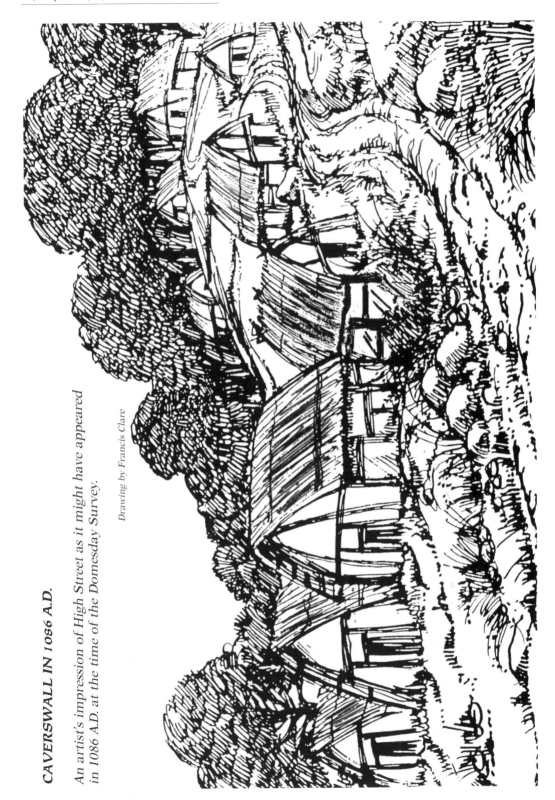

CAVERSWALL IN 1086 A.D.

An artist's impression of High Street as it might have appeared in 1086 A.D. at the time of the Domesday Survey.

Drawing by Francis Clare

seems to have lingered on into the twelfth century and is illustrated by the stories of violent and bloody conflicts which, if legend is to be believed, raged around Bucenhole and Asche.

Early in that saga of hate an arrow sang through the damp air of a misty autumn afternoon and drove deep through a minstrel's tabard to find his heart. The minstrel's body splashed into the stream which drained the steep-sided valley below Asche near the point where the modern main road crosses the course of the self-same stream. The minstrel had been on his way to sing at the table of the de Halle family. The Saxon arrow which whispered through the autumn murk bore a cruel message to the Norman minstrel and left an evil memory. To murder a christian minstrel on the eve of the sainted Martin's day was a foul act causing the minstrel's unshriven soul to prowl restlessly through the mist shrouded clough doomed forever to seek the peace of the quietly dead. No local used the clough on such evenings.

Political and personal rivalries continued to flourish. The de Caureswelles by virtue of their power and status were too strong to challenge but to the north-west the contending powers of the Abbot of Hulton, the Saxon Audley of Heighley and the Norman Sir Leon de Layne of Asche Halle were constantly at odds over the control of the wild forest lands which sprawled between their holdings. The curse of the church, the strong arm of Audley and the Norman might of de Layne held the area in an uneasy state of truce.

De Layne's greatest fear was for his beautiful daughter Clare who, since the death of his wife, had provided the only splash of feminine brightness in his dour world. A constant stream of suitors ebbed and flowed around the stout wooden bailey and its fortifications. Each new arrival disturbed the peace of Sir Leon's mind, each subsequent departure left him rejoicing in Clare's continued presence but increasingly perplexed as she rejected a sequence of worthy suitors.

The secret of Clare's apparent determination to remain a spinster lay in the clough below the tower wherein walked the spirit of the long dead minstrel. There, at a secret trysting place, she met frequently her true love Harold, the son of Lord Audley, her father's most bitter enemy. The friendship between the youngsters had blossomed into love, a love which seemed fated both by virtue of the intense enmity between their fathers and by her impending, politically necessary betrothal to Rupert Beeston, a powerful ally whose support would make possible a final, conclusive assault upon the Saxon stronghold at Heighley.

Distressed by the thoughts of the consequences for her lover of such a powerful alliance she whispered the story of the plot to Harold.

The betrothal feast was set for the eve of St. Martin's Day.

At the height of the festivities the Saxons struck using the haunted clough to approach the hall unseen. Harold seized Clare in accordance with their prearrangements and hastened with her to the security of their trysting place where he left her, swearing to return when Rupert had been killed and the Norman power broken.

Despite the advantage of surprise the Saxons failed in their initial onslaught and in struggling to re-group for a second assault lost Harold to a Norman axe. In the full fury of his grief Lord Audley charged at the head of his men and carried the tower by storm. Unable to find his daughter and fearing the worst, with the triumphant Saxons pounding at his door, Sir Leon ordered the bailey to be fired and perished in the flames.

Seeing the sudden flame through the naked, mist shrouded branches, Clare watched the smoke weave menacing shapes across the troubled autumn sky. The screams of Norman fugitives, the turmoil of pursuit and slaughter and the sudden silence of death caused Clare to cower beneath the sheltering bushes, fearful lest she be slain as a Norman before Harold returned.

Added to the terror of the conflict was the menace of the minstrel's myth which she and Harold had carefully nurtured to protect their secret. A raw day passed followed by a second, more bitter night which brought terror and deepening madness as wolves, maggot-pies, kites, ravens, crows, foxes and badgers tore savagely at the charred and bloody corpses. Eventually hunger and the madness of fear brought death to Clare as she shivered in the bitter, damp, frost-bearing air which came pouring down from the ice-crusted pools of the moor.

Her pathetically torn and broken corpse was found by a party of warriors and village men from Caureswelle who came, too late, to see if anything could be salved from the disaster.

1150 A.D.

THE SAXON GROWS MORE LIKE THE NORMAN

By the middle of the twelfth century the cultural divisions between Saxon and Norman were beginning to blur. Greater prosperity, the extending influence of the church and the increasing desire of the secular gentry to lay up treasure in heaven had begun to interact. One manifestation of this interaction was the employment of itinerant masons to add certain embellishments to the fabric of the church. Among their labours was the production of a magnificent tympanum depicting the 'Ascent of Alexander' worked in the warm reddish brown sandstone of the area. Carefully instructed by Walter de Kareswelle the masons fashioned a scene depicting Alexander borne triumphantly aloft by griffons. Walter lavished much money upon this project fetching in a particularly skilled master mason from Canterbury to provide a quality of execution and finish transcending the normal standards of the area. Secretly he saw himself as the figure being borne majestically heavenwards conveniently forgetting the unhappy fate of earlier aspiring aeronauts. More openly he took pride in the growth and prosperity of his village and

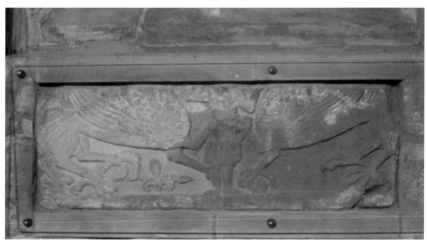

A fragment of the Tympanum.

saw the triumphant motif of the tympanum as a testimony to his achievement and a constant reminder of the cultural standards of his household.

The remains of the tympanum were finally removed from obscurity in 1978 and are now displayed at the east end of the north aisle of St. Peter's Church.

Above: a reconstruction of the whole stone

In 1155 A.D. Walter de Kareswelle, having obtained the consent of his Lord, gave to the Canons of the Priory at Stone the income deriving from his half share in the Church at Stoke. Goods and money which had been part of the wealth of the village since the Domesday Book went to secure for Walter a place in paradise. Yet the wealth of the village was sufficient to withstand the loss for, in the years since Domesday, fortune had favoured the industrious and Walter clearly felt the time propitious to take some steps to protect his soul in the hereafter.

The donation is recorded as follows:

'Anno Domini Anno I Henry II   Robert de Stadford gives greetings to all his friends, French and English. Know ye all, now and hereafter, that for the salvation of my soul and the soul of Alice my wife and the souls of my forebears, parents and friends, I have given and granted as an alms to the Church of Saint Mary . . . by its petition and free assent . . . Likewise I grant and confirm to the said Church half of the Church of Stoke which is of my feoff which Walter de Kareswelle with my consent gave to it as an alms, also the land of Erdewic which is of my feoff, which William Giffard, who held of me gave as an alms to the canons of Kinild in reparation for the harm which he inflicted on them, and to secure his absolution.'

The approval of Robert de Stadford to the donation was essential because he was over-lord of Walter de Kareswelle who held his lands from Robert who, in turn, held the shire from the King.   It was this chain of interdependence coupled with King John's love of hunting and his indefatigable Angevin energy which brought the King to Kareswelle during hunting expeditions with which he lightened the burdens of his royal progress through England

.The arrival of the monarch must always have constituted a strain upon the de Kareswelle purse for such visiting was intended to be one way in which a medieval monarch could impoverish and so control potential foes. It seems possible that John had a special affection for the area. The forest stretching north from Cannock Chase offered good hunting. The area contained within the Potteries Basin was identified as a New Forest during this period. Most particularly however did John seem to find pleasure among the monks of Croxden for it was here that his heart was buried when this most misjudged of English monarchs breathed his last.

To commemorate his visits to Kareswelle later owners of the Castle commissioned a carved overmantel for the castle banqueting hall which depicts the King in pursuit of a common but dangerous foe, the wild boar.

Such visitations brought a flurry of excitement to the hard, routine labour of the daily round and the seasonal rhythms of the land. It was adherence to the routines of the common task which laid the foundations for the wealth of the de Kaverswelles and in turn brought profit to the villagers. If the poor people provided the muscle power then Walter provided the necessary guidance. Common industry and resolute leadership had brought wealth and confidence to the village. The abstract evils of the forest were no longer feared. The hazards of the untracked waste beyond the known limits of the

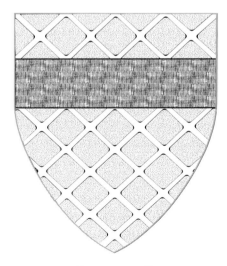

Caverswall

forest fringe were sufficiently respected to inhibit travel far beyond the demands of the daily round. Human foes in the shape of the leper, the footpad and the unglamorous outlaw were feared with good reason. More than one girl child disappeared in mysterious circumstances as she wandered off in search of a lost beast or a patch of sweeter black-berries. Lepers were fortunately few in the relatively isolated areas around Kareswelle but occasionally they did move through the parish soliciting alms, constantly shunned and hastily rejected, finding Christian charity only at the religious houses at Stone, Hulton, Dieulacresse and Croxden. No villager wished to meet such repulsive and deformed crea-tures in the depths of the forest where they wandered aimlessly till death brought a merciful release from the loathsome sickness.

The church had done something to shake loose the primitive shackles which had bound the minds of the villagers with superstitious dread but it had signally failed to destroy the belief of the villagers in witchcraft. All of the villagers used white magic frequently, most had recourse to black magic not infrequently and all lived in fear of its use by way of reprisal. The church sought to fight such practices with visions of a concrete heaven and a concrete hell illustrated crudely but graphically in the words of sermons preached and homilies proclaimed by the lord's priest or by some travelling friar who would rest and speak beneath the great oak tree in the village square.

At the close of the thirteenth century Walter's descendant William de Kaverswelle, feel-ing death's hand upon him took further steps along the pathway trodden by Walter. In 1291 the church of St. Peter at Kaverswelle was one of the four most affluent churches in the Deanery of Alton and Leek. Between them the four contributed no less than £29 in taxes, a substantial sum in 1291. In that year the income of St. Peter's was appropriated to the Priory at Stone. Two years later William transferred to that same body the power to appoint clergy. Thereafter the parish priest was no longer a vassal of the local lord but a man free from secular curbs and so able to bring to the life of the village a new, signifi-cant, social and political influence.

Slowly the church began to extend its hold upon the lives of the villagers of Kaverswelle.

The Chartulary of St. Thomas records the wording of one action by which William sought to ensure the heavenly fate of his own soul and the souls of his family.

'By gift of William de Kaverswelle advowson of the church Kaverswelle. By gift of William de Kaverswelle two messuages and two crofts in Kaverswelle.

I, William, Lord of Kaverswelle gave to Friar Nicholas, Prior of St. Thomas, two messuages with crofts in Kaverswelle. Witnesses Lord William Wyther, Lord Phillip of Draycote, Lord William Coyne. We, Robert of Kaverswelle, son of Robert, and William his brother, gave six shillings sterling to God and the Church of St. Thomas. Witnesses Lord Robert de Kaverswelle, Lord William Mererell, Walter of Hangate.

To all the faithful in Christ who shall see or hear, by this Charter Lord William de Kaverswelle gives greetings in the Lord. May you all know that I gave, granted . . . for myself and my heirs to Nicholas, Prior of St. Thomas the Martyr near to Stafford and to the convent of that same place and to their successors, as a free gift for the benefit of my soul and the souls of my predecessors, one piece of land in the territory of Kaverswelle below 'le Roug Croft', lying along the water called Bliye and extending as far as the croft which belonged to Norman the plumber, with the houses built on it, and with the advow-son of the Church of Kaverswelle, which church they and their successors may hold for their own use for ever, without claim or contradiction from me or mine. I have granted to these same and to theirs free passage beyond my new fishpond and an adequate road from the raised road which passes through the middle of the village of Kaverswelle be-tween my garden and the house which belonged to Thomas the steward beyond the said pond as far as the land of the said Prior and Convent, for going and returning with a two-horse or a four-horse carriage, and their ... of all kinds, and of carrying out all their other needs, whatever they may judge expedient by the same without any contradiction or hindrance from me or mine, for ever. This is to be held and possessed on my own and my heirs' behalf by them and their successors as a free gift with all rights for ever, and I, Lord William de Kaverswelle. Witnesses Thomas of Lee, John of Cocton, Hamund a cleric, and Abus of Drengeton and others.'

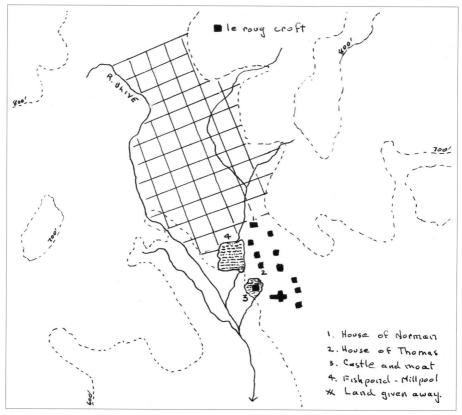

Sketch map to show the land between 'le Roug Croft' and 'the water called Bliye'
which was given away by William de Kaverswelle in 1291 A.D.

The map suggests how this gift might have related to the village of the day. The track from Stone approached from the south, crossed along 'The Dams' entered the village square and then swang north. The land in question was a substantial stretch of damp, pasture land lying between the modern road and the river. Land whose local name of Billy Nuns perpetuates a donation made almost 900 years earlier.

The local name of this area is 'Billy Nuns' and seems to commemorate William's gift, the name appearing to have survived, possibly in various forms, since the 13th century. The course of the 'Water called Bliye' is marked by the trees and bushes in the middle distance

The 'Water called Bliye'. This old postcard of the river flowing through 'Billy Nuns' shows the 'misfit' nature of the river and explains why the area was so quick to flood in wet weather. The land William gave away lies to the right.

WILLIAM de KAVERISWELLE HIGH SHERIFF OF STAFFORDSHIRE 1260AD

The office of sheriff is an ancient one. It derives from the office and duties of the shire reeve. The shire reeve was the king's representative in an area. His principal duties included the management or farming of the king's estates of which there were twenty-two in Staffordshire alone. In addition he was responsible for the collection of all fines imposed on offenders, the implementation and enforcement of royal instructions issued as writs and responsibility for holding the shire courts on behalf of the monarch. The legendary wickedness of the Sheriff of Nottingham in the tales of Robin Hood gives some idea of the extent to which people were prepared to believe that the sheriff could abuse his powers and profit by either sharp practice or downright dishonesty. Perhaps of more significance is the fact that over one third of the grievances noted in Magna Carta related to the abuse of the office of sheriff. Over the centuries Caverswall has been home to citizens who have held that office on eleven occasions. William de Kaveriswelle held office twice, in 1260 and 1268. Peter Caveswell held office in 1376.

A brief outline of William's work in the year 1260 will give some idea of what was involved and also serve to indicate a little of the working life of a leading county personality.

The process began and was rendered formal when the monarch pricked William's name among those recorded on a parchment. The intention was to provide a clear and unalterable record of those chosen by pricking a hole against the preferred name. William was then declared to be High Sheriff of Staffordshire and Shropshire. The practice of pairing counties was introduced in 1204 and lasted until 1344. It was reintroduced for one year only in 1377. The area allocated to William extended over at least two and a half thousand square miles all of which had to be covered on horseback. During his shrieval year William would have been expected to visit the king's estates, check on the work of the royal bailiffs, ensure that the building or repair of roads and bridges had been well and properly done, check that any work on the clearing of the forest cover was being done efficiently and in the correct locations and generally to ensure that the king's writ ran throughout the area. The money necessary to finance these ventures was taken from the king's revenues and had to be accounted for at the end of the year. (The word used to describe this blend of income and expenditure was 'farm'). Towards the end of 1260 a royal messenger would have arrived bearing a Writ of Summons from the king.

The writ read as follows:-

> Henry, King of the English
> To William de Kaveriswelle

> Greeting,

> See, as you love yourself and all that you have, that you be at the exchequer on the morrow of the Feast of Trinity and have with you whatever you owe of the old farm or of the new and specifically

the debts of the following.......... (Here would be listed details taken from the so-called Pipe Rolls or financial records, of those persons in some way indebted to the king) And you shall have with you in monies, tallies, writs and quittances or they shall be taken from your farm.

The arrival of this message would have prompted the final stage of the tax collection process with all concerned being notified of what was due and when it would be collected. At the same time a party of the sheriff's men together with two or three of the king's knights would travel the area to check that all the work for which the sheriff claimed reimbursement had been completed. This party would probably be joined by others wishing to travel to London in connection with financial matters and who were anxious for the sort of protection that William's party could provide.

The principal coin was the silver penny. As the coins were collected they were counted and tied securely in leather bags which in turn were stowed in wicker panniers called hanapers. An accurate record was kept by means of wooden tallies. Eventually a party comprising a cart carrying a box of silver pennies, the relevant tallies and provisions for the journey; a strong well-armed escort, Sir William himself, his clerk and any additional hangers on, would leave the castle. The journey had to be carefully timed. If William arrived one day late he could be fined one hundred shillings for each shire. If two days late the fine was doubled, if three days late his belongings could be confiscated and if four days late he risked prison and the loss of his estates.

On arrival William was required to report to the Doorkeeper of the Exchequer House. The Doorkeeper would then report the arrival of William de Kaveriswelle to the Barons of the Exchequer. They in turn would order heralds into the street to announce the arrival of William so that anyone who owed, or was owed, money was aware of his arrival. Meanwhile the chest of pennies would have been unloaded and taken into the Chamber of Receipt where they were counted. Forty-four shillings worth (a total of 528 pennies) would be taken at random from the total and sealed in a special leather purse called the pyx. These would be set aside for assay or checking to ensure that they contained a full pennyworth of silver for the practices of clipping and sweating were widely employed by dishonest persons. The whole would then be counted, divided into bags containing either £10 or £20 and finally stored in a massive oak chest lined with iron plates and secured by triple locks. William would receive a receipt in the form of a wooden tally recording how much he had paid.

In due course William would be called to present his accounts to the Barons of the Exchequer. The meeting took place around a table ten feet long and five wide covered by dark russet cloth divided into squares and columns by a series of chalk lines . The columns represented tens, hundreds and thousands. Among those present was a person holding the office of Calculator. As the accounts were discussed and agreed he would record the sums involved by placing counters in the appropriate column. Others present would include the King's knights who had toured Staffordshire to check on the quality of work done and the accuracy of any claims made. William would then be interviewed, perhaps over several days, before the accounts were finally agreed. If any deficits were found either in the accounts or in the quality of the silver pennies assayed William would be required to make up the deficit out of his own pocket.

When all was settled and agreed William was free to return to Kaveriswelle.

Beyond the village limits stretched the cool, green shade of the forest. A vast expanse which comprised a blend of towering oaks, fallen and rotting tree trunks, sprawling ferns and tangled undergrowth. The needs of the villagers and their beasts for kindling, fodder, bedding and building materials had tended to produce a cleared zone around each community in the area beyond the confines of the village proper so that a shrewd observer could sense the proximity of an inhabited area before he actually saw the dwellings simply by noting the absence of dead timber, fern and the like.

Such pockets of cleared ground and thinning forest surrounded the village at Kaverswelle, the halls at Westone, Asche and Holm and the scattered hovels at Werynton, Efes, Kerr, Ticca's Hyll, Cuccu's Hyll, Hecregard's Wick and Waesse-walle. The dwellers at each of these sites tended to be men of quick temper. To carve a living from the unyielding and never wholly neutral forest required tenacity and industry. To hold it required, at times, a strong arm and a ready blade.

Occasionally the law's delay offered a less immediate solution to a dispute. It has been suggested that

'the great bulk of the medieval plea rolls is a monumental testimonial to the litigiousness of the English people'.

It might equally well be argued that the same mass of records offers evidence of a desire to seek peaceful and honourable solutions in a less than law abiding age. The wealth of material which exists making reference to the de Kaverswelle family is sufficient to indicate the range of the family's interests and activities. The following examples are taken from 'The Staffordshire Historical Collections'

In 1227 the priest, Robert de Kaverswelle, attempted to extend his prebendary by misappropriating a messuage (dwelling) and 5 $\frac{1}{2}$ acres of land in Penkridge, his landgrab was thwarted and the 'said Robert is in misericordia'.

Lands were acquired by lease and by marriage, thus Sir William was able to extend his influence by marriage to Lady Chandos a wealthy widow.

In 1258 following Welsh disruptions of Shropshire and Staffordshire and a seeming attempt by Philip of Tamworth to recruit a mercenary army of Welshmen a number of powerful lords were required to act as sureties for the peace of the area, among them was William de Kaverswelle.

By 1278 William was in Bruges acting as one of a jury of peers hearing the case against Robert de Buckenhale who was held for the death of one Robert de Brichehulle; de Buckenhale was acquitted of the charge. Next William appears, or rather fails to appear, to answer a debt for £9 9s owed to the executors of a will.

Allegations of fish poaching, a serious offence when fish represented a vital source of fresh food, actions for neglect of land brought rather harshly against a widow, leases involving the transfer of lands, houses and mills and charges over failure to deliver lands gifted as portions of a dowry all appear between 1294 and 1310 A.D.

Another fascinating insight into the affairs of the family may be gleaned from exemptions granted to the people of Kaverswelle because their Lord attended in person when the King went to war. By so doing the 'common people' archers, men-at-arms and hobelars (serfs) were excused service and so could be left at home to work the land. From such records it is apparent that the Lord of the Manor of Kaverswelle served most readily when a call to arms was heard, ably supported by a number of his relatives. In this way the honour of Kaverswelle was represented at Sluys, Calais and Crecy, in Scotland with Hugh le Despenser in 1337, in Germany in 1339/40 again with le Despenser, under Bartholomew de Burghersh in 1342 and at Melun in France in 1346. In consequence of the family service at Melun Thomas de Kaverswelle was granted a free pardon for all *'homicides, felonies, robberies',* a fairly frequent royal gesture but one offers an interesting gloss on the seamier side of an apparently noble family for this same Thomas appears frequently in law suits as the guilty party.

Perhaps the exemption dated 1347 summarises everything.

'Writ to the Treasurer and Barons of the Exchequer to supersede all demands on William de Kaverswelle for men-at-arms, or hobelars, or archers on account of his lands and tenements, the said William having served personally in the expedition.

Dated 19th December.' [6]

The expedition was that led by Edward III which saw the followers of the King gain much plunder, financial reward through the payment of ransoms and acquire much military glory at Calais and Crecy.

In 1272 Adam de Werynton sued James de Aldthelegh for the return of two parts of a burgage (a holding of land for which rent was paid) and four acres of land, land which had been forfeit by Adam for his part in supporting the forces which opposed Edward I at Evesham in 1265. Others preferred to settle their disputes by violence, in 1346 Adam de Hall and his son Bertred were sued for *'beating, wounding, ill treating and robbing'* one John Burgylon.

During this troubled period in the history of Kaverswelle more than one corpse was found at some isolated spot within the parish.

Life was hard, savage and turbulent. Families like the Kaverswelles, Weryntons, Buchenhales, de Halles and the Holms fought to expand their communities, increase their wealth and protect their holdings. For such families, supported by their kindred, tenants and serfs, skirmishes between retainers over the rights of grazing or warren, the theft of the odd load of hay, timber or peats or the impounding of a stray beast were part of a way of life. For lesser mortals such behaviour; the quick, too heavy blow struck in anger or a desperate act of theft meant at best a discreet disappearance into the forest and at worst a fine, physical punishment or mutilation.

The villages were very much responses to the physical environment. The sun mattered most. At Kaverswelle the village snuggled beneath a south facing slope of sandstone which seemed to shelter the dwellings from the bitter winds of winter and to hold the warmth of the sun in summer. Adderley had developed upon a long and gentle south facing slope rising from a narrow, damp valley and the undulating forest floor to the south- west. In Buckenhale the village had developed around the banks of a stream in a south facing valley. Here, although arable land was somewhat restricted, the de Buckenhales lived rejoicing in the isolation and near inaccessibility of their home.

At Asche the de Halles had adopted a flat south-westerly shoulder of land just below the crest of a long sloping climb towards the bleak, damp moorlands of the 'wet-lea'.

Westone, the home of the Cuney family lay on the southern side of another mass of sandstone and had the advantage of almost constant exposure to the sun since the land fell away on all sides from northeast to north- west. The site was warm but exposed and this may well explain why the village never really flourished. At Waesse-wall the home of the Weryntons faced south, looking out over the broad expanse of the forested valley beyond. Yet the site was never a happy one for it was set too high, too near the edge of the moorland and was too frequently a prey to cold winds and winter frosts.

Only Holm failed to conform to the general pattern. Latecomers among the Norsemen had been able to select sites with a sunny exposure but the settler at Holm chose instead a tongue of dry sandstone rock jutting out into the damp and marshy valley floor. Facing north-east and exposed to north-westerly winds the site must have been, despite the cloak of forest which enwrapped it, bleak, damp and cold.

Water was the second key factor in the location of the settlements in the area. The passage of hundreds of years and the consequences of zealous husbandry and drainage, the removal of the forest cover and the increasing demands made upon the water re-source have all served to alter the drainage pattern and to lower the water-table which in turn destroyed the original water source for each site. Even so, by studying the contour pattern of the locality it is possible to identify the site of a probable water source so assisting in the tentative location of the early settlement.

The forest provided timber for building, kindling, for domestic use and game for the pot. The fern clad floor, the tangled bushes and the seasonal fruits offered bedding, food and a rhythmic variation to the diet of man and beast alike. The river banks and marshy areas provided rushes for plaiting, thatching and floor cover.

The key factor in the settlement pattern appears however to have been the existence of an extensive area of relatively level land which was well drained and covered by a light, readily tilled soil. It was in this respect that the sites at Westone and Kaverswelle scored. By the close of the thirteenth century those two sites in particular had begun to prosper at a level above that of their neighbours and Kaverswelle was home for the most prosper-ous group of dwellers in the area.

Despite extensive overbuilding the basic features of the sites can still be discerned in the contemporary landscape. The settlement at Asche lay upon and between the sites currently occupied by the Ash Bank Hotel and the Ash Hall. The Werynton's home lay in the vicinity of the area now occupied by the library, schools and church. Holm stood slightly to the northwest of the present village.

Kaverswelle was very much as is the present village. It had a choice of three streams one springing from the locality of the present Yard Farm, one from the vicinity of St. Filumena's School and the other flowing from the vicinity of Fair View. The valley of the Blithe and the expanse of flat land beyond the present church combined with the cherished south-erly exposure to produce a most favoured site.

The presence of entrances to farm yards opening directly onto a major road in the heart of a village is often proof that the associated farm is of considerable age; often medieval in origin. This farm entrance lies opposite St. Filumena's church and must have been closely associated with the castle. Was it the site of the Lord's demesne?

1293 A.D.

A MARVEL WHEN IT'S DONE

High summer in Kaverswelle. Beneath the cool umbrella of the lofty oaks the green dampness seemed to throb with insect life. The moist air was heavy, laden with the humid, rotting stink of leaf mould and the pungent reek of the undergrowth. Scattered along the forest fringes stood the substantial bee skeps of the villagers, their inhabitants adding to the throbbing, humming mass of insect life which hovered, moved and twisted across the pollen heavy, nectar bearing blooms of the undergrowth.

The industry of the bee was a byword among the villagers who never tired of quoting *'He that hath sheep, swine and bees, sleep he, wake he, he may thrive'.* Honey was highly prized by the villagers who used it extensively for sweetening or bore it to the still room to aid the processes of fermentation using it as an essential ingredient in mead and metheglin. Beeswax served as the base for candles or, when mixed with violets, was used as a salve.

Trampling among the waist-high ferns the long, flat-sided, coarse-boned, lop-eared, agile, omnivorous, evil-tempered swine rooted, snuffled and chopped at any remotely edible morsels churned from the moist earth by their questing snouts. Swine, like bees, were highly valued as a source of easy wealth. *'A swine doth sooner than a cowe bring an ox unto the plough'.* The young swine herds lolled in the shade of the oak trees waving handfuls of fern fronds to keep off the savagely biting clegs.

Beyond the shelter of the forest trees the heat was intense. In the fallow portion of the great field the stunted village cattle grazed steadily swishing their tails against the flies

Ancient ridge and furrow, the legacy of the great open field which once fed the village

whose attentions had brought bloody streaks to the cheeks and forearms of the herd boys. A few beasts had clustered in the scant shade offered by the church wall against which stood a crude, scratch sundial with a wooden gnomon. The herd boys glanced constantly towards it as the shadow crept slowly towards the third scratch.

Among the strips bearing the stubble of barley and oat crops the men of the village toiled, slowly manoeuvring the cumbersome wooden ploughs drawn, in some instances, by ponderous oxen in others, by their wives. Beast and woman alike strained against sweat stained harness as they hauled the ploughs through resistant earth. Sweat oozed from every pore, the body stink hanging heavy in the still air. Tickling, biting flies sought eyes, nostrils or lips before drowning to a choking, cloying death in a gobbet of sputum ejected from a fly choked throat.

Those strips devoted to the year's wheat crop lay motionless, the scrawny, golden stalks interspersed with rank weeds. The lines of the field were broken only by the fencing, earth dykes and lines of stones used to delineate the holdings of individual villagers.

To the west of the village the sun's rays danced with a sullen sheen upon the glassy surface of the millpond. The motionless waters seemed part of the stone faced earthwork

The face of the dam as it was in 1960 showing the ancient hedgerow

of the new dam which held them in check. Long had the villagers toiled, hauling earth and stones to close the mouth of the broad valley so that a great reservoir of water to serve both mill and castle moat could be created.

Along the north side of the rush-lined pond straggled the thatched hovels of the villagers, their tiny vegetable plots running down to the water's edge. Only the clacking mill-wheel and the steady splash of water broke the heavy silence.

Dam, stone church, castle, village, fields and forest all bore evidence of the lordship of William de Kaverswelle, twice Sheriff of the County of Stafford and a man to be reckoned with. A distant descendant of Ernulf the Norman, a loyal subject of Edward I, a shrewd businessman and a hard taskmaster.

The eight hundred year old hedgerow which bordered 'The Dams' in 1960

The meadow beyond the dam.
This picture gives some idea of how the land sloped naturally to create an area of open, flat land which would be flooded to create the great medieval pond.

THE de KAVERSWELLE FAMILY

Records suggest that the leading family in the village bore the name of de Kaverswelle, spelt in various ways, from before 1100 AD to almost, or possibly just after, 1400. The first recorded member of the family to bear the name seems to have been Henry de Caureswelle who flourished around 1100 and may well have been a direct descendant, probably the son, of Ernulf de Hesdin.

In 1155 Walter de Kaverswelle gave half his share of the income of the church at Stoke as an alms to the church of St. Mary. The gift was made to the Canons of the Priory at Stone.

Walter de Kareswelle not only installed the tympanum which once graced the , now lost, west door but made various donations to churches elsewhere. In part these gifts were intended to secure for himself a place in heaven, in part they were to help his lord, Robert of Stafford make reparation for harm done by one of his followers, William Giffard.

Walter is mentioned in records for 1155 and again in 1166. He had a son, Robert, whose own sons were William and Thomas. Thomas married a daughter of the Chetelton family. He figures in the Assize Roll for 1190 where he is recorded as Thomas de Kersewell and is one of the knights deputed to elect XII people in order that a large session might be held. A 'large session' was a gathering convened to settle disputes over land. In this case the argument was between Osbert of Fotesbroc and Radulph de Dulverne.

Thomas appears to have had a son, Robert, who, in 1227 was appointed the next prebendary by Elias of Bristol, Dean of Penkridge and appears upon Caverswall's list of incumbents against the year 1230. The entry R.... persona de Kaveriswelle is interesting because it identifies the origin of the word parson. A persona was the person who could sue or be sued, on behalf of the parish. Overtime the word was degraded to parson.

Walter also appears to have had a daughter, Philomena, since an entry in the Assize Roll refers to Philomena, daughter and heiress of Caverswall

The most influential member of the family was William de Kaverswelle. The inscription on his tomb translates freely as "William of Caverswall here lye I, That built the castle and pooles hereby." His sepulchral slab now much worn lies in the church on the north side of the sanctuary. His wife was named Joan, his daughter Eleanor. In 1291 William de Kaverswelle gave the church near to Stafford an area of land lying between the village, Roughcote and the River Blithe. The popular name of this area, Billy Nuns, reflects that gift. William served both as High Sheriff and as a judge. As High Sheriff his duties included the maintenance of the King's Peace, the punishment of offenders and the collection of the crown's revenues. In 1262 William was one of the sureties, a guarantor of the public peace, appointed after a multitude of Welshmen, disturbed the peace in Warwickshire and Staffordshire.

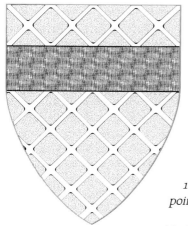

From 1290 onwards William's son Richard, was prominent in public life and served as one of the first representatives from Staffordshire in Parliament.

A grandson of William, also named Richard, held similar office in 1341. This Richard seems to have been born about 1285, His mother was Scholastica, a daughter of Robert de Hasting. Richard was married in 1309 to Joan the heiress of Sir William de Ercall. He was knighted in 1315 and died in 1324, His preferred home appears to have been High Ercall in Shropshire.

Legal records for 1310 reveal the existence of one, Henry de Kaverswelle. He had stood as member of the court of justice in 1298 and appears again, this time as witness in 1310. Similar evidence points to the existence of a Roger de Kaverswelle in 1319.

At roughly the same period Roger the son of Robert de Kaverswelle and Thomas his son had to pay a fine, effectively they lost bail money, when Agnes the widow of Nicholas de Dulverne failed to appear in court and so lost her plea by default. Agnes had appealed to the County Court after Richard Roper of Abbots Bromley and three others beheaded her husband.

In 1346 Thomas de Kaverswelle was granted a free pardon for all homicides, felonies and robberies because of the service done by his family in the wars with France. A year later William de Kaverswelle was excused the demands of the war levy because he chose to serve in person, with the king, during the French wars. He was probably motivated less by high minded patriotism than by a desire to partake of the rich spoils such campaigns offered.

The last member of the family was Sir Peter de Careswelle who died sometime after 1398. Sir Peter married Mary of Ercall in 1359, they had no children. In 1376 he served as High Sheriff and in 1380 entered Parliament, he served again in 1382 and 1384. At a slightly later date a priest with the name John Careswelle was sued by the Bishop of Coventry and Lichfield to render account of his time as receiver of the Bishop's money. He failed to appear and a warrant was issued for his arrest.

THE De KAVERSWELLE FAMILY TREE

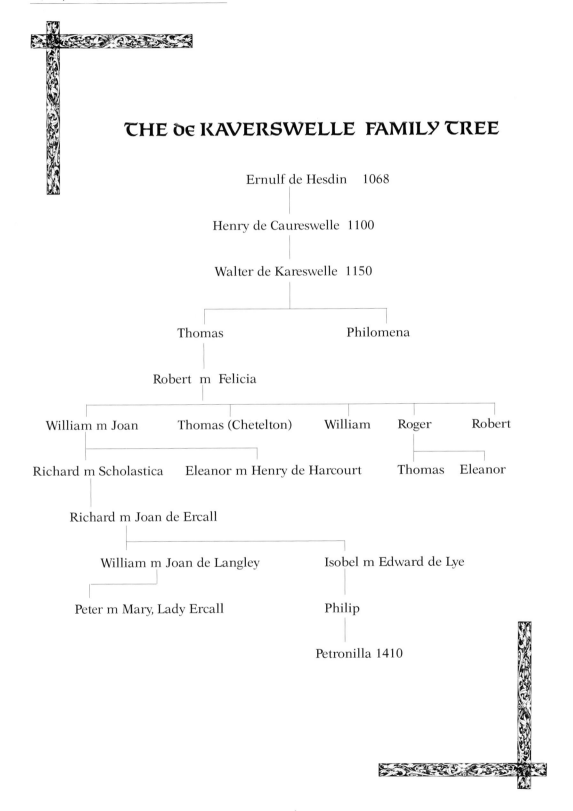

Ernulf de Hesdin   1068

Henry de Caureswelle 1100

Walter de Kareswelle 1150

Thomas   Philomena

Robert m Felicia

William m Joan   Thomas (Chetelton)   William   Roger   Robert

Richard m Scholastica   Eleanor m Henry de Harcourt   Thomas   Eleanor

Richard m Joan de Ercall

William m Joan de Langley   Isobel m Edward de Lye

Peter m Mary, Lady Ercall   Philip

Petronilla 1410

William had dominated the village for so long that he seemed as much a part of it as the forest which cloaked the surrounding countryside. As arrogant and high-handedly acquisitive as his monarch, William had fought and won both profit and renown under the royal banner in France and Scotland. Few men could stand against him in his ire for the majesty of his wrath and the ready strength of his arm were well known. It was the profit from his shrewd dealings with the abbots of the great Cistercian sheep ranches at Croxden and Dieulacresse that had aided the prosperity of his village. It was much of that money which had financed the red stone church, the great dam and the crenellated manor house which well merited its local title of 'castle'.

William's wisdom and the knowledge gleaned from his travels had led to the introduction of new practices like the dunging of the land, careful draining in wetter areas, the rigorous weeding of growing crops and the more varied use of crop rotations. Such practices had served to bring profit to his tenants and higher crop yields to his fields. Some of those tenants it was true, bore physical evidence of the ferocity with which William enforced the forest laws. Others feared his harsh angry voice and burning eye but all conceded that the village had prospered and that individuals had been treated fairly during William's rule. Indeed they acknowledged that it was his bullying and driving which had forced them into extending their own holdings by clearing patches of forest for their own use. The process of assarting was well advanced in Kaverswelle, all but the most indolent had some worthwhile stake in a plot on the forest edge and could show profit therefrom.

William was accounted a hard man, a stern taskmaster, a demanding but just lord. Shrewd and far sighted for the age, he was feared in the Shire, respected in his village and dying in his chamber. With surprising suddenness his last great fight was over. The heavy jaw slackened, the furrowed brow relaxed, the scarred hands unclenched and the deep set eyes lost their soul. As a dribble of saliva began to course through the untrimmed stubble of the jaw, tense no more, William de Fenton began to recite the ritual prayers at time of death commending William's soul to Mary's bosom as he gently closed the staring eyes.

The villagers buried their lord at the foot of the chancel steps, marking the grave with a large, grey marble slab inlaid with brass upon whose face were incised a long cross fleur and two shields surrounded by a marginal and incised inscription which at once paid tribute to their lord's achievements and bespoke their appreciation of his life:

'Hic jacet Wills. de Kaverswelle miles castri structor: eram: domibus forsis: que cemento: virus: dans operam: nunc clandor in hoc momento:'

which, being translated, proclaims:

'Here lies William of Caverswall who built the Castle, residences and dams in Stone and that having given work to the living is now enclosed in this monument.'

The local stonemasons who had better reason than most to love William resolved to produce, as a love boon, corbels in the shape of heads worked in stone. These were added to other older ones fashioned by their predecessors. In one they sought to capture the power and strength of their lord and paymaster. Those heads now peer truculently from the walls of the south aisle.

Even at this distance in time the ravages of the passing years have failed to destroy the power in the faces. In the strongest face every residual line bespeaks the power and tenacity of the man who made the village. The sepulchral slab may still be seen set in the floor of the north side of the sanctuary.

With the death of William and Richard de Kaverswelle still under age, the custodianship of the Castle passed briefly to Theobald de Verdun and shortly afterwards was assumed by the King's officers. By 1295 Richard was not only of age, but by virtue of his

lineage, had been summoned to London as one of Staffordshire's two county representatives to that father of the modern legislature, the Model Parliament of 1295. The thought that one of England's first Members of Parliament dwelt in Caverswall and rode out past the church, through Black Birch Hollow and thence to Forsbrook, Tutbury and London is an exciting one.

Is this William de Keverswelle?

The East Window and Altar of St. Peter's church. The sepulchral slab which marks the last resting place of William de Keverswelle lies to the left of the picture beneath the radiator and the candlestand.

1320 A.D.

MERRIE KAVERSWELLE

John de Smallys counted himself well blessed to have been awarded the living of Kaverswelle. His holding was a substantial and prosperous one. To the north his parish was bounded by the line of the high ground running eastwards from Wetlea More. The More yielded peats which were a precious source of fuel to the people of his parish and which would burn on his own hearth as part of the village tithe. Below the More the villagers of Ayssch were also of his flock as were the dour, Odin worshippers of Holm and the dwellers in the moated farmhouse at Simfield. To the west his influence extended into the hovels at Adderleye nestling in lands once subject to the stringent forest laws and still thought of as the New Forest. To the south the ague ridden, damp stained hovels at the marshy spot called Meer lay below the heathy ridge of sandstone which rose against the southern sky in the great heave of a forest clad shoulder and sprawled away eastwards. To the east the parish boundary wove a somewhat uncertain way northwards from the marshy valley of the River Blithe through the low, rolling tree clad hills towards Dulverne.

The heart of the parish was the village of Kaverswelle where the work of William still lived. The substantial, fortified manor house well merited the title of 'castle'. The stone built church stood proudly at one end of the village square dominating the village to the west and overshadowing the great field to the south. The field was extensive and for the most part well-tended. The gleaming mill pond, its busy mill and the straggle of thatched hovels along the high street with their neatly worked and heavily stocked domestic garden plots all spoke of honest endeavour and steady toil.

From the village clearly defined pathways ran into the surrounding forest. The trail to Dulverne climbed sharply up the steep slope and served as a road for beasts trailing to and from the high meadow or 'heanley' where good summer grazing was to be found. Constant use had already served to etch the path deeply into the soft sandstone rock so earning it the local name of the 'holh' or hollow. The road to Fotesbroc was the major roadway of the village and snaked away past the great field before climbing up into the wooded hill-slopes to the east. Between the trail, the church and the river sprawled the strips of the village field. Already the field showed the characteristic undulations typical of land which had been under cultivation for over 700 years. The only other pathway in the village wriggled between the dwellings which straggled along the edges of the mill pond turned into the square and left it along the top of the dam which linked the higher ground upon which the village stood to the tongue of higher ground to the west. This pathway proved to be something of a hazard on dark nights and even, for the unwary, in broad daylight, so a hedgerow had been encouraged partly as a windbreak, partly by neglect and partly as a guide to travellers. The depth and extent of the huge pond was such that death by drowning was a real threat to people who had no true skill in swimming.

The line of these early pathways can still be traced in the lines of the modern road system. The undulations in the great field are still visible in front of 'Heath View' whilst the site of the mill pond now contains the in-filled area of the recreation ground and the site of the new village hall. The hedgerow which ran along the northern side of the dam, whose presence is still recorded in the name of 'The Dams' was dated, in 1963, to approximately 1250 A.D. containing as it did eight major woody stemmed species. It was destroyed in 1975.

The present roads enter the square offset against each other possibly for purposes of defence, possibly for protection against the wind. Probably however the true reason is to be found in a combination of the lie of the land, the location of the dam and the hapazard mode of building current until modern times. There is little truth in the story that the serpentine form of the high street reflects a form of defensive design. It wanders in an attractive manner simply because people walking about their own business, or cows ambling to be milked do not walk in a straight line, indeed cannot do so. However that is one of those delightful pieces of 'history' which get remembered and so it should be, for it helps to draw attention to the elegance of this central village thoroughfare.

The upper end of the old Saxon 'holh' or 'hollow way' up onto the high meadows or 'hean leah' which were used for grazing.

EASTER 1325 A.D.

FOUR GOOD LEGS TO MY FATHER'S CHAIR

In five years John de Smallys had learnt much about his flock and not the least part of that knowledge was the fact that they had no love of theological debate. In consequence his sermons tended to be brief, relevant, simple in tone, realistic in content, well spiced with rural imagery and, on occasion, brutally direct. By such homilies and his own unswerving example he sought to do God's work and to demonstrate rather than voice, God's message. However, his Bishop had sent word that his priests should strive to raise the levels of theological awareness among their flocks and so John was laboriously struggling to reduce to simple and comprehensible terms his concept of the soul. The task was not an easy one and not infrequently his mind sought inspiration from his predecessors finding wry comfort in the fact that William de Fenton could probably have escaped with a few vague, poorly latinised sentences larded with Anglo-Norman about the soul flying to Mary's bosom and no embarrassing questions about its nature. As his mind shaped a sentence he sat conning it and let his mind roam over the possible reactions of Giles the Smith, Bartholomew Brassyngton, Allan Slynne, William Radcliffe and the rest of his flock. Sadly he shook his head knowing that his task was nearly impossible for he knew beyond doubt that many of his carefully chosen words would fall on rocky ground.

Pensively he rehearsed his sermon:

'As the Feast of the Resurrection draws near I wish you to consider your soul, that gift of the Lord your God which raises you above the beasts of the field and brings vital, human life to that mortal clay we call the body.

As you use or misuse your body so you mould and shape your soul as Giles the Smith moulds hot iron. The soul takes its life and shape from the body it inhabits, in that sense the soul is the body. The things which the body does, experiences, enjoys and endures are given meaning through the senses. (He paused, surely that would trouble all of them?) The meaning that the senses give to experience is shaped by the mind, it is the intelligence that makes pleasure or pain a part of the soul. Because Man is an intelligent creature he can use his brain to shape his soul by conquering his animal passions with reason.

It is this power of man to shape his soul, to save his soul or to cast his soul into the eternal torments of hell that raises man above the beasts of the field and the forest. When a beast does wrong it corrupts its soul. When your cow, Allan Slynne, strays and devours your neighbour's cabbages it steals, it sins, it destroys a part of its soul until it has no hope of salvation, no prospect of repentance. (Not only was the logic unfair but who could fault a starving cow for such a theft if the cowherd dozed?) This evening Master Slynne when you reach the ale-house door you will be able to make a choice. You may pass by and help to save your soul by using intelligence to conquer bodily passions. You may enter for refreshment and leave when refreshed to walk steadily homeward having met and conquered temptation.

You may enter for refreshment and remain for debauchery and so help yourself to lose your soul as you stagger home, splay-legged like the gleeman's bitch. You may choose, your starving, straying beast may not. (Perchance that was a little severe but Master Slynne's name was fast becoming a by-word in the village and a timely check might save him)

Are you not all better than your beasts? Why then by your actions do you choose to discard that which raises you above them?

Think my people, the beast lacks a soul because it has no choice. You have a choice, you may choose! Will you not choose Christ and the Blessed Virgin? By your thoughts, by your actions, by your prayers you may save your souls and so you should for when the body dies the soul remains in life.

When death sets free your soul to receive its rewards or punishments what merits and demerits will be marked against it in the book of your life?

Think, each one of you, of what will happen when your body is conveyed to its last resting place and your soul flies heavenward to receive its reward. Some of you will encounter obstacles in your path, some of you will find obstacles so vast because you have corrupted your souls that, though those souls are set free of the body that destroyed them, they will sink straight to hell.

For some, less tainted with life's sins that last swift flight to happiness may be delayed until their debt of sin has been repaid. How long that delay will seem when weighed against the rich rewards to come.

For those whose earthly deeds have earned God's great rewards the soul's flight will be swift and sure to that last great happiness which is the true man's end.

The soul so sped finds that its greatest gift is its own true happiness in God. That wondrous prize is God's great reward for life's torments and life's terrors here on Earth. Life's true happiness is found only beyond the grave in that lasting peace which we must earn through earthly, charitable deeds. That peace we must seek through the resurrection of our Lord by strict obedience to His word and by a stern observance of His laws.

Take God into your hearts, into your lives, into your works in order that you may choose aright and save your immortal souls from the searing fires of hell.'

In his mind's eye he could see the crowded church, the baudy tabards of his flock's 'Sabbath best', he could smell the odour of bodies, hear the rustle of feet in the rushes on the floor and feel the warmth in the spring sun slanting through the windows. Deliberately he gauged the probable impact of his words upon the minds behind those faces. It was heavy going at the start but finished with more power and fire than it began. He could almost feel a surge of pleasure as he thought of himself delivering the latter portion of the sermon, perhaps the Bishop had a point after all.

If his flock seldom listened to and but rarely wholly understood the meat of his sermons then perhaps it was the quality of his own performance, the fire of his delivery that mattered. Ah well, that he could control and would !

1327 A.D.

IF GOLD RUST...

The Subsidy Roll for 1327 offers a guide to the names and relative wealth of those who owned property in the parish in that year. The Roll records the names of those parishioners who were sufficiently wealthy to be required to pay a subsidy or property tax upon land and goods in order to provide financial sinews for the Scottish wars of King Edward III.

The Roll reads as follows:

CARESWELL

	s	d	
De Joh 'e de Chetewynd	iij	vj	
Ric'o fil Willi		xviij	(Perhaps Richard son of William de Careswell)
Thoma Roberd		xij	(Perhaps Thomas Roberts)
Will'o filio Coci		xiiij	(Perhaps William Cocis son of Wm. Cooks son)
Henr' Sichet		xij	
Will'o Coynee	iij		(William of Coyney)
Rog'o filio Galfridi		viij	
Rob'to de le Herdinges		xvj	(Robert of Hardiwick?)
Ric'o de Aderleye	ij	vj	(Richard of Adderley)
Ranulph' filio Make	ij		(Ranulph son of Make)
Henr' de Wodewalle		xiij	(Henry of Washerwall)
Will'o de Ayssch	ij		(William of Ash)
Joh'e de Ayssch	ij	vj	(John of Ash, Wills brother?)
Joh'e de Tuttesovere	ij		(John of Tittensor?)
Rad'o Robert		xviij	
Rob'to de Holm		vj	(Robert of Hulme)
Ranulph de Wolfdale	ij		(Ranulph of Wolfdale)
Rog'o de Walton		xij	(Roger of Walton)
Henr' filio Thom	iij		(Henry, son of Thomas Roberts?)
Petro filio Rog I	xij		(Peter son of Roger of Walton)
Will'o Elot			
Will'o filio Willi	ij		(William son of William, but which one?)
Rob'to filio Henrid	ij		(Robert son of Henry?)

	Summa	<u>xis viijd</u>	pb [7]

In 1327 Parliament deposed Edward II who was imprisoned in Berkeley Castle and subsequently murdered. Was De Joh'e de Chetwynde steward for Richard or perhaps William of Careswell, who was otherwise engaged?

Among those recorded can be detected men possessing names rooted deep in the Saxon past of the parish. Cuccu who gave his name to Cuccu's Hyll has become Coci whose son William stands as progenitor of the modern Cooks and Cooksons. The names borne by Richard of Aderleye, Rob'to de Holm and the two men of Ayssch give some indication of the extent of the parish in addition to confirming the antiquity of those families which still bear the surnames of Hulme, Adderley and Ash. The references to Walton and Tittensor, if so it be, suggest a past and perhaps continuing involvement with the Priory at Stone whilst relics like 'Galfridi' and 'Make' are reminders of the Danish immigrants who settled at Hulme and Normacot just as the christian names of Henry, Roger, Ranulph and William bespeak the French or Norman influence. The presence of Henr' de Wodewalle and the absence of the de Werynton family may indicate that the Werynton line had come to an end or may, just possibly, indicate a closer identification with the Washerwall area.

The relatively high level of the subsidy paid by Will'o Coynee suggests that the manor house at Weston was prospering and confirms that the community had already acquired the suffix of 'coyney'.

The Coyney Family

The founder of the Coyney family, given its duration it is tempting to call it a dynasty, appears to have been Robert Coyne to whose son, Walter, passed the manor of Weston - sub - Kevremont (since called Weston Coyney) at a date before 1240.

Robert had two sons, Walter to whom passed the manor of Weston Coyney and Robert described as 'of Hulme'. The Hulme branch died out after 1345.

In 1292 John Coyne received Wetley Moor as part of his wedding settlement when he married Margaret Erdinton.

One of the earlier references to the Coyney family occurs in the Subsidy (tax) Roll for 1327. There Will'o Coynee was worth three shillings and was the second wealthiest man in the area.

In 1343 Sibilla the wife of Robert Coyne received back gifts of land made prior to the death of her husband Robert.

Robert Coyne of Weston Coyne sold the manor of Nethercroft in Warwickshire to Sir Richard Wigston, knight, in 1539.

Thomas Coyney who was baptised at Caverswall in 1615 had three daughters Ellen, Mary and Jane.

In 1686 the Coyney family had a crest and were recorded in Plot's History of Staffordshire as 'esquire'. This suggests that the head of the family was probably a justice of the peace.

In 1736 Ellen Coyney was fined £200 as a nonjuror and her husband William Gower was fined £211 17s

6d. A nonjuror was one who refused to swear an oath of allegiance to William and Mary and the Protestant succession.

There is a memorial to Edward Coyney dated 1772, in the nave of St. Peter's Church.

In 1790 Walter William Hill assumed the arms and name of Coyney.
All of the evidence suggests that the family were prosperous farmers.

The street named The Moat suggests that the first Coyneys lived in a manor house surrounded by a moat. They may well have taken the name"Cuney' from the corruption of the early name for the village - Weston -sub-Kevremont in Weston Cuney.

The change in the spelling from Coyne to Coyney seems to have taken place between 1540 and 1557 but the village name was being spelt Coyney as early as 1473.

Later generations lived in Weston Coyney Hall which was situated where the present Village Hall stands.

In 1811 a Mr. Walter Hill Coyney acted for the order of nuns who leased the castle. He may even have purchased it himself before leasing it to the nuns.

Elizabeth Coyney, daughter of William was abbess of a convent at York in 1820.

In 1825, the same Walter Hill Coyney was one of the founders of what was to become the present St. Peter's Church of England Primary School.

Walter Hill was an Anglican who met and married a wealthy Catholic orphan, a Miss Mary Catherine Coyney the family taking the name of Hill Coyney. The couple agreed that any daughters of their union should be brought up as Catholics whilst any sons should follow their father's faith.

In 1851 the family was represented by Charles Coyney who is reported as being resident in Weston-Coyney Hall in White's Directory.

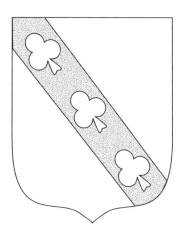

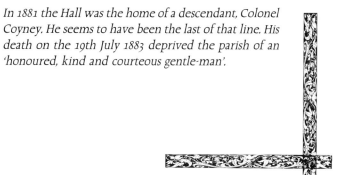

In 1881 the Hall was the home of a descendant, Colonel Coyney. He seems to have been the last of that line. His death on the 19th July 1883 deprived the parish of an 'honoured, kind and courteous gentle-man'.

Proud of his parish John de Smallys was not one to let standards slip, his watchword was *'if gold rust what shall iron do?'* And with all his heart he strove to keep rust from his flock. His eye was keen, his tongue sharp and his energy unflagging; like Chaucer's priest he was:

'A holy minded man of good renown
There was, and poor, the Parson to the town
He did not set his benefice to hire
And leave his sheep encumbered in the mire
Or run to London to earn easy bread
By singing masses for the wealthy dead
Or find some brotherhood and get enrolled
He stayed at home and watched over his fold.' [8]

By 14th century standards the prosperity of his flock was not insubstantial. The neat village and the generally well tended fields spoke eloquently of industry and wealth. Around the church a number of carefully worked sepulchral slabs gracing stone tombs proclaimed both wealth and the time necessary for such work. During John's incumbency improvements to the fabric of the church were mooted and implemented. With an increasing congregation and a generous Lord some extension of the church seemed both necessary and possible, debate continued until the decision to add a north aisle to the nave was taken.

John de Smallys must have been the prime mover in this work for his Lord, Sir William descendant of Sir Richard de Careswelle spent much of his time abroad fighting at Sluys in 1340, Crecy in 1346 and at Calais in 1347. Whilst the precise dating of the extension incorporating the provision of the north aisle does not appear to be possible it is just probable that it may have been undertaken as some form of thank-offering to God for the safe return of Sir William from the French Wars.

The north aisle, of course, remains whilst several of the sepulchral slabs may still be viewed built into the fabric of the church particularly above and inside the door and in the floor of the aisle. Etched deep into the external walls of the north aisle may be seen the marks of those masons who extended the building.

Such wealth, prosperity and activity meant extended involvements and such involvements inevitably meant lawsuits of the type which, in 1346, saw Henry de Careswelle suing Prior John for a toft at Forebridge in Stafford. Even so the return of Sir William and his fighting men rich with the pride of victory at Crecy and Calais and bearing

Stonemason's marks visible on the wall of St. Peter's church.

plunder won during their marches and campaigns seemed to augur well for a village whose daily round seemed a little less onerous than heretofore. Yet among that plunder and in the travel stained clothing may have travelled the deadly fleas which were already wreaking havoc among the people of the Continent.

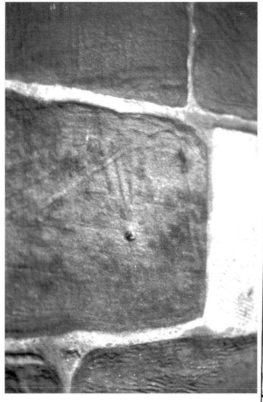

The last vestiges of a medieval, scratch sundial still visible on the wall near the vestry

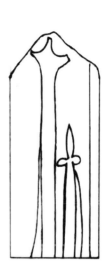

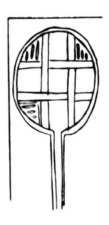

Right:
Some of the designs on medieval sepulchral slabs which have been built into the walls and flooring of the church.

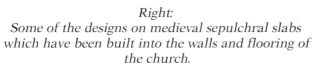

THE COYNEY FAMILY TREE

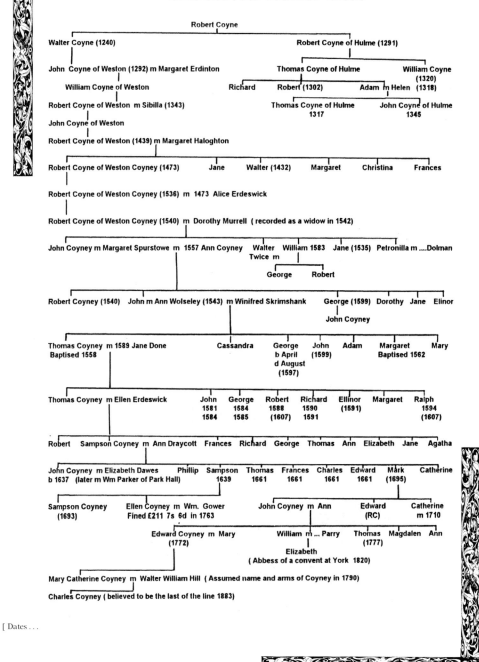

Robert Coyne

Walter Coyne (1240) — Robert Coyne of Hulme (1291)

John Coyne of Weston (1292) m Margaret Erdinton

Thomas Coyne of Hulme — William Coyne (1320)

William Coyne of Weston

Richard — Robert (1302) — Adam m Helen (1318)

Robert Coyne of Weston m Sibilla (1343)

Thomas Coyne of Hulme 1317 — John Coyne of Hulme 1345

John Coyne of Weston

Robert Coyne of Weston (1439) m Margaret Haloghton

Robert Coyne of Weston Coyney (1473) — Jane — Walter (1432) — Margaret — Christina — Frances

Robert Coyne of Weston Coyney (1536) m 1473 Alice Erdeswick

Robert Coyne of Weston Coyney (1540) m Dorothy Murrell (recorded as a widow in 1542)

John Coyney m Margaret Spurstowe m 1557 Ann Coyney — Walter — William 1583 — Jane (1535) — Petronilla m ....Dolman

Twice m — George — Robert

Robert Coyney (1540) — John m Ann Wolseley (1543) m Winifred Skrimshank — George (1599) — Dorothy — Jane — Elinor

John Coyney

Thomas Coyney m 1589 Jane Done Baptised 1558 — Cassandra — George b April d August (1597) — John (1599) — Adam — Margaret Baptised 1562 — Mary

Thomas Coyney m Ellen Erdeswick — John 1581 1584 — George 1584 1585 — Robert 1588 (1607) — Richard 1590 1591 — Ellinor (1591) — Margaret — Ralph 1594 (1607)

Robert — Sampson Coyney m Ann Draycott — Frances — Richard — George — Thomas — Ann — Elizabeth — Jane — Agatha

John Coyney m Elizabeth Dawes b 1637 (later m Wm Parker of Park Hall) — Phillip 1639 — Sampson — Thomas 1661 — Frances 1661 — Charles 1661 — Edward 1661 — Mark (1695) — Catherine

Sampson Coyney (1693) — Ellen Coyney m Wm. Gower Fined £211 7s 6d in 1763 — John Coyney m Ann — Edward (RC) — Catherine m 1710

Edward Coyney m Mary (1772) — William m ... Parry — Thomas (1777) — Magdalen — Ann

Elizabeth (Abbess of a convent at York 1820)

Mary Catherine Coyney m Walter William Hill (Assumed name and arms of Coyney in 1790)

Charles Coyney (believed to be the last of the line 1883)

[Dates . . .

68

1348/49 A.D.

TIMOR MORTIS CONTURBAT ME

The summer of 1348 had been warm, the crops were well advanced, the grass in the meadows stood tall and lush. The scrawny beasts which, in spring had been so weak that the villagers had been forced to carry them bodily out to pasture, had put fat on their spindly bones and had acquired a gloss to their coats. The hens were laying on at least one day in three, most of the geese had produced four or five goslings apiece whilst the hens had done sterling duty by producing between six and eight chicks each. The sows had managed second litters and the dovecotes throbbed with white, feather fluttering life.

Above the hum of the village rose the clamour of the masons extending the north aisle of the church. The rumble of carts hauling stone, the brisk clatter of the mason's maul, the squeal of the pulleys and the brittle sparkle of the hammer and chisel served as a constant reminder of the expanding size and work of the church.

The arrival of a wandering mason caused a stir in the village. He was greeted, tested and admitted to the resident lodge at the hour of the evening meal. He talked late into the night about his past work, the previous places of his employment, the skilled craftsmen he had known and the great plague which was stalking Southern England. That plague which:

The Nail Head or 'dog tooth' ornament shown here is typical of Early English masonic decoration

'in men and women alike first betrayeth itself by the emergence of certain tumours in the groin or the armpits, some of which grow as large as a common apple, others as an egg, some more, some less which the common folk called gavocciolo. From the two said parts of the body this deadly gavocciolo soon began to propagate and spread itself in all directions indifferently; after which the form of the malady began to change, black spots or livid making their appearance in many cases on the arm or the thigh or elsewhere, now few and large, now minute and numerous. And as the gavocciolo had been and still was an infallible token of approaching death.' [9]

The Lodge retired to bed that night in shocked silence, each member a prey to black thoughts, subdued and apprehensive. The visitor left the following morning, striding away through the dew damp forest to seek employment among the abbey builders of the north.

A Decorated window in the North Aisle dating from the time of the plague.

The reeve, the vicar and the bailiff traditionally met at the far end of the main street following a custom introduced by William de Careswelle as a means of ensuring that his chief officers could see and be seen. They gathered at the point where the street petered out to become a slender forest trail, dropping down a slight slope and splashing through a small stream before weaving away among the ferns to the old rough cote where lived Agnes whose senility and near madness had earned her the reputation of being a witch. This reputation was enhanced by her pale blue, strangely blank right eye which glittered sightlessly in the dirt-lined, brown and wrinkled face contrasting sharply with the bead-like orb which occupied her left eye socket.

Agnes figured in the thoughts of all three men that morning. Alan Slynne had a sickly cow with sore feet, a blistered tongue and foam flecked lips. Rumour had it that Agnes had cast her evil eye upon it when last she walked to the village. The reeve was sceptical, that form of cattle sickness was far from unknown and occurred where Agnes had not walked. The bailiff was worried, his village could not afford the loss of even one cow, to his mind Agnes was a luxury which, for all her potions, charms, medicaments and philtres his village could ill afford. The vicar was perturbed. He served his God with all his heart, his villagers came regularly to Mass but he knew that among those squatting among the rushes of the church floor or leaning against the walls and pillars of the church were those to whom Beelzebub was no enemy and to whom Agnes with her demented cackles, odious potions and almost sibylline utterances was a more ready source of

The base of the most easterly pier in the North arcade is Early English. Does it belong to the nail head patterning adjacent to it? Were the two separated during some of the 'restoration' work?

comfort than Holy Mother Church. Agnes obsessed his tidy mind. The isolation in which she lived, the harm she was doing to her own soul, her poverty and degradation all offended his sense of duty, yet the threat she posed to his own hold on the minds of his flock was, he acknowledged, a real one. It was a threat difficult to define and so, the more difficult to defeat.

The long slow walk back into the village was almost a pleasure. In the mist-bright beams of the morning sun the round, thatched hovels, the rectangular mud and wattle cottages, the varied roofs of reed, thatch or hide which straggled down the gentle slope to the village and housed the 40 or so families of the village seemed almost pleasant. In winter the juxtaposition of goats, sheep, hens, pigs, the occasional cow and people all sheltering beneath the same roof and lying on the same soiled, straw covered floor in an atmosphere of stinking, smoke clouded damp had a different impact upon the visitor. All of the villagers moving about their daily tasks bore some evidence of skin disease. Rashes, scabs, blotches, scars, boils, eye infections, scurvy and the like were all accepted as a part of life by people who had not heard of bathing, washed intermittently and subsisted upon a diet of poor quality, lacking a constant supply of fresh green vegetables. Some of them bore evidence of poorly healed broken bones in the shape of deformed limbs, many showed clear proof of rickets whilst almost everyone suffered from some disorder of the teeth and gums.

Away to the right of the walkers the mill clacked busily, reminding them of the work which needed to be done on the face of the dam. A heron fished stealthily along the reedy shallows its slow, lofty leg action barely rippling the surface of the pond. An occasional fish leapt clear of the water, falling back with a resounding splash as it tried to dislodge the lice working beneath its scales. Already the stench of the castle moat was beginning to lie heavy on the steadily warming air, for, after the custom of the time the moat served as a defence, a gutter, a sewer and, on occasion, a well.

> 'My privy and well drain into each other
> After the custom of Christendie
> Fevers and fluxes are wasting my mother
> Why has the Lord afflicted me?'

In the square the sun-dried cart ruts had begun to crumble into a fine dust which lifted around their feet as they walked. The bailiff and the reeve noted with quiet satisfaction the bulk of the castle which dominated the village and the air of industry surrounding the home farm with its dovecote, orchard, ricks, barns, stables, byres, henhouses and pigsties. Beyond the church they could see the sprawling, open field dotted with the shapes of the villagers at their labours. If they resented that portion of the wealth of the village which went in tithes to the church they kept those thoughts to themselves for the hold of the Church upon the minds of men was immensely strong and whilst earthly greed might resent the exactions of the Church dread of the possible hereafter made cowards of most men in 1348. John de Smallys reflected with silent pride upon the way in which the bulk of the church, the sward of the churchyard and the hum of masonic activity seemed to dominate and invigorate the village.

Standing beside the west end of the church they discussed the affairs of the village. The poor standard of husbandry apparent in the strips worked by Thomas Radclyffe and Simon Coci was noted as was the dilapidated state of Alan Slynne's fencing. The distribution of boons, 'wet', 'dry' and 'love' for harvest-time was discussed as was the business of the next manorial court.

Briefly their discourse turned to relaxation. John de Smallys spoke of the intentions of the stonemasons to produce a mystery play-cum pageant based on the theme of the coming of the Three Kings to Herod, a venture which would serve as a useful vehicle for their masonic skills besides providing the central element in the village fair. The problems of containing cockfighting and bull baiting within reasonable bounds were discussed as was the need to curtail the excesses of violence likely to attend upon an impromptu game of football between the masons and the villagers. Leaping, archery, wrestling, casting the stone both with and without a sling, quarterstaff contests and bowls all figured in their discussion of the manner in which the revels should be ordered. Humour intruded as they recalled how successful had been John of Coynee in five times winning the prize for grinning through a horse collar, his broken nose, toothless gums and twisted eyes giving him a major advantage over his fellow competitors. As they spoke their minds encompassed the strident, gaudy panoply of fair days with the gaily tinted booths, crude but humorous jesters, sweetly voiced minstrels and itinerant cheapjacks whose private lines of communication seemed capable of bearing the news of such fairs far beyond the confines of village society. They thought of the tumultuous and abandoned merrymaking, the riotous and sensual aftermath as the day drew to its close, the dangers likely to arise from the opportunities such a gathering would give for the settling of old scores and the need to ensure the safety of all concerned. Each rejoiced privately in the fact that his status in the village would enable him to end the day amid the more restrained albeit equally coarse and bawdy delights of the castle to which building the leading citizens would withdraw when the hilarity in the village became abandon as the soft shades of evening created a shroud of warm velvet for the more secret celebrations which were inevitable as ale worked its magic upon mind and body alike.

Their business completed the officers turned back into the village. On the scaffolding along the nearly completed north aisle a workman swayed unsteadily and as they watched, collapsed onto the planking and then slid slowly off the edge, landing heavily among the grave mounds. His flushed cheeks, tortured breathing and rolling eyes denied their first angry thoughts of drunkenness.

Simon Coci collapsed next, his cheeks flaming, his breath wheezing in shallow gasps between vomit flecked lips. Those who carried him home found red boils sprouting beneath his armpits and in his groin. Recognising the signs of which the itinerant mason had spoken they fled in panic to the flea infested insecurity of their own hovels.

Late summer merged into early autumn through a nightmare of terror, pain and death. Some died with bitter relief like Walter the Cooper who had never found life a joy. Others died hard like Bartholomew Brassyngton a worker and fighter throughout his life. Agnes the Witch died savagely at the hands of a group of villagers who held her responsible for the wrath which had fallen upon the village. The partially harvested crops, untilled plots and rank vegetable gardens told their own sad story. Of all those who died during that colourful autumn of 1348 only Agnes was spared the burning fevers, tearing thirst, agonising boils and evilly odorous black pus which oozed from them at the point of death.

The gay leaves of autumn crinkled untrodden in the Square and rotted undisturbed beneath the rains and snows of winter. With the quickening warmth of spring came relief from the pestilence. The village emerged from its stupor. The untilled, uncut fields; the starved and sickly beasts; the overgrown pathways; the derelict buildings were all tragic evidence of a plague which had carried away almost one third of the village's population. The churchyard at Careswelle seemed to be heaped high with the bare soil of untidy grave mounds giving the impression that some vast mole was at work thrusting the soil well above the pathway leading into the church itself.

The height of the present churchyard above its pathways and the adjacent highway is eloquent testimony to the consequences of burying in one place over a prolonged period of time; its present levels are not the direct consequence of the Black Death alone.

At first the memories of death faded slowly, then with increasing rapidity as it was realised that the same amount of work remained to be shared between fewer families. Those who survived discovered that from death had come wealth.

1350 A.D.

THE NIGHT IS DONE

With the shortage of labour wages began to rise, men began to move in search of work. The size of land holdings increased and more than ever the larger landholders looked to enclosure and sheep to offset the economic burdens under which they were labouring Steadily the Lord of the Manor began to consolidate and enclose his holdings. The labourer began to seek to escape his boon obligations by a small payment in cash or kind, his lord became both ready to accept such settlements and more eager to pay for work when it was needed on a similar cash basis. Lands held for rent or tenancies taken up for a cash payment became commonplace. Labour services languished. The more prosperous and industrious small men began to follow the example of their lord. The less fortunate or more indolent began to fall by the wayside and were forced to hire themselves out as paid labourers. As bondmen absconded to the nearby towns the fabric of the old parish society began to disintegrate. Such fugitives sought the protection of a greater lord, took the tonsure or entered the monasteries at Croxden, Dieulacresse or Hulton as lay brothers.

Old patterns of land ownership, old relationships, long standing agreements were forgotten, neglected or deliberately flouted giving rise to periodic outbursts of inter-family strife, animosity, unrest and violence.

Just such an outburst occurred in 1381 when a long smouldering dispute over land tenure between William Alcok, Vicar of Careswelle and Peter de Careswelle exploded into violence. William Alcok supported by a group of armed and evilly inclined hirelings broke into Peter de Careswelle's private orchard brazenly driving in William's beasts that they might graze upon Peter's haycrop and ostentatiously felling trees to demonstrate William's dominion. Despite being sued by Peter who appears to have been a law-abiding man the feud lingered on until at least 1398 when William was again called to account. The dispute appears to have ended with the death of Sir Peter de Careswelle in 1398 when ownership of the Castle passed to the Marchyngtons through Sir Peter's daughter.

Such unrest helps to explain the presence of moated sites within and around the parish. For the prospering landowner the moated farmhouse was at once a symbol of prosperity and a very necessary stronghold against both his neighbours and the marauding bands of lawless rogues who roamed the countryside.

At Simfield, at Hall Hill farm and at Weston Coyney on the site now occupied by the road known as 'The Moat' stood moated farmsteads like squat, pugnacious guardians of the surrounding tillage. The best surviving local example of this feature, if the landscaped moat around the castle is excluded, lies just beyond the boundary of the parish on the southern side of the road to Barlaston from Rough Close where, even today, the farmhouse surrounded by its water-filled moat recalls a turbulent and savage past when a citizen's reasonable fears were such that:

'They have made bars to bar the door crosswise and they have made wickets on every quarter of the house to shoot out at, both with bows and with hand-guns.'[10]

By 1418 William Alcok, that turbulent and militant priest had been succeeded by a local man, John Careswelle, and the village had toiled and brawled its way into the reign of Henry VI.

Although violence was commonplace people were still prepared to resort to the due process of law particularly if the villain of the piece was Mother Church. Thus, in the reign of Henry IV, Thomas de Marchyngton who acquired the Castle and estates through marriage to Petronilla cousin to Sir Peter de Kaverswelle found it necessary to invoke the process of law against Ralph, Prior of Stone, alleging that he

'had unjustly desseised Thomas de Marchyngton and Petronilla, his wife, of a rent of 13s 4d in Walton.'

The Prior counter-claimed that the land from which the money sprang had been granted to the Prior by Sir Peter and produced a deed to prove it. Thomas and Petronilla then challenged the authenticity of the deed but lost.

By 1426 Petronilla had remarried and we find her second husband, William Venables, also going to law this time to sue Hugh Erdeswyk armiger

'for a third of 40 messuages, 1,000 acres of land, 60 acres of meadow, 200 acres of wood'[12]

claimed as dower of Petronilla having been given her by Thomas Marchynton.

In 1443 Petronilla was suing her son, William, who had inherited Kaverswelle for an account of the money which he had received on her behalf from the estate. Seemingly at this time Petronilla was resident at Kinderton and appears to have become a litigious and grasping woman, a worthy descendant of the mercenary Thomas. She was well matched in marriage to William Venables who was proving himself to be

'the most mysgoverned man in England'[13]

and the subject of frequent complaints about his violent and menacing behaviour.

It is on record that in 1433 Asche paid a tithe to Stoke Church this could indicate that geography in the form of the higher, drier and more level route to Stoke was beginning to influence travellers or wayfarers and local orientations more effectively than the circuitous high, dry route to Caveswelle or the more direct but marshy, forested and rugged route past Holm and the old rough cote where the spirit of old Agnes still walked.

By the middle of the 15th century unrest was rife. Society was a prey for armed bands and grasping landlords, complaints about the despoilation of property, infringement of rights and a general disregard of the claims of the weaker abound. Even the greater men were not free from such assaults for in 1480, Nicholas Montgomery, Lord of Kaverswelle brought a suit against:

'William Verney of Uttoshather, mason, for breaking into his close and house at Kaverswelle and taking the goods and chattels to the value of 40s.'[14]

A people nurtured on the myths, legends and factual achievements of the Hundred Years War could look to the prowess of the yeoman with his longbow and mumble against baronial oppression. Apparent and rampant injustice at home was less easy to bear than wealth squandered abroad. Popular discontent was widespread and rumours of the revolt of the Kentishmen under Jack Cade ran across the face of the land like a forest fire. Slowly the nation slid towards civil war until August 1453 when an outburst of Henry's hereditary insanity proved sufficient to trigger off the Wars of the Roses.

For some men the fear of death was a source of mental anguish:

'Unto the Death goes all Estates
Princis, Prelatis and Potestatis
Baith rich and poor of all degree
Timor Mortis conturbat me.
Since for the Death remeid is none
Best is that we for Death dispose
After our death that live may we
Timor Mortis conturbat me. '

THE MONTGOMERY FAMILY

In 1102 the Montgomery family, in alliance with Robert de Belleme, fought against Henry 1.

Philip de Montgomery was chief forester or warden of Cannock Chase. He acquired the office in 1284 but in 1293 was jailed for fraudulence and abuse of office. At the time his daughter Margaret was a minor; when she reached her majority and married John de Swynnerton the stewardship of Cannock Chase passed to her husband.

Between 1403 and 1408 Nicholas Montgomery was chief forester of the Forest of Needwood and constable of Tutbury Castle.

A Nicholas Montgomery, presumably the son of the aforementioned Nicholas, is recorded as the owner of Caverswall Castle in 1480 when, in a lawsuit, he sued William Verney of Uttoshather, In 1482 he served as High Sheriff of Staffordshire and was named as a Commissioner of the Peace by Richard III (1483-85).

His son, John, seems to have inherited the Caverswall estate. He died sometime before 1514 leaving a daughter and heir Dorothy and Elizabeth his widow. They married a father and son; Elizabeth married John Giffard and her daughter married John's son Thomas. Both marriages took place in the same year.

John Montgomery had no male issue. He was recorded as a member of the king's household at the age of 76 years and still carrying out duties for which he was paid 200 shillings a year. These payments ceased in 1542 suggesting that his wife died in that year. It would seem that she had received that sum, paid on a half yearly basis as a form of pension following the death of her husband.

For others earthly wealth, rank and power was all and it was those others who dragged Careswelle into the conflict. Careswelle's allegiance was to the dark rose of Lancaster through the manor's association with Tutbury, the chief seat of the Duchy. Although there is no immediate evidence of involvement it is difficult to believe that no men of Careswelle were present at Blore Heath on 22nd September 1459 when the forces of the sombre rose were sadly worsted by those of the white. The news of Bosworth Field, the accession of Henry Tudor and the marriage of the light rose with the dark brought some assurance of peace to the parish despite its Lord's inclination towards the deposed monarch, Richard III. Yet the influence of the dispute lingered long adding to the normal vicissitudes of life.

The power of the de Careswelles which had begun significantly with William de Careswelle and his *'Licenses to Crenellate'* in 1275 had come to an end in 1398 with the death of Sir Peter. Thereafter the castle and its attendant wealth had been inherited or acquired largely through the distaff side. This had tended to mean that each succeeding owner had looked closely at the ageing castle, its maintenance needs and running costs before deciding whether to live therein. Succeeding generations had variously neglected or enhanced the building and had been prepared with ever greater readiness to accept a financial adjustment in respect of dues, duties, boons and tithes.

Through Petronilla, daughter to Sir Peter, the castle passed to the Marchyngtons and then in varied succession to the Montgomeries, the Giffards, the Ports and the Hastings who were the Earls of Huntingdon. The last gentle occupation of the Castle appears to have commenced about 1515 when Dorothy Montgomery married Sir Thomas Giffard and moved into the 'goodly castle' with its *'Pooles, Dams and Houses of Office being all of Masonry.'* (The 'House of Office' was the toilet).

There may be a simple explanation for the absence of the names of the incumbents between John Careswelle in 1418 and Nicholas Bolyvant in 1533 but all in all it is difficult to escape the conclusion that between 1400 and 1500 the economic stresses which followed the Black Death, the political turmoil which afflicted the nation, the national problem of recruiting clergy of the requisite calibre and the changing attitudes of the leading families all combined to diminish the parish. As the might of the old feudal nobility decreased and the great family dynasties began to peter out a new class of dominant parishioner began to emerge. The parish came to know the wealthy and industrious yeoman farmer by whose efforts the face of the parish was being reshaped. It was this group of men who were at last able to turn their eyes and hands to the last great waste land in the parish, the damp, lofty and brooding expanse of Watley More.

1535 A.D.

THE WORK THAT LIES UNDER HIS NOSE

As always when his mind was troubled Nicholas Bolyvant had left the village and climbed to the highest point of his parish. There, among the bilberries, heathers and darkly damp peaty soils he walked, feeling the stiff breeze on his face and watching the towering galleons of cumulus cloud surge across the sky. The wasteland beneath his feet tainted the air with the odour of sour decay and sprawled away in all directions giving a strangely dark cap to the generally green land below him. Reaching south-westwards the darkness of the moor stretched almost to Holme, westwards it dipped out of sight down towards Ash, eastwards the desolation clawed its way over the farthest ridges whilst northwards it rolled unbroken in a sea of brown towards Chedylton.

Wetley Moor, now protected, was once a source of both peat and conflict between villages

Beyond the sparsely wooded darkness of the moor lay the undulating verdure of the forest among whose still largely trackless wastes wild swine, wild cattle and the vicious wild cat still roamed. The bear and lynx had long since disappeared from the parish but Nicholas knew that it was not many years since that a wolf had been seen in the parish and it was believed that they roamed still in some of the more remote localities.

Clearly identifiable islands of cultivation broke the blanket of the forest seeming to lie in holes driven into the mass of the forest cover. Over the pasture land and among the peripheral trees moved sheep, their *'golden hooves'* and rapacious teeth pushing back the forest cover by the slow but relentless destruction of seedlings, saplings and scrub.

To Nicholas Bolyvant, Vicar of Careswall, the sheep represented both wealth and anguish. Wealth in fair measure had accrued to some men in England from the keeping of sheep but all men who farmed s h e e p - l a n d seemed to profit therefrom. Yet that profit had not been easily won and the constant friction between

Cotton Grass, Eriophorum Angustifolium, and not as local lore believes, cotton plants brought back from the Americas by two 'Werynton worthies' who served in the army during the War of Independence.

sheepfarmers and tenant cultivators which stemmed from the land hunger of the age had caused more than one heated and bloody skirmish in the parish since Nicholas had arrived in 1533.

It was that same land hunger which was the cause of the activity on the south facing slopes of the moor below Werynton. Here and there on the slope where the valley trees gave way to the heathy moor men, women and occasionally children were at work toiling away to win a small pocket of arable land from the inhospitable moor.

Here a man was laboriously ditching a selected area throwing the soil onto the outer edge of the drainage trench to make a low earth bank. There two children were systematically working over a finished square clearing stones and lumps of coarse gritstone from its face and piling them along the earth bank in the form of a very crude dry stone wall. Elsewhere swathes of dirty smoke from the burning heather seared the fresh blue sky whilst in other plots sheep nibbled busily, their teeth completing the final stages of clearance their droppings returning nutrients to the soil for thus it was that the *'golden hoof'* converted waste to tillage.

Nicholas knew the strain of toil himself; his 30 acre holding of glebe land demanded much of his own time, energy and sweat for he spent most of his week as a small farmer. Even as vicar of a relatively prosperous parish and as private chaplain to Sir Thomas Giffard and his wife, Dorothy, he was still forced to rely upon his own physical efforts for much of his real income. His neighbours contributed to the income of the church with obvious reluctance for, like yeoman farmers throughout the nation,

'the tithe sheaf goes against conscience for each had rather spend the value upon his reapers and ploughmen than bestow anything to the maintenance of a parson.'

Yeoman niggardliness notwithstanding, Nicholas was not too popular in his parish. Unlike his industrious parishioners he did not publicly subscribe to or even demonstrate the popular belief that *'immoderate sleep is rust to the soul.'* His grasp of dog Latin was sufficient to mark him as a scholar and man of culture yet insufficient to mark him as so highly educated that the doors of higher county society were opened to him. He was also a target for that local form of the great religious discontents which were sweeping across Europe for he well knew that the recent unruly and vicious depredations instigated by the Abbot of Dieulacresse had not helped the Catholic cause in the area. As parish priest Nicholas had, on more than one occasion in the past, offered absolution or indulgence for a 'donation' whilst his 'understanding' with his housekeeper had not gone unremarked in the parish. Yet he was no better and no worse than his contemporaries throughout England. Indeed there were those who held that Catholic faith and duty was strongest in the northern counties and in Staffordshire in particular where clerical vows of poverty, obedience and chastity were deemed to be most carefully observed, at least by the standards of the times.

However, Nicholas had worries which extended beyond his own parish. Messengers from the diocese had brought news of what was to become known as the Reformation in Europe. This had been followed by news of the developing conflict between Henry and the Roman Church over Henry's desire to divorce Katherine, his Queen. The most recent despatch had brought news of something called the Act of Supremacy which held that

'the King is and aught to be the Supreme Head of the Church in England as far as the laws of Christ would allow.'

For opposing this high-handed diktat Fisher, More and a number of Carthusian monks had been burnt. Rumours were already rife that the next target of the King's covetous wrath would be the monasteries whose manifest wealth and apparent corruption had long been the target of criticism; whose usefulness was now openly doubted and whose role in succouring, supporting some claimed, destitute wayfarers was commonly held to greatly encourage that vagabondage which represented such a menace to isolated dwellings, small villages and even to the law and order of townships.

He gazed round, his mind in a tumult. His eye traced the line of the forest-fringed track which led from Dieulacresse in Leek to the Priory at Stone, he picked out the junction between that track and the similar one which linked the Abbey at Hulton with that at Croxden. Already the point at which the two trails crossed had become something of a meeting place in spring and autumn when farmers, craftsmen, merchants and labourers came together to barter their surpluses and the products of their skill for necessities or even the rare luxury which a good year meant that they could afford. At such meetings old contracts of employment were renewed or new ones entered into. Beyond the dark smoke of the burning heather writhing plumes of woodsmoke marked the dwellings at Careswell, Holme, Westone Coney, Werynton, Buckenhale and Ash. Drifts of a dirty black smoke rose from a potter's kiln at Adderleye, seeming to foul the clean,bright, clear air which smelt slightly of rain to come. Somewhere off to his right a curlew bubbled. In the air above and somehow behind him an invisible skylark poured its song in a shimmering cascade of notes upon the surface of the moor. Above Werynton a kite hovered, its forked tail flexing as it searched for carrion, as Nicholas watched it seemed to become an avenging angel louring upon his parish and suddenly he knew with a sharp, hateful certainty that his time there was short.

Wetley Moor still exists as rather more than a square mile of peaty heather, bilberry and cotton grass. As the highest local landmark it still offers marvellous views although building development is at once encroaching upon its bounds and placing the pedestrian viewer at a disadvantage by restricting his line of sight. Even so eastward can still be seen the Weaver Hills and the Churnet Valley; to the northward lie the Morridge, Meriton Low, Hen Cloud and the Roaches, Shutlings Low, Macclesfield Forest and Biddulph Moor; westward beyond the Potteries Basin lie Delamere Forest, the Welsh Mountains and the Shropshire Wrekin whilst southward ridge after whalebacked ridge tumbles and climbs away towards Cannock Chase.

The evidence of the labours of generation after generation of local folk to reclaim the moor can be seen in the field patterns which surround it. Elsewhere in the parish the fields are of generous size but around the fringes of the moor particularly north-east of Washerwall, north of Brookhouse Wood and north of Great Eaves tiny fields marking the first stage of reclamation can still be detected. In other localities elongated fields can, to the discerning eye, offer evidence of how dividing walls have been removed to create larger units.

The process of reclamation was still going on in the 1940s but has now ceased leaving a residual crown of protected moorland as an increasingly attractive reminder of an arduous and turbulent past.

The history of Wetley Moor is indeed a troubled one. Its turves were a most precious form of fuel and peat cutting rights on the moor were so highly prized that each adjoining community had some claim upon its area.

In the early years of the sixteenth century the moor or 'more' as it then was, appears to have covered some 610 hectares (1,500 acres). Of this area some 130 hectares (320 acres) belonged to the Manor of Weston and were held by one Robert Cuney. A further 275 hectares (680 acres) belonged to Careswell whilst the residual area on the northern slope was claimed by the Manor of Chedylton. Between each parcel of land boundaries were at best ill defined and at worst, subject to occasional 'adjustment' usually in the absence of the other party. More than once a local priest found it necessary to rebuke members of his flock by preaching a sermon upon the theme of Deuteronomy 27 v 17 *'Cursed be he that removeth his neighbour's landmark'*, generally to scant avail.

Shortly after his arrival in 1515 Thomas Giffard of the castle granted the right to cut turf on Wetle More to Thomas Browne and other tenants of the town of Careswall[15] whenever they pleased. The wording of the licence, *'time out of mind'*, suggests the formal confirmation of a longstanding practice. In 1529 Browne took his social superior, Robert Cuney, before the Court of Star Chamber complaining that Cuney and others named had, *'riotously and with force'* taken and held six wagon loads of turves which had been cut by the men of Careswall and that subsequently the same Robert Cuney, members of his family and others, had *'feloniously and at night burned and destroyed'* a further twenty wagon loads.[16] Cuney's reply was that the complaint was untrue and that the incidents had taken place on his area of the moor. The Court found in favour of Browne and the men of Careswall.

A similar outbreak of violence occured in 1540 when *'forty and over riotous and evil disposed persons, with force and arms, in a manner of war, did break and enter into waste ground or moor called Watley More being parcel of the Manor of Chedylton.'*

It was after one such affray that a body was found near the area in dispute. Whilst an affray was deemed to be a fairly harmless part of life an affray with bloodletting was more serious. To cause death in such an incident was an act which imperilled mans immortal soul as well as his mortal carcase and earthly possessions. The corpse was irreligiously interred at the spot where it fell. The locality was subsequently referred to in whispers as *'deadman's grave'*.

The spirit of that unfortunate soul slain in the dark of the moon is said still to walk on bleak winter evenings seeking a christian burial which he can never gain. There is a grim irony in the fact that 400 years after the christian minstrel was buried at Buckenhale on the western slope of the moor another murder on the eastern side should provide a second spectre to torment travellers on the darkest evenings of the year.

1539 A.D.

COLD IRON IS MASTER OF THEM ALL

The calibre of the contestants in such feuds may be assessed from contemporary texts and from the Muster Roll for 1539.

Of the men of the better kind, the true yeoman farmer, it was said:

'Though he be master he says not to his servants 'Go to the field but Let us go' and with his own eye doth fatten   his flock and set forward all manner of husbandry. He is taught by nature to be contented with a little; his own fold yields him both food and raiment, he is pleased with any nourishment God sends.' [20]

At home such a worthy would boast a comfortable and well furnished dwelling by the standard of the times and
'a chandler's treasure of bacon, links and pudding in the chimney corner'.

Abroad such a man believed in
'rising early in the morning and being up, he hath no end of motion'.

The nature and industry of the honest yeoman farmer whose life was the essence of the parish in 1539 is not difficult to deduce from the above.

The men of the lesser kind were much less well endowed, their homes were scanty hovels, their fare modest, unvaried and meagre. If the better men in the parish lived well their social inferiors scrabbled a livelihood and eked out a squalid existence in conditions but a little removed from that endured by their medieval forebears.

The Muster Roll for 1539 is interesting in three respects. Firstly it reveals an absence of many of the names carried by noble or gentle families earlier in the history of the parish. They have been overtaken by the yeoman families of the parish. Secondly the list records names which can be traced back to the Saxon settlement of the parish and followed forward to the present day, John Cocke is clearly a descendant of Cuccu and an ancestor of the contemporary Cooks. Indeed with somewhat bettered spelling the Muster Roll might almost be an extract from a contemporary electoral roll. Thirdly the list of weapons available for mobilization gives some indication, when supplemented by the ubiquitous knife, of the type of weaponry likely to be employed in an 'affray'.

To manage a bill required both height and strength, it is reasonable to assume therefore that men described as 'abulmen' (able men) and 'bilmen' (bill men) were the biggest and strongest men in the village.

The absence of the violent and turbulent Cuneys is not without interest.

Such war gear offered, at least, personal protection in an age when men took pleasure in inflicting and withstanding pain and the baser, sadistic instincts of man were given free reign: each man carried and was quite ready to use, a rapier, dagger, staff or cudgel depending upon his degree.

The Muster Roll reads as follows: [17]

John Gyfford, Phillip Draycotte, Thomas Gyfford

Edmund Hulme	a jacke and sallett
Wylliam Holme	a bowe
Thomas Brassyngton	a bow and arrows
Ric. Hulme	a bowe
John Cocke	a bowe

John Coke	}	
Ric. Ratclyff	}	be able men and archers but
Ric. Sebrigge	}	thei have no harnesse
Laurens Holme	}	

Robert Senton	horse and harnesse	}	are bylmen redy
Homfrey Adderley	horse and harnes	}	furnyshed withe
John Hollens	horse and harnes	}	horse and harnesse

John Hulme	a bowe and a shef of arrows	}	
William Hulme	a salett and a bill	}	are abulmen and
William Devell	a pair of splents	}	bilmen havyng
Robert Hulme junior	a salett and a bill	}	such harnesse as
William Ratcliff	a bill and a pair of splents	}	expressid
Ruff Coke	a jacke	}	

William Brassyngton	an abulman and bilman but have no harnesse

In translation:

Jack	-	a doublet or defensive garment padded and quilted with strips of leather.
Splents	-	armour for the arms.
Salet	-	a light steel cap with a projection behind to protect the nape of the neck.
Harness	-	any kind of necessary and appropriate armour and equipment (a horse's harness was usually described as 'furniture'.)
Bill	-	a pike with a long handle and a spear head with a bill hook on the reverse edge often reaching 18 feet in length, which was used to drag a man off a horse.

THE GIFFARD FAMILY

The Giffards trace their descent from Walter Giffard who fought beside William the Conqueror at Hastings. Walter was the son of Osborn de Bolebec and was one of the commissioners appointed by William the Conqueror to compile Domesday Book.

The family was a power in the land throughout the ages. William Giffard was Bishop of Winchester, Godfrey was Bishop of Worcester and Chancellor to Henry III, Walter was Archbishop of York. In 1235 Hugh Giffard was Constable of the Tower of London whilst his son, Alexander travelled with the Crusade of 1240.

Thomas Giffard was born in 1491 and married Dorothy the heiress of Sir John Montgomery in either 1514 or 1515. The lands attached to the castle at Caverswall passed to Thomas Giffard upon his marriage and he lived there until 1539.

It is tempting to wonder if it was Thomas who was responsible for the family motto of "Take breath, pull strong", advice given to Sir John Giffard by his son in 1513 when Sir John's captive leopard had escaped and was menacing a woman and child. The words, murmured in French, were sufficient to curb Sir John's tensions and allowed him to kill the leopard, in mid spring, with his crossbow.

In February 1539 the family moved to Brewood.

Thomas Giffard served as High Sheriff in 1529, 1530, 1535, 1553, 1554 and 1560. He died in May 1560 at the age of 69 years.

His first daughter Elizabeth married Sir John Port and with her the Caverswall estates passed to the Port family.

From this point forward the fortunes of the Giffard family went into decline largely because of their unswerving adherence to the catholic faith. William Giffard went to France, became a Jesuit and subsequently Archbishop of Rheims. The Giffards played a leading role in preserving the life of King Charles II after the battle of Worcester.

In the early 1760s Thomas Giffard obliterated the whole village of Chillington in order to extend his parkland.

The Giffard family mostly remained Catholic until 1861 when it was said that both they and the majority of their tenants were staunch Catholics.

In 1996, John Giffard, a direct descendant of Walter Giffard became Chief Constable of Staffordshire.

GIFFARD OF CHILLINGTON

1540 A.D.

HERE IS MORE GAIN THAN GUESSED

It was late in the day when the small group of riders clattered into the village passing the sprawling field and the church before swinging left to the Castle. Sir Thomas Giffard came forth to greet them and spoke warmly to their leader.

That night before he retired to bed John Leland penned the following words for his Itinerary:
'the castle or preaty pile of Cawseurl iii miles by north fro Stone a Priori Channons sumtyme belonging to the Montgomerihes now to the Giffards.'[18]

As a surveyor of the libraries of the doomed monastries, acting for his royal master Henry Vlll he had taken upon himself the task of recording his observations during his travels for, as he related to Henry, he had become:

'totally enflamed with a love to see thoroughly al those partes of this your opulente and ample Realme that I had reade of you the aforesaid writers yn so much that al my other Occupations intermitted, I have so traveled yn your Dominions bouthe by the Se Costes and the midle Partes, sparing nother Labor nor Costes, by the space of these Vl Yeres paste, that there is almost nother Cape, nor Bay, Haven, Creke, or Peere, Rever or Confluence of Rivers, Breches, Waschis, Lakes, Meres, Fenny Waters, Montagnes, Valleis, Mores, Hethes, Forestes, Chases,Wooddes, Cities, Burges, Castilles, principal Manor Placis, Monasteries and Colleges, but I have seene them; and noted in so doing a hole Worlde of Thinges very memorable.'[19]

The following morning he offered a few words of kindly wisdom to Sir Thomas advising him not to identify himself too closely with the dispossessed clerics whose library had been lodged at Caveswall for safe keeping until the King's men should come to collect the books. They parted with mutual good wishes and a profusion of thanks, Leland acknowledging the generous courtesy of his host and Sir Thomas expressing his ill concealed pleasure at having been selected as an agent of the King's works whilst hiding his deeper more Catholic feelings about the actions of his Majesty.

During this period the village seems to have declined. The Gyffards appear to have been rather ineffectual personalities who were dogged by ill luck. Dorothy died shortly after their arrival to take up residence in the Castle; with her death the heart seemed to go out of her husband. The great and costly castle slid imperceptibly into a state of disrepair. Social divisions in the parish became more clearly marked, some throve and prospered, others struggled and sank. The ancient mill pond had silted up to become a weed and rush choked morass. Its passing had gone almost unnoticed as the new wooden windmills began to supplant the older water mills. The windmills with their great wooden arms beating the skyline were a symbol of the ways in which urban money and a new technology were changing the face of the parish. Increasingly, prosperous townsmen were investing their money in some skilled local craftsman, or some able artisan was branching out on his own to tap a specialised aspect of the local market; each, by so doing, was helping to set up a small cottage based industrial centre which in turn attracted labour from the traditional rural practices.

1549 A.D.

YOU HAVE SHOWN ME THE ROAD

For most dwellers in the parish of Careswell the upheaval which was to become known as the Reformation had meant little. It had been illustrated by the passage of the Royal Commissioners in 1538 on their way to dissolve the monasteries at Croxden, Hulton and Dieulacresse. The villagers had noted with awe and shivered with foreboding at the cruel features and arrogant demeanour of Dr. Thomas Leigh who led them. They had given more overt attention to the deposed Gregory Scarlett who had replaced Nicholas Bolyvant taking up in every respect where Nicholas had left off but had reserved their most curious scrutiny for the new arrival John Wildeblod, priest, representing the new Church of England.

The introduction of Cranmer's English Prayer Book on Whitsunday 1549 produced a few minor brawls in the tavern but the Vicar, John Wildeblod, was cast in the mould of his predecessor John de Smallys, he knew his flock and they knew him, such feuds soon died. For most of John's folk life was still a matter of self sufficiency and barter. Their diet was still meagre, monotonous and lacking in real sustenance. It did little to promote resistance to disease and nothing to fill the coarse and ill- fitting clothes which hung, dirty and verminous, about the gaunt frames of the villagers whose faces revealed further evidence of dietary deficiency. Cracked lips, rough skin patches, inflammation of the eyes, poor teeth, sallow complexions, spots, rashes, eruptions and the pock marks of disease all told their own sad story. For such souls deprived of energy and vigour by the poverty of their diet day followed day in a wearying, predictable round of drudgery sweetened but slightly by the knowledge that a man might rise by his own efforts.

The yeoman farmer was in better case than his labourers. Not only could he call upon the security of his own holdings but the richer and more plentiful diet derived therefrom made him healthier and more active. Besides his heightened physical and mental vigour such a man could call upon accumulated knowledge in the shape of a wealth of rural lore to guide him in his work.

Such wisdom served to shape his daily round and provide discourse with his neighbours who would be advised to

'Rub your poultry with the juice of rue or herbe grasse and the weasels shall doe them no hurt, if they eat the lights or lungs of a Foxe the Foxes shall not eat them.' [20]

When buying a horse each knew that:

'Many men will protest and sweare that they are sound when they know the contrary, onley for their private gaine'

'There be three kindes of men, the horse-master, the corser and the horse-leche. And when these three be mette if you add a poty-carye to make the fourthe ye myghte have suche a foure that it were harde to truste the best of them' [20]

Most men knew that a 'full bullock yard makes a full stocke yard' but equally none would deny that 'the best dung for the ground is the Maister's foot and the best provender for the house the Maister's eye'.

Around such fact, fiction and fancy the life and prosperity of Careswell revolved in the middle of the sixteenth century.

The village on an autumn night. Above each hovel climbs a meagre wraith of peat smoke etching slender columns of greyness against the star bright sky and filling the raw night air with the warmly sour tang of smouldering peat. Against the southern sky made somewhat brighter by the absence of trees and the level openness of the field the great stone bulks of church and castle draw strange, dark outlines beneath the stars. Beyond that bulk, beneath the grotesquely tilted constellation of the Plough the vast open field slumbers, rimed with frost. Ice crisped leaves nestle and curl around the dark naked tree rising tall from the rutted earth of the Square. Somewhere in the bright darkness a baby squalls with hunger and is comforted by its mother. A cat tenses its muscles as a mouse ventures out into the stone flagged desert of a floor in the castle kitchen. From the window of the vicar's cottage, scarcely richer than the rest, the fitful, fretful gleam of a candle flickers and flares as the priest, muffled against the sleep disturbing cold, ponders his text.

The last, dull coldness before dawn steals across the village presaging the brightening eastern sky and the whitening frost of daybreak. Slowly the east pales into a brittle, bitter, blue tinged greyness casting brief dark shadows around the slumbering hovels. Somewhere in the greying mistiness a man coughs, clears his throat and spits violently. A cockerel shatters the morning peace and is answered by another and then another. In the steaming warmth of the byre a restive cow lows tentatively. A dog barks, a plough-team ponderously jangles through the village and milkmaids bustle in their dairies. Porridge pots begin to spit and splutter filling each dwelling with a sense of warming hunger. Gradually the village brightens into day and wakens into life.

Labourers plod slowly through the cold air towards their work. A beggar rolls out of a hayrick and shivers as the colder air cuts through his rags. An axe rings on timber and an empty wain rumbles through the village square, splashes through the muddy stream its heavy wheels shattering the brittle glass of the ice which encrusts its shallows and disappears towards the moor. In the field beyond the church a plough steadily turns the rich, dark earth following the pattern of ridges and furrows created by generations of ploughmen serving the needs of Careswall.

The clangour of the church bell summons the faithful to prayer and briefly holds the ear of the faithless. Chickens are fed with a scanty scatter of corn, swill splashes before hogs and on the opposite side of the square from the church the tavern door is thrown open and the landlord relieves himself as he surveys the village scene.

Gradually the warming rays of the sun begin to pierce the crisp air, frost melts, mist forms briefly and then clears as the grass dries and the day brightens. The beggar walks warily into the high street surveyed with just suspicion by the villagers who note the long staff which will be used to angle a drying garment from a bush or even a money pouch thrown carelessly upon a stool before an open window should the opportunity offer. A dog snaps bitterly at the beggar's heels as he pauses to break his fast at the spring whose tinkling waters sparkle just off the square. Housewives pound away seeking to make butter and cheese from the accumulated thin milk of their poor beasts. A labourer pauses in the rhythm of his task, lays his billhook on the grass, dips into his wallet for bread and swigs rough ale from a small earthen jar.

In the castle kitchen trenchers are scraped and napkins folded, knives are scoured and the mighty wooden table set with salt and ale. The poor folk settle to their brief meal of thin gruel or tenacious porridge. The better folk enjoy fresh bread and firm, moist cheese, a mainly vegetable stew and crisp home-picked apples and pears. Briefly the village pauses in the fleeting mid-day warmth of an autumn sun.

Refreshment and a brief rest taken, the village resumes its normal round. The priest abruptly leaves his glebe and hastens to the pallet of a dying woman, the dirt of toil still grained into his knuckles. Grazing cattle stray through the churchyard, a group of noisy children chatters out of the village in search of edible berries and in the barn-yard of the home farm a hen announces its triumph with a proud cackle of relief. Slowly the sun casts lengthening shadows across the square and a sudden chill breeze stirs the languid air and bespeaks another cold night. The current of humanity which had flowed out-wards from the village at dawn begins to ebb back into the welcoming shades of the village. Returning labourers bear the casual fruits of their absence a faggot of wind blown sticks, a bundle of dry bracken, a kerchief of mushrooms and the indisputable marks of wearying labour.

The village darkens and voices raised in ale elevated mirth begin to ring across the stillness of the evening air. Belated, the huge, peat laden wain returns the turf cutters grimed and sweat streaked from their toils. Doors close, weak candles gleam and weary bodies sink in eased extension to the floor, aching muscles relax in sleep and night returns once more.

Taken from 'The Tudor Housewife' by Alison Sim.

The 'bucket and chuck it' approach to the disposal of waste water before proper drainage systems were developed, waste water was poured into a 'sink' from which it would drain away without creating a muddy patch.

The will of Sir John Wyldeblode -
Clerke and Vicar of Caverswall

*T*he original of this will and the associated inventory showing the possessions of Sir John Wyldeblode is held in the Lichfield Diocesan Joint Record Office. I am indebted to one of Sir John's descendants, Roger Wildblood, for supplying me with a transcript.

Sir John Wyldeblode (spellings vary) became Vicar of Caverswall in 1538 and served until at least 1554. 'At least' is necessary because the records are unclear about the status of Walker who is recorded as incumbent in that year. The will was written on Christmas Eve 1561 and the inventory was prepared on the 4th. January 1562. The precise date of his death is not known.

John Wyldeblode represented the new Church of England. His appointment in 1538 came at a time when Henry VIII. was striving to create his new church. Political influences within the hierarchies of the church and state ebbed to and fro as Henry sought to achieve a unity of opinion. He applied force, he used reason, he resorted to subterfuge. By 1545 Cranmer had produced a new litany the use of which was made obligatory in August of that year. At that point tensions existed between the extremist views of the protestant zealots and the cautious supporters of Henry's movement towards the creation of a church which would embrace all of his subjects. When Mary entered London in 1553 following the death of Edward VI the pendulum swung back towards Catholicism and it may be more than coincidence that Sir John's tenure may have ceased shortly after Mary abandoned her early pretence of moderation by restoring Catholic bishops, annulling the ecclesiastical legislation of her predecessor and achieved a reconciliation between England and Rome in 1554.

Of his background little is known. Around 1560 there were between 9,000 and 10,000 parishes without a priest. In one sense, given the uncertainty which surrounded religious life this is not surprising, on the other hand the position did offer status and a living to bookish persons who might otherwise have had to cast round for a way of earning a pittance. The bulk of this shortfall has been attributed to the reluctance of bishops to appoint persons other than university graduates to priestly office. The title 'Sir' is of little help. It was often placed before the Christian name of priests, sometimes for contemptuous or ironic effect. He may well have been university trained given the date of his appointment and the fact that Caverswall was reckoned to be a good living. At worst he would have been one of those 'honest, sober and wise men such as can read the Scriptures and the homilies well unto people' later advocated by Elizabeth as a way of filling the vacant posts. The fact that he was a stipendary in Stafford in 1533 suggests that he was university trained.

To discharge an effective ministry through such tense and troubled times was no easy task. Prime requisites would have been personal courage, Christian commitment, tact, humanity, a sense of human decency, persuasiveness and an ability to compromise without sacrificing his principles.

That Sir John possessed a wry sense of humour and a secure understanding of the common man may be deduced from his wish that *there be a penny dole to every person that cometh to my funerall*. Was he anxious to have a good send-off or was he determined to get as many as possible into the church on this last, one occasion?

His wish to spread his worldly goods as widely as possible suggests both generosity and a realistic appreciation of what individual needs were, people seem to get that which is likely to be most use to them.

His references to *corne and ley in the barne*, would seem to confirm the presence of a substantial tithe barn, if not the one along the side of the churchyard adjacent to Dove House Farm.

Does his gift of *my cowe called Fairhead* (today, Beauty?) for the *fallo* (as in fallow deer, a speckled soft, fawn colour) *cowe I had of him* reflect a debt being repaid perhaps from a time when the priests own herd was diminished? or does it reflect some form of understanding about stone removed from the castle walls during the time that Browne was its custodian? or an unexpected gesture of appreciation?

The will also confirms the role of the priest as a farmer of the church glebe and highlights the relatively modest and highly functional nature of private possessions at that time. Did the priest not possess his own bible or religious texts? Possibly not. Were they, perhaps, buried with him?

Interestingly the gift of *a yonge heyfer to John Cunye that is dwellynge withe me* draws attention to an item in the Coyney family tree. John Coyney married Ann Wolseley of Wolseley Bridge who seems to have died in 1543. Her wedding portion was 600 marks. John Coyney was still alive in September 1609.

Why were two men *dwellynge with him*? John Cuyne and John Furnivalle are both so described. Yet, if it is the same John Coyney who married Winifred Skrimshank after the death of his first wife in 1543, his children were still being born in and after 1562. Does *dwellynge with me* have a different interpretation, perhaps suggesting support for the Christian ministry? Did they, perhaps, succour him at the end of his life? Are the variations in the wording significant? John Furnivalle *dwellith with me* but John Cuyne is *dwellynge with me*.

The Will of Sir John Wyldebolde 1561

In the name of the Lord Amen.

I Sir John Wyldebolde clerke Vicar of Caverswall beynge of perfaite mynde but sycke in bodye do make my last wylle and testament the xxiiij th. day of December in the syxeth (?) year of the regn our Soverayn Ladye Elizabeth by the grace of god of England, France and Ireland Quene, defender of the feith etc. And where I have (?) the coyce I do give to Rauffe Browne my cow called Ffeyzehed (Fairhead or Beauty) for the fallo cowe I had of him.

Item -   I gyve to John Furnivalle that dwellith with me my redde cowe and the yonge black cowe

Item -   I gyve to Thomas Wyldeblode my black cowe called Ffenell (?)

Item -   I gyve to Jane Massye my little redde cowe

Item -   I give (sic) to Mr. John Cunye that is dwellyng with me my yonge heyfer I gyve the said Thomas Wyldebolde a mattress ij coverlets ij peyze of shets / one bolster and a few peces of pewtervessels

Item -   I gyve Hugh Wyldebolde my brother my best gowne

Item -   I gyve the said Jane Massye one ffether bed ij coverlets ij peyze of shets and all my fflax hempe and my tawe (wool awaiting carding) that is dressed

Item -   I gyve Marerye Russheton my servant iijs iiijd

Item -   I wylle that the resydue of my goods I be honestly brought whom by the discrecion of my (sic) executors hereunder written and that there be penny dole to evry person that cometh to my buryall / And after my funerall expeces and my debts payde I wholly gyve all the resydue of my goods cattalls movable and unmovvable / and also my corne and ley both in the barne and upon the grownde to the said John Ffurnivalle that dwellith with me

Also I make my trusty fryende and kynysman John Wyldebolde of Etone Hugh Wyldebolde my brother the said John Ffurnivalle that dwellith with me my executors of this my last will and testament praising them to cause this my wylle to be performed/

me that this was the present wylle of the said John Wyldebolde these beynge wytness Rauffe Watson Wyllam Coke Wyllm Browne Rauffe Browne Jane Massye and Margery Russheton

The use of the long i to give a j tends to be confusing. The practice was adopted to prevent unscrupulous persons from adding an additional penny or i here and there, thus iij means three.

The Inventory of the goods of Sir John Wyldebolde attached to his will 1562

This is the inventozye indented of all the goods of John Wyldebolde Cleke late Vycar of Cazyswall praysed the iiijth. day of Januarye Ao Domn: 1562 by indifferent men Willm Dave Thomas Ares and Rychard Thacker

			£	s	d
Imprimis	6 kyne pzce	vj I	6	0	0
Item	1 lyttle heyfer	xs		10	0
Item	6 swyne more or less	xs		10	0
Item	a lyttle mare	xiijs iiijd		13	4
Item	geese, incke and hoznnes	iiijs		4	0
Item	viij coverletts bett and worse	xs		10	0
Item	xiij peyze of shets and an od shete	xxvs	1	5	0
Item	ij ffetherbedds and iij mattresses	xxvjs viijd	1	6	8
Item	iiij bolsters	iiijs		4	0
Item	iiij pillowes	iiijs		4	0
Item	ij blankets and ij towyll shetts	vs		5	0
Item	j pan j potte a lyttle potte	xxxs	1	10	0
Item	all pewter vessell	xxvjs viijd	1	6	8
Item	all maner ironware as broche or spygott gowbeats, brondent tongs and axe and snachatherz	xiijs iiijd		13	4
Item	all maner wodden vessell	vjs viijd		6	8
Item	corne and hay in the barne	xxxvijs	1	17	0
Item	corne on the grownde	xijs		2	0
Item	in redye money	ijs		2	0
Item	his apparell	xxs	1	0	0
Item	ffleshe and malt in the house	xs		10	0

(Sir John Wyldebolde left an estate valued at £19 9s 8d in an age when a labourer received 4d or 5d a day or about £6 10s 0d a year. The labourer's wage was barely enough to ensure survival and required him to manage effectively his own cottage garden or smallholding after he had finished work for the day. No wonder the average life expectancy was only about 38 years. At the same time Sir John was bequeathed 12 pence to pray for one of his parishioners, Ralf Adeley.)

1556 A.D.

IT IS NOT GIVEN FOR GOODS OR GEAR

The departure of the Giffard household in 1542 took away the last gentle family from the castle and removed from the village those essential traditions, social influences and standards which together had represented the last supports of a declining gentility in parish society. The same departure also removed the main source of patronage from the church. The benefits which had been derived from gentle patronage can be detected in the inventory of church goods, vestments, plate and possessions taken in the reign of Edward VI.

In the possession of the church at Careswall the following items were recorded:

Fyrste 2 belles in the stepull, a sanctus bell and a hand bell.

Item A sacring bell, a cross of coper with a banor to the same.

Item 2 sensors of brasse, on cruett, on towell.

Item 2 vestments, on of blewe chambler, thother of taffeta silk with all things thereto belonging and a rockett.

Item 2 coopes, on of redd silk, thother of checked cruelle.

Item 2 corposes with cases, 2 alterclithes and on surplis.

Md. John Aston and Gilbert Rowley, Churchewardens there delyvered to Richard Forcett, surveor, on challes of silver, with a patent parcelgilte.

Md. Edward Clark delivered to Richard Cowper, surveor, a vestment of whitte justian with all things to hit and 36 shillings.

Md. delyvered etc. to Edmond Clark and Richard Hone. Churchwardens there, 2 belles in the stepull, a sanctus bell, 2 Iynen clothes for the Holi Communyon Table and a surples for the ministre to menestre with, safely to be kept untill the kinges Majtus pleasure to therein furder knowen &c.

1570 A.D.

WARLOCKS HAMPERED OUR ARMS

The new prayer book and the new order of service sat lightly enough upon the villagers. The compulsion to attend church, the threats of house search and the disarming of recusant families which increased steadily after the excommunication of Elizabeth in 1570 throve on the tensions nurtured by Mary and the Popish threat of Spain and sat more heavily upon the consciences of the yeoman of Careswall. By 1552 only the name of *'William Maxfield of Mere gentleman'* appeared upon the list of local recusants.

Perhaps the key to this relatively easy switch of faith lies in the rural spirit which had never really been subjected to a dominant influence for good between 1418 and 1533. Perhaps it lies in the failure of Nicholas Bolyvant and Gregory Scarlett to provide a credible Catholic presence. Perchance it reflects the anglican zeal of John Wildeblod and his successors. Possibly it lay in a fear of the powerful grip of the Commissioners and a common loathing of Spain. Most probably the secret is to be found in the uncritical, receptive and innately superstitious minds of the villagers.

The medieval dread of the forest had disappeared to be replaced by an omnipresent fear of witchcraft. The hold of the church had lessened in the sense that its influence no longer held the folk in thrall but had intensified in the sense that those who were truly committed were ready to burn for their faith. Among those upon whom faith sat most lightly there were many who, in accordance with the spirit of the age, stood ready to oppose any enforced change by might of arms. In general, however, the parishioners of Careswall held the church in such slender regard that they still begrudged giving anything *'to the maintenance of the parson'.*

Superstition was rife. It was generally believed that ghosts walked, witches still burned on occasion and were, rather more frequently, hung. Astrology, chiromancy, cartomancy and necromancy were popular among the higher social orders but among the people of Careswall more dread was afforded to the malevolent spirits represented by Robin Goodfellow, Gull, Grim, Pinch, Patch, Hag, Sib, Tib, Lick, Lull and the others of their kind who wrought constant domestic and agricultural havoc around the parish. Addled eggs, curdled cream, aborted calves, broken harness, lost knives, spilt milk, burnt bread, sour ale and the rest were all blamed upon the mischief worked by these sprites.

Some of these spirits were clearly in the employ of those who depended upon hired labour:

'I, that am called Pinch, do go about from house to house. Sometimes I find the doors of the house open. That negligent servants have left them so, I do nip him or her, that with my pinches their bodies are as many colours as a mackerel's back, ... sometimes I find a slut sleeping in the chimney corner when she should be washing of her dishes or doing something else which she hath left undone; her I pinch about the arms for not laying her arms to labour.' [20]

Others, however, appear to have sided with the employee for Gull, who also served as the fairies' midwife claimed:

'When mortals keep their beds I walk abroad ... many times I get on men and women and so lie on their stomachs that I cause them great pain for which they call me by the name of Nightmare. 'Tis I that do steal children and in place of them leave changelings. Sometimes I also steal milk and cream.' [20]

Against such sprites the teachings of the church offered little help, indeed, very little assistance was sought for such presences did at least offer an excuse to the careless, idle, slovenly or foolish and provide a threat for use by the goodwife..

Day followed day with very little variation. 'Feasts', 'Ales', holy days and the traditional landmarks of the farming year alone brought relaxation and joy to the lives of the villagers. Visitors were relatively few although messengers to the castle, itinerant priests, frequently of the old persuasion and recruiting officers bent on persuading some stout local lad to trail a 'puissant pike' to some distant war were accepted as part of the general social fabric whilst travelling entertainers and the pedlar with his bundle of trinkets, geegaws and a bottomless fund of gossip and good humour were enthusiastically welcomed.

The arrest and imprisonment of a beggar brought a more vicious thrill of excitement to the village when he appeared in the stocks. Such sturdy idlers were abhorred and feared by all. Rural settlements like Careswell, Holme, Ash, Adderleye and Werynton lived in dread of the terror of the tramp. The presence of a single sturdy rogue was usually sufficient to frighten some small donation out of the weaker villagers in the hope that he would then leave quietly. The arrival of a group of ruffianly vagabonds posed a more serious threat to the village and could lead to some bloody upset before the intruders were driven off. All in all however the mere fact that people could be prevailed upon to make some form of tribute coupled with the opportunity for nimble fingers and quick wits to work among unguarded goods and possessions was sufficient inducement to persuade such rogues to risk a bloody back, a bored ear, a battered face or a spell in the stocks. To people who prized, if they did not always adhere to, the virtues of godliness, industry, loyalty and cleanliness the plague of vagabonds was anathema.

If pelting the beggar offered one relaxation the villagers found others in riding, shooting with the bow and perhaps, even the gun. Vaulting, running, leaping, wrestling, dancing, singing and quarterstaff bouts could all be witnessed in and around the square and the churchyard on days of relaxation. The bloodier sports of bull baiting and cock-fighting were highlights of such days and held pride of place in the area between the tavern and the bank of the former mill pond where they were enjoyed by all. Less popular but equally certain was the game of football which almost invariably exploded at the end of the day of leisure when the men of Weston, Adderleye and Holme joined issue with the stalwarts of Werynton, Careswell and Dillorne.

Such occasions fast became:

'a bloody murdering practice . . . For doth not every one lie in wait for his adversary, seeking to overthrow him and pitch him on his nose, though it be upon hard stones, in ditch or dale, in valley or hill, or what place soever it be he careth not, so he can have him down. And that he can serve the most of this fashion he is counted the only fellow, and who but he? So that by this means sometimes their necks are broken, sometimes their legs, sometimes their backs, sometimes their arms, sometimes one part thrust of joint, sometime another, sometimes their noses gush out with blood, sometimes their eyes start out and sometimes hurt in one part, sometimes in another. But whosoever scapeth away the best goeth not scot-free, but is either sore wounded and bruised, so as he dieth of it, or else scapeth very hardly. And no marvel for they have sleights to meet one betwixt two, to dash him against the heart with their elbows, to hit him under the hip and to pitch him on his neck, with an hundred such murdering devices. And hereof groweth envy, malice, rancour, choler, hatred, displeasure, enmity and what not else and sometimes fighting, brawling, contention, quarrel picking, murder, homicide and great effusion of blood.' [20]

With the tree as one goal and the church wall as the other the village square must have seen some lively and bloody encounters when the people of Careswell took their ease.

During the 16th century the face of the parish changed markedly. The islands of cleared and cultivated land around each settlement had been extended considerably, even so the overall appearance was still one of an extensively wooded countryside. Areas of open pasture on the higher lands at Park Hall and Roughcote offered a smooth, sheep nibbled sward fringed at the lower levels by lofty standard oaks beneath whose canopy the ferny forest floor was being pushed back and converted into yet more pasture by the combined efforts of man and beast. These areas tended to extend over much of the higher ground between Westone Cuney and Holme and along the whole area between the eastward extension of what is now Handley Bank, through Caverswall Common to Windycote and Cellarhead.

Drainage works had tended to produce a drier valley than ever before but even so the great sprawling floor of the valley occupied by the River Blithe was still a spreading, tussock fringed morass. On the slopes of Wetley Moor small, formal fields were beginning to appear but the great wasteland with its sparse, stunted, wind-twisted trees was still a dominant, forbidding feature. Beyond the settlements lay a haphazard mixture of enclosed fields of various sizes and the great, open hedgeless strips legacy of a past age. Around each settlement the tracks were rutted with deeply etched wheelmarks which would set rock-hard in a dry summer and become deep quagmires in a wet winter. Beyond each settlement these trackways petered out into a network of tree and fern fringed trails which merged with the major routeways through the parish.

The main network of such roads was simple to define. One trail ran from north to south taking advantage of the higher ground on the eastern side of the valley. Two slightly broader trails ran from west to east, one to the north and one to the south of the parish. That to the south hugged the higher land south of the marshy patch well named Mere. The more northerly route climbed eastward along the fringes of the Moor again taking advantage of the higher, drier ground rising from Brookhouse to Windycote. A similar but much lesser trail ran from Adderleye to Weston Cuney and thence to Careswelle crossing the trail formed in the days when Dieulacresse Abbey in Leek had contacts with the Priory at Stone close the the spot at which the Weston Inn now stands. It would be an injustice to call such trails 'roads'. They were in reality at their widest no more than one cart's width and at their most scanty no more than the sort of track which intermittent passage on foot through undergrowth leaves in its wake. Any traveller through the parish could count on getting wet feet, or wetting those of his beast several times during his journey.

The only stone buildings in the parish of any consequence were the church and the decaying castle. Some, like the moated manor houses had significant stone foundations supporting their half-timbered superstructures. Some along the fringes of the moor had walls of rough- hewn gritstone but the great majority of dwellings were simple, rectangular thatched huts with walls of wood and wattle enclosing one or two rooms, adjoined by an assortment of animal shelters for those beasts not sufficiently cherished to be permitted to share some part of the family's living space.

The population of the parish at this date can only be guessed at even when supported by deductions drawn from such sources as hearth tax returns, surviving ecclestiastical censuses and the like.

In Cafhere's day the 'village' was his family and retainers say, not more than ten souls. In 900AD the 'parish' probably contained no more than 80 or 100 persons all told. By 1086 A.D. the village itself must. have contained not fewer than 45 souls and not more than 90; with a parish figure not much higher than about 240 persons. By 1340 A.D. this figure appears to have stood at rather less than 100 persons higher but fell almost to its Domesday level with the onset of the Black Death and the turbulence of the following century. For the middle of the 16th century an average life span of about 30 years seems to be not unreasonable bearing in mind the implications of both longevity by Tudor standards and the level of infant mortality. If a figure of four or five persons per household is taken as an average drawn from a community whose family unit size would have ranged from the single person unit represented by the widow to the lusty brood sired by the yeoman farmer anxious to ensure the prosperous survival of his stock, a parish figure of between 270 and 300 souls for 1570 seems feasible.

By households such a total might have been grouped into somewhere between 67 and 75 families. Of these households between twenty three and twenty seven appear to have been concentrated around Caverswall. Meir, Werrington, Hulme, Bucknall, Weston Coyney and Adderley appear to have varied between four and six households with a scatter of single houses of tiny groups of two or three at sites like Cookshill, Roughcote, Eaves, Ash and Kerry Hill.

In Careswell village very little had changed in plan since the days of John de Smallys. The heart of the village was its square, its soul was the church whilst the castle and the surrounding fields were its sinews. Around these vital organs the dwellings of the people had moved sporadically as a family died, a dwelling became uninhabitable or prosperity heightened aspirations but with all, such tissue growth and change had not altered the general plan of square, main street and major buildings, only their precise locations had varied.

The castle was a steadily decaying hulk, its farmlands tenanted and worked by the family of that Thomas Browne to whom Sir Thomas Giffard had granted rights of turbary in 1515. The Brownes had been loyal tenants but with the departure of the Giffards in 1542 and uncertainty over the obligations to be honoured following an expired lease loyalty had been swayed by self interest. The industry with which they worked the land and reaped the harvest was coupled with a resolute determination to ensure that the rightful owners should never wish to return to the castle maintained at personal expense. Necessary repairs had been ignored or skimped, stonework had been cannabilised, the drying moat had become a dumping ground for all forms of village waste whilst rank grasses and insidious weeds had begun to overwhelm the surrounding pathways and rise up the walls.

Somewhere about the year 1540 Sir John Port scholar of Brasenose College and a future Sheriff of Derbyshire, married Elizabeth the daughter of Sir Thomas Giffard and so acquired the estate at Caverswall. He and his wife had three daughters the eldest of whom was to marry George Hastings, the fourth Earl of Huntingdon.

THE PORT FAMILY

The Port family was neither as old nor as noble as the Giffards but their ancestry contained a proud merchantile tradition based largely on the city of Chester but with extensive interests in Lancashire and Derbyshire.

Sir John Port married twice. His father had played an important role in the establishment of Brasenose College, Oxford. John had been educated there and served as a lecturer for some time. He was knighted in 1547 and acquired Caverswall through his marriage to Elizabeth Giffard in 1539. They had three daughters. It seems unlikely that the family spent much time in Caverswall for in 1542 the family was engaged in a legal dispute with two men, Richard Harper and Simon Starkey about land leased to them in Caverswall.

Sir John married for a second time upon the death of Elizabeth and died in 1557.

If Sir John Port and his wife ever actually lived in the Castle it can only have been for a brief time between the departure of Elizabeth's father and the leasing of the castle and estate which seems to have been effected by 1542 for the records show that:

'*On the Octaves of St. Hillary 33, HVIII (1542). Between Richard Harper and Simon Starkey, complainants, and John Porte amiger and his wife Elizabeth, deforciants, of a moiety of the castle of Cariswalle and of a moiety of 200 messuage, 40 tofts, 200 gardens.*'[21]

With the marriage of Dorothy Port to George Hastings the estate once again changed hands as part of a marriage dowry and once again the rightful owners were very much absentee landlords. It was the Earl of Huntingdon and his wife who leased the estate to farmer Ralph Browne.

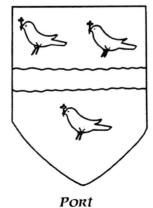

PORT

THE HASTINGS FAMILY

The first recorded member of note was Sir Henry de Hastings who died in 1250. He married Ada daughter of the Earl of Huntingdon who was the younger brother of the Scottish King, William the Lion.

His son also Sir Henry de Hastings, was summoned to parliament by Simon de Montfort in 1264 whose party he supported in the Barons' War (1263 - 67), he died in 1269.

During the war Sir Henry fought at the battles of Lewes and Evesham. From June to December 1266 he held Kenilworth castle against King Henry III.

His son John served Edward I in Wales and Scotland and may well have met members of the de Kaverswelle family during those campaigns.

The Lord Hastings who was executed by Richard III was the grandfather of George Hastings who was created Earl of Huntingdon in 1529. His descendants held that title until 1789 when the 10th. Earl died.

Dorothy one of the daughters of Elizabeth Giffard and Sir John Port married George Hastings, the fourth Earl of Huntingdon. In addition to his wife he acquired 200 messuages (either sites of property or buildings with associated areas of land), 10 cottages, 6 tofts, 40 gardens, 40 orchards, 400 acres of land, 300 acres of meadows, 600 acres of pasture, 200 acres of wood and 100 acres of furze and heath in Caverswall. This property was the source of legal action between George Hastings and Thomas Chiswell in 1592. This suggests that lands at Caverswall had been leased to one or more parties for some time.

The Earl and his wife did not settle in Caverswall. A farmer, Ralph Brown, leased from the Earl the castle, a messuage, a dovecote, a watermill, 60 acres of wood, 300 acres of furze and heath, 20 acres of moor and 20 acres of marsh in Caverswall. The lease ran from the feast of St. Michael 1582 for 25 years at an annual fee of £11. 6s. 8d.

1600 A.D.

THE NOISE OF FETTERS BREAKING

On New Year's Eve 1600 the bulk of the parish was in good heart. It was a yeoman parish whose wealth was fairly vested in the land, whose beasts were well fed and carefully tended, and whose private dwellings were well maintained. Yet as a yeoman parish it lacked leadership, the Brownes were probably the first family, if such a concept existed, they held the most land, claimed the greatest income and carried the greatest weight but only in a practical sphere, they were maintainers rather than leaders; the state of the castle, church and churchyard proclaimed to the thoughtful observer that such modest leadership was not enough.

The mental horizons of the people of Careswell were traditionally marginally wider than those of their neighbours. The horizons of the 'common man' were, of necessity, shaped by the needs of the body, the physical demands of incessant toil, the simple need to explain the inexplicable, the physical and mental problems of travel far beyond the limits dictated by basic needs and a dearth of even moderately reliable sources of information. For a great majority of the villagers a lack of education, the lack of a saleable skill, a lack of means and a lack of will meant that their world was encompassed within the landmarks of Wetley Moor, the forested wastes beyond Adderley, the great ridge beyond the Mere and the neighbouring villages of Foresbrook and Dillorne. Yet the involvement of a constant sequence of castle owners with both county and national affairs, their ownership of estates elsewhere necessitating a certain coming and going of messengers and the proximity of a number of religious houses had served to ensure that the villagers of Careswell had some modest awareness of the world outside. Each community possessed a hinterland of consciousness and contacts which meant that news passed albeit erratically and uncertainly from place to place by means of a variety of chance encounters.

Such channels of communication bore to Careswell news of great political moment; stories of wealth being won from the wool trade and strangely garbled news of the lives and deaths of great and infamous men. Such news however served to provide no more passing interest for a parish bent upon toil, survival and advancement than was necessary to enrich an idle hour in the tavern or beneath the tree on a balmy evening.

1606AD

TAKE OF ENGLISH EARTH

The arrival of the travellers from a place called Wolverhampton caused a substantial stir in the village. The party was led by the agent of the Hastings family and comprised a group of men before whom the normally proud and arrogant bailiff behaved obsequiously. They took the best rooms at the tavern which meant ousting the landlord from his own, insisted upon a complete change of bed linen and bedding, eschewed the common table with its set meal at five pence per head and threw the house into disorder by demanding the provision of good meals to be served privately to them in their chambers. Their calm acceptance of the landlord's hastily calculated charge of two shillings per head for such treatment astounded him and raised problems, for the cuisine at Careswell was very much of the five penny variety. The strangers accepted the charge of three pence per horse at grass with out demur but insisted upon the provision of decent oats, straw and shelter. A boy with a cart was hastily despatched to Mr. Barber at Weston Coyney to fetch a load of his finest oats and cleanest hay. The agent then summoned Ralph Browne the farmer and sometime tenant of the Hasting lands to a meeting with the strangers. Browne arrived in his own time as befitted the most powerful man in the village and left some twenty minutes later looking pensive and shorn of bombast.

When the group walked across the Square the village came to standstill. The appearance of each member, his clothing, confidence, self assurance and lively interest in the things around him were all of a type not seen in Careswell before. On succeeding days they studied the castle with care, rode over the parish and spent long hours in quiet but intense debate in the chambers they had sequestered. Finally, they reappeared and surveyed the Square. The one known as Mathew Cradock pointed to the angle where The Hollows entered the Square, looked carefully at the position of the early morning sun and gave a series of firm and incisive instructions to the agent. That done the reckoning was paid, the horses called for and the party left.

The Stone House

Between them Browne the farmer, the landlord and the domestic servants knew enough to piece together the story.

Mathew Cradock was an exceedingly wealthy wool merchant, the owner of vast estates with extensive business interests in Wolverhampton and Stafford. His father, it was rumoured, was even richer, was called George and had been responsible for building the new Shire Hall in Stafford between 1586 and 1590 and had been bailiff of Stafford in 1589. The Cradock family, through George, had purchased the Castle from the Earl of Huntingdon. Browne had been subjected to a severe snibbing for his neglect of the fabric of the Castle despite his plea that the formal lease had long expired..

The women whispered that George Cradock had married a Leek girl called Jane Yolley or Jolley and that they had travelled a lot to London town when George Cradock had been discharging his duties as Member of Parliament. Mathew Cradock had been born in 1580, was 26 years old and was married to Dorothy the daughter of Lord Greenway from somewhere called Berkshire.

Cradock

All marvelled at the news that such distinguished persons were intending to live in the village and that was certain because Mathew Cradock had ordered the immediate building of a big stone house in the Square in which he might live whilst the Castle was being rebuilt. At the thought of the Castle being rebuilt heads were shaken in wondering amazement and the village hung in suspense. Farmer Browne applied himself zealously to the task of rearranging his affairs and marking clearly the livestock which belonged to his family.

The Browne family first begins to figure in parish records in the early years of the 16th century. By 1585 these yeoman farmers had risen to a sufficiently high level to be able to lease from George Hastings and his wife Dorothy, the lands belonging to the Castle. At this time a large dovecote stood where Dove House Farm now stands. In the time of Ralph Browne such a feature was a commonplace on every large holding for it was from that stock of domesticated doves that the owner's family drew birds for the table. Ralph Browne was industrious and able. Contemporaries claimed that he was also cunning and deliberately permitted the Castle to decay in order that its owners would be less than eager to return and dispossess him. Evidence exists which shows that his lease expired in 1607 leaving a period when formal control of the property was uncertain for almost twenty years. What Ralph did during that period will never be known.

The parish registers contain many references to the Browne family and it is apparent from the number of monuments which exist within the Church that after the arrival of the Cradocks the Browne family continued to prosper. That they were parish benefactors there can be no doubt for a wall tablet in the Church records that:

'John Browne late of Caverswall Gent: and Ralph Browne his father late of the Meir and Cookshill Gent: left for the poor of this parish forever 14 acres of land called the Stevenstiches, out of which two pounds ten shillings is to be paid yearly forever, to the minister for two sermons, one upon the 24th June and the other upon 12th December.'

THE BROWNE FAMILY

The Brownes, later spelt Brown, were yeoman farmers of the class whose industry was the mainstay of rural England in the sixteenth century.

Although Ralph Browne was condemned by his contemporaries for allowing the castle to fall into disrepair in order to dissuade its owners from returning to live there tablets in the church indicate that the family was prosperous and generous in its gifts to the parish. Indeed evidence suggests that he may have been wronged in relation to his alleged neglect of the castle.

Ralph Browne had three daughters, Margery (1559), Marie (1569) and Grace (1570) and four sons John, the eldest, William (1574), Thomas (1576) and Ralph (died 1625).

Thomas is recorded as patron of the parish of Caverswall in 1618.

An ordnance survey map for 1877 reveals traces of what seems to be a water control system beside the area of ridge and furrow beyond the church. Evidence of those works is still visible. It is possible that those remains represent part of a water meadow system introduced by the Browne family during their dominance as farmers during the second half of the sixteenth century.

A wall monument dated 1670 bears a rather unusual epitaph which seems, by one interpretation at least, to convey good wishes to the living members of the Browne family for it reads:
   'Anno Domini 1670 Blest here and near in peace doe rest All they of those that are deseased.'

Then follows a list of names, the tablet has been damaged but ends with the words:
   'The two first Brownes of Caverswall were but all the rest were of the Meere. The fourth made this in memory of parents . . .'

The baptismal registers record that Ralph Browne had three daughters, Margery, Marie and Grace and four sons, John, William, Thomas and Ralph.
   The Vicar, Ralph Turner, had also been the target of some severe criticism. Mathew Cradock had made it abundantly clear that he wished to worship in a worthy church and had rated Turner, whom he had descibed as *'nothing better than an ignorant household*

servant',[23] for the near dereliction of the church, the unkempt appearance of the church-yard and the abysmal quality of his sermons.

Mathew Cradock enlisted the skills of John Smythson in the rebuilding of his castle. The south front was to be built anew incorporating the traditional features and qualities of the Jacobean age and eschewing the new fangled Palladian innovations of Inigo Jones. The new dwelling was to be built on the north side of the castle mound, the back of the house rising four storeys high from the bottom of the moat. The principal rooms were to be on the south side prefaced by a high terraced garden designed to catch the full warmth of the sun. The whole was to be approached over a double arched bridge and entered through the arch of a twin turreted gate-house. As much as possible of the earlier castle was to be retained. The stinking and choked moat was to be drained, cleared, puddled, rebanked and refilled. The bailey was to become a terrace, the flanking towers were to be converted into garden pavilions. The curtain walls, no longer likely to be needed for defence, were to be lowered to give generous views over the surrounding countryside. The stone so released was to be used initially for the new and first stone house to be built in the village. The west tower was to be rebuilt and rewindowed. The whole castle was to be enriched within by the extensive use of the finest oak panelling and embellished without by choice and elegant plants.

Mathew Cradock was intelligent, wealthy, widely travelled and well read. He knew well of the truth behind the writings of William Harrison:

'How wonderfully is the beauty of the gardens annexed to our houses increased with flowers and variety of costly and curious workmanship and with rare and medicinable herbs.'

Whilst the house was to be testimony to his vision, wealth and status, pride demanded one last gesture, upon the forged hinges of the oak doors at the entrance to the Moat Bridge he had stamped 'M.C. 1625' recording the completion of a project which had been launched some ten years earlier.

Despite Mathew Cradock's concern to beautify his castle one of the prime concerns of the villagers was the collection of peat from Wetley Moor. The peat was cut from the ground in small blocks leaving water filled trenches and blocks of exposed peat resembling the area shown.

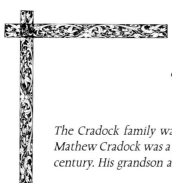

THE CRADOCK FAMILY

The Cradock family was well known in the south of the county in the late 16th. century. Mathew Cradock was a prominent citizen of Stafford during the second half of the sixteenth century. His grandson also Mathew Cradock became the first mayor of Stafford in 1614.

Mathew (senior) died, probably in 1584, although 1586 and 1592 are possibilities, leaving his son George the heir to immense wealth.

George Cradock had been responsible for the building of the Shire Hall in Stafford between 1586 and 1590. The family had extensive business interests in timber and wool as well as range of wider and overseas interests.

George Cradock married Jane Jolley from Leek and in 1580 their son Mathew was born. Mathew in his turn had married Dorothy Greenway and in 1627 took over the affairs of the castle when his father purchased it from the Earl of Huntingdon. The Earl had leased the castle to Ralph Browne a yeoman farmer who, according to his contemporaries, had allowed the castle buildings to fall into disrepair in the hope that the owners would not regard it as a residence and so extend the lease. This may be an injustice since the initial lease ran from 1582 for twenty-five years giving an expiry date of 1607.

Church records show that the church was rebuilt by the Cradock family during the period 1628 to 1630. Engraved hinges on the doors at the entrance to the Moat Bridge bear the inscription M C 1625. Property Transactions dated 1638 and held in the William Salt Library at Stafford refer to a stone house built at the site of the castle, evidence which points to the present day Stone House. The available evidence points to the termination of an earlier lease in 1607, a period of uncertainty during which some of the stone was removed followed by extended sale negotiations and a major period of rebuilding starting somewhere around 1615. The date of 1625 on the hinges suggests completion of the work on the castle before work on the church began in 1628.

Mathew Cradock put money and energy into rebuilding both the castle and the church. In the church he had the original pointed arches pulled down and replaced with rounded ones the better to accommodate the new clerestory windows. The doors were replaced and a new altar table provided.

Mathew Cradock evaded the responsibilities of knighthood and in consequence was fined £50 by Charles I. Other offenders were fined as little as £5 or £10.

When he purchased the Caverswall estate Mathew Cradock also acquired lands in Dilhorne and Ipstones. He was regarded by those responsible for the records which appear in the Parliamentary History (Vol.II) as a capitalist and appears to have bought into the East India Company to the tune of £2,000.

As a Puritan and a Parliamentarian he found his personal friendship with the brave and outspoken, staunchly Royalist Parkers of Park Hall a source of worry. Mathew Cradock died in 1636.

His son George died suddenly in 1643 only a year after he had been appointed a Captain of Foot in a force created to try to keep the county quiet. The death of George is recorded on a wall memorial in the church which makes interesting reading. It states that … George Cradock was assaulted by death in the meridian of his age not far off from his castle … Did he die of a heart attack? Was he lodged in the Stone House which seems to have been used for quarantine purposes in an age when many diseases, including smallpox, were efficient killers? His death left his mother and his wife Mary, who was eight months pregnant, to look after a castle coveted by both sides as a possible strong point in the Civil War which was dividing the country. With the end of the Civil War Dorothy sold the castle to William Jolliffe of Leek another Parliamentarian, and moved to London.

Her three daughters all married well. Their marriages are recorded on a memorial in the Chancel. Dorothy married Sir Robert Slingsby, Elizabeth married the Right Honourable Robert, Lord Cholmondeley and Mary married Sir John Bridgeman.

The Castle, the bulk of the building shown reflects the
work carried out by Mathew Cradock

As the work on the house drew towards its conclusion Mathew Cradock turned his attention towards the church. The new Vicar was Alexander Howe, a Bachelor of Divinity from Oxford. Although he held Caverswall in plurality with Draycott in the Moors where he had been Rector since 1614 his parish had seen little of him. The news of his acceptance of the incumbency of Careswell had been welcomed partly in the hope that such a scholar could only be an improvement upon the unregretted Ralph Turner and his successor Richard Barrow. Unfortunately, these hopes were soon dashed and local opinion became so bitter against 'Mr. Howe' that in 1629 the Bishop's Visitation produced the brief but damaging comment that:

'Mr. Howe, Vicar, is noted by many in our parish to have obteyned the Vicaridge of Careswell by symony.'

Even a radical and rather insensitive reshaping of the Church between 1628 and 1630 failed to attract the Reverend Howe back to his duties most of which were discharged by his goodly, not overly wise but diligent curate Richard Bentley. In 1637 Richard Marchenton assumed the curacy, a fleeting reminder of the days now past when the Marchentons had been lords of the castle. In acknowledgement of his lineage and apparent zeal George Cradock, son of Mathew, authorised some further but small scale improvements to the church so completing the building which was to cater for the spiritual needs of the parish for the next century and a half.

However a sadder and more genuine purpose underlay these final reconstructions for in 1636 Mathew Cradock, saviour of the village who had rebuilt the Castle *'even to beauty'* had drawn the last dark breaths of death. These final adjustments to the fabric were intended at once to provide a suitable location for the marble tablet to be erected to his memory and to bring his plans for further work to an end.

The work of Mathew Cradock and the tablet erected to his memory remain to this day. The Castle although shorn of its wet moat is much as he left it, the tablet is still visible in the chancel of the church.

In purchasing the Castle the Cradock family acquired land at Dillerne and later in 1633 at Ipstones. They also brought themselves into the obligations of knighthood for in Volume II of the Historical Collections of Staffordshire's Parliamentary History it states:

'Charles I heavily fined knights for non-appearance. Under the feudal system it was compulsory for everyone who held a knight's fee, to be received in the Order of Knighthood or in default to pay a fine to the King. Mathew Cradock of Caverswall £50.0s.0d.' [24]

Mathew Cradock as a Puritan and a Parliamentarian must have regarded such a fine as a modest price to pay for being freed from the obligations of knighthood and the burden of loyalty to a monarch whose politics he detested. Such a sum must have represented but a drop in his financial ocean; an ocean of wealth which allowed him to invest £2,000 in the funds of the East India Company in 1628.

The wall tablet erected by his son George reads:

'Here lies buried Math: Cradock Esq: whose wife was Elizabeth daughter of Ric. Rowler (of Shropshire) Esquire. His children were George, his first born (whose wife was Dorothea daughter of John Sanders Doctor of Medecine), and his only daughter Mary who was married to John Lilday. The son raised this marble monument to his father, (the son) for whom the father had first built a splended house. It is not for me to say whether the father was more provident, or the heir more mindful of his duty.

Both were worthy, the father of his son and the son of his father. If only the world had been as worthy of both.'

This tablet in company with a number of beautiful and unusual wall monuments and

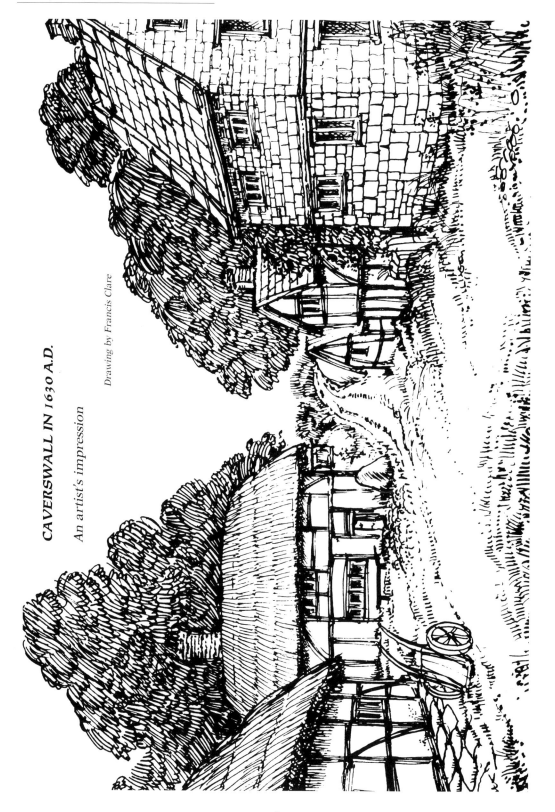

CAVERSWALL IN 1630 A.D.

An artist's impression

Drawing by Francis Clare

memorials may still be viewed in St. Peter's Church.

During the second decade of the century another member of the *'nouveaux riches'* appeared in the parish. George Parker had married Grace Bateman of Huntington and in seeking a country seat had discovered the properties owned by the Coyneys at Weston Coyney. The transaction was speedily completed and the Parkers moved into the Coyney home which was still situated in the substantial moated farmhouse which once dominated the area where 'The Moat' now is.

George Parker and George Cradock were of an age, their wealth, backgrounds, status in the parish brought them together despite their differing political allegiances.

Since the two Georges were friends and Mathew Cradock was an ardent Parliamentarian it is not inconceivable that George Parker sat with his friend George Cradock listening to Mathew's account of incident in Parliament in 1621 when the Puritan members had clashed with the monarch. Perhaps they walked on the incomplete terrace of the half finished house as Mathew recited with quiet fervour how the members had attacked monopolies, impeached Bacon and finally had felt so strongly that they had recorded in the journals of The House a protestation of their right as representatives of the people to speak freely on all subjects. The scarcely suppressed angry bitterness of Mathew's voice seems to echo down the years as he told, with graphic coldness, of the King's action in tearing the offending page from the book and hurling it to the floor in gesture of contemptuous defiance. To the puritan parliamentarian Mathew Cradock, with his businessman's knowledge of the sources of wealth and a true understanding of the changing balance of power in society, such an act must have been both a proclamation of unbelieveable economic ignorance and a declaration of war.

Perchance it was after this discussion that George Parker and Grace were invited to dine with the Cradocks in order that they might try the latest aid to refined eating, a device called 'a fork' which had appeared in the higher social circles of London about ten years earlier and was designed to replace the fingers at table and so spare the clothes.

To such well read, far travelled, for the age, and practical men the state of the parish in the early 1630s must have been a source of concern. Movement through the parish was not easy, of the roads it had been said:

'In the clay and cledgey soil they are often very deep and troublesome in the winter half.'

In order that such problems might be overcome Parliament had laid the duties of highway maintenance clearly upon the parish so that:

'all sorts of the common people do employ their travail for six days in summer upon the amendment of the roads.'

Human nature being what it was and still is and road travel meaning so little to the 'common people' of Careswell it comes as no surprise to discover that observers were able to note with sadness that:

'the rich do so cancel their portions and the poor so loiter in their labours that of all of the six scarcely two days work are well performed and accomplished.'

The process of the consolidation of agricultural holdings and the progressive enrichment of the arable farmer must have gladdened their hearts. Even the Brownes whose industry and ability had, in the ultimate, saved them from removal from the 'in-desmesne' holdings had been encouraged to consider the possible use of the new fangled draining machines, ploughs and manures. The Cradocks had transferred turnips and potatoes from their garden plots where they had been grown as curiosities to their fields beyond the church where they were cultivated as a root crop. They even endorsed the general view of pigs:

'They are troublesome, noysome, unruly and great ravenours, the Husbandman's Best Scavenger, and the Huswife's most wholesome sinke and in the dish so lovely and so wholesome that all other faults may be borne with.'

John Browne put it more bluntly in true 'Carsa' fashion:

'The hog is never good but when he is in the dish.'

Although ignorant of cattle breeding they knew the value of the rugged long-horned Staffordshires as beef cattle and spoke of driving them to market in Wolverhampton where the Cradock business interests offered easy access to the urban markets.

They also brought a new sense of purpose to the village. Having first initiated the restoration of the church fabric the Cradocks provided a magnificent altar table in 1633 as another clear statement of their faith. The hedge along The Dams was cut back and the path opened to Weston Coyney. The rebuilt church and its tidy yard, the orderly fields with their unusual, newly planted and much encouraged hedgerows, the neater, better maintained wooden farmhouses were all proof of a new vitality in the parish. Self help or individual enterprise had led, despite occasional lean years, to a steady improvement in the lot of the villager.

Contemporary scribes wrote glowingly that things *'be marvelously altered in England'* and made reference to *'the multitude of chimneys recently erected;' 'the great amendment of lodging'* as the flock mattress replaced the tick infested straw pallet and commended *'the exchange of vessels'* as *'treen platters and wooden spoons'* gave way to *'pewter ware and silver or tin spoons.'*

Outside the home praise was lavished upon:

'Our orchards which were never furnished with so good fruit nor with such variety as at present. For beside that we have the most delicate apples, pears, plums, walnuts, filberts . . . so we have no less store of strange fruits as apricots, almonds, peaches and figs.'

The Parkers and the Cradocks must surely have striven to bring such features of the southern shires to Careswell parish. They may well even have drawn coal from that part of the parish in the vicinity of Winterfield Lane where mining was still taking place at the end of the 1950s.

Yet life was far from a round of ease and glamour and comfort. Sanitation was abysmal at all social levels. During the Civil War the Royalist leaders and their ladies were accused, during their sojourn in pro- Royalist Oxford, of fouling stairs, corners, passageways, and rooms with their excrement although this may have been deliberate propaganda. Pepys was able to record in his diary for 20th October, 1660:

'going down to my cellar to look, I put my foot into a great heap of turds, by which I find the Turner's house of office is full and comes into my cellar, which doth trouble me.'

Clearly most dwellings had a 'proper place'. In 1515 when Dorothy Montgomery brought her husband Sir Thomas Giffard to the 'goodly castle' reference was made to *'Pooles, Dams and Houses of Office being all of masonry'* [25] These indispensable facilities varied from crude earth closets in the poorer dwellings to vents which opened straight into the moat of the castle.

Life for the peasant and the yeoman alike must have been squalid and foul by modern standards. Medical care was non-existent, well tried local, natural remedies were often the only potential cure for most ailments. Days were long, life was hard, homes were verminous. For the poor life, only marginally better than that lived by generations of their forebears in the parish, was still a dour struggle and far from 'merrie'.

The feud between King and Parliament rumbled on until 1640 when the Totmanslow Hundred in which Careswell still lies, was required to produce Ship Money amounting to £468 - 16s - 11d. This Royal imposition brought concern to the parish. Shorn of the influence of his father and able to watch events from closer at hand than many of his countrymen and concerned for the peace of the area, the early inclination to Parliament of George Cradock had given way to slightly pro-Royalist tendencies. He and George Parker had much to lose if the war came and in company with many of their kind found a sad conflict of opinion within their own minds. North Staffordshire would clearly declare for the Parliament; the strongly rumoured Catholicism of the King and his financial impositions apart, they and many of their own class felt a fundamental, precautionary, conservative loyalty towards the King and the stability the monarchy seemed to represent.

In a desperate effort 'to keep the country quiet' a military force was to be raised which would keep the peace. George Cradock's name was recorded as one of the 'Captaines of Foote' within the Hundred whilst George Parker was designated a 'Captaine of Horses'. Their co-signatory on a document requiring the Totmanslow Hundred to raise, train and exercise twice weekly some 135 foot and 35 'carbynes' was a yeoman farmer, John Hollins of Careswell.

Against this back-drop of uncertainty the life of the parish and its leading families moved on. George and Grace Parker produced two sons, William who was to inhabit Park Hall and Thomas who moved to Leek. George Cradock and his wife produced their 'pair royal' of incomparable daughters, Dorothy, Elizabeth and Mary in 1640, 1641 and 1643 respectively. The Brownes laboured steadily and quietly, by sheer merit and industry maintaining their status as the leading yeoman family of the parish.

In 1643 tragedy struck for, when Dorothy was eight months pregnant with Mary, her husband George was 'assaulted by death in the meridian of his age, not far off from his castle'. There is a suspicion that the cause of death may have been smallpox but there is a strangeness about the wording which suggests that George Cradock may have suffered a heart attack perhaps in the fields near his castle.

In the chancel of St. Peter's Church there is a lovely mural monument in the Renaissance style which serves as both epitaph and record of the family history.

'George Cradock Esq: for his great prudence in common laws, was thought well worthy to be Beau Clerk of the Assize of this Circuit, did take to his wife the most amiable and most loving Dorothy, daughter of Job Saunders, doctor of physic, by whom he had a pair royal of incomparable daughters, to wit, Dorothy, Elizabeth and Mary. It is easy to guess that he lived in a splendid degree, if I shall recount unto you that Sir Robert Slingsby, Baronet, married Dorothy, the Right Honourable Lord Cholmondly married Elizabeth, and Sir John Bridgman married Mary. But to our grief George Cradock was assaulted by death in the meridian of his age, not far off from his Castle, lately built, even to beauty, by Mathew Cradock, his father, who lies interned near this place. And dying of the Smallpox the 16th April 1643 he took himself to the private mansion of this tombe erected for him by Dorothy his obsequious wife where he now rests under the protection of an essoine until he shall be summoned to appear at the last great and general Assizes.'

The term 'pair-royal' is a slight misnomer since correctly used it means 'triplets'. However it could also mean 'three of a kind' and may well bear the more subtle interpretation that the daughters were so alike in beauty, charm, temperament and kindliness that they could have been cast from the same mould.

1643 A.D.

THIS SIN OF WAR

Civil War brought new tensions to the parish. William Parker, son of George, declared for the King and took command of a local company of foot in the service of King Charles. George Cradock, less a zealous parliamentarian than his father, was havering, uncertain in his allegiance but inclining to the King, when death struck. His widow seeking solace and support as her time drew near sought true comfort and consolation with the Parker family, friends of long-standing. She found herself a widow, mother of three baby girls, the youngest scarcely a month old and, in the eyes of the Parliamentary Committee at least, the defender of Caverswall Castle, a potential Royalist stronghold in the heart of Parliamentary North Staffordshire. Suddenly friendship with the brave and outspoken Parkers became a threat.

THE PARKER FAMILY

The patriarch of the family was George Parker who died in 1675 aged 84 years. It was he who bought and rebuilt Park Hall. He was an ardent loyalist and an able lawyer.

In 1642 the High Sheriff and the Justices of the Peace for the County met to devise a strategy for keeping the County quiet as the nation moved towards war. George Parker was appointed Captain of Horse for the Hundred of Totmanslow. His near neighbour, George Cradock of the castle at Caverswall was appointed a Captain of Foot at the same time. The joint initiative came to nothing and neighbourliness came to an end when hostilities broke out and George Cradock declared for the Parliament.

George, nicknamed Buffcoat Parker because of the dress worn by his company of foot soldiers, fought at Hopton Heath, Marston Moor, Naseby and Worcester. He was captured and imprisoned first on the Isle of Sheppey then at Stafford Castle. He returned to Park Hall and his own lands at the Restoration.

Sir Thomas Parker (1695 - 1784) was a barrister who became a judge and a Privy Cousellor.

The Parkers suffered a severe blow in 1791 when, after a prolonged dry spell Park Hall caught fire. The family moved into temporary quarters at Rough Cote Hall and subsequently built a new hall which was situated at the western end of the present lake.

In 1825 Thomas Hawe Parker of Park Hall helped to establish a primary school on the site where St. Peter's C.E.A Primary School now stands. He acted as one of the founders and sold the site of the school to the founders for the sum of £10 'lawful money.'

An Extract from the Parker Family tree

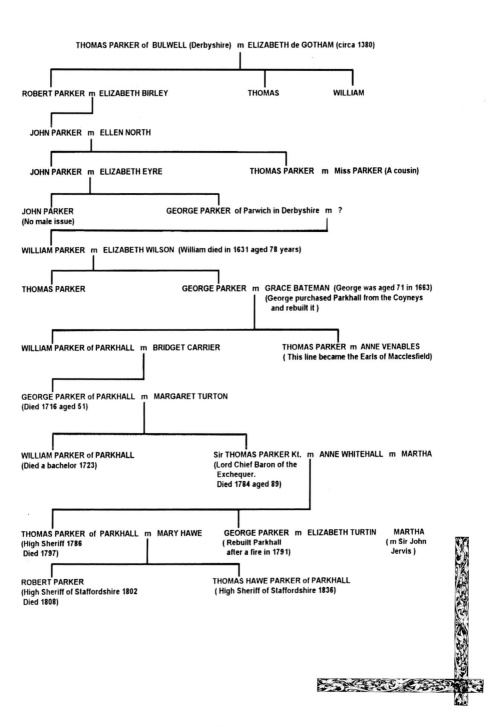

THOMAS PARKER of BULWELL (Derbyshire) m ELIZABETH de GOTHAM (circa 1380)

ROBERT PARKER m ELIZABETH BIRLEY   THOMAS   WILLIAM

JOHN PARKER m ELLEN NORTH

JOHN PARKER m ELIZABETH EYRE   THOMAS PARKER m Miss PARKER (A cousin)

JOHN PARKER
(No male issue)   GEORGE PARKER of Parwich in Derbyshire m ?

WILLIAM PARKER m ELIZABETH WILSON (William died in 1631 aged 78 years)

THOMAS PARKER   GEORGE PARKER m GRACE BATEMAN (George was aged 71 in 1663)
                                          (George purchased Parkhall from the Coyneys
                                          and rebuilt it)

WILLIAM PARKER of PARKHALL m BRIDGET CARRIER   THOMAS PARKER m ANNE VENABLES
                                                        (This line became the Earls of Macclesfield)

GEORGE PARKER of PARKHALL m MARGARET TURTON
(Died 1716 aged 51)

WILLIAM PARKER of PARKHALL   Sir THOMAS PARKER Kt. m ANNE WHITEHALL m MARTHA
(Died a bachelor 1723)   (Lord Chief Baron of the
                                    Exchequer.
                                    Died 1784 aged 89)

THOMAS PARKER of PARKHALL m MARY HAWE   GEORGE PARKER m ELIZABETH TURTIN   MARTHA
(High Sheriff 1786   (Rebuilt Parkhall   (m Sir John
Died 1797)   after a fire in 1791)   Jervis)

ROBERT PARKER   THOMAS HAWE PARKER of PARKHALL
(High Sheriff of Staffordshire 1802 (High Sheriff of Staffordshire 1836)
Died 1808)

The Committee at Stafford was not slow to act. Military districts were delineated and levies made upon them requiring each, according to its means, to support a group of officers and men and at the same time to provide men for the armies of the Parliament. In this way the villages were to be garrisoned and controlled by Parliamentary troops.

The setting sun was throwing long shadows across the Square and sharpening into a pattern of silver and dark the waters of the castle moat when the sound of chanting was heard coming from the direction of the hamlet at Mere. Urchins who scurried off to see what was the source came panting back, fear written across their faces, with the message that 'an army of puritans' was coming! The rhythmic chanting grew louder and across the marshy valley of the Blythe splashed a horseman and 20 file of foot. The column moved forward purposefully, across the meadows below the Castle and up onto the pathway which ran along the top of the dam. The tramp of their feet and the hymn on their lips seemed to fill the quiet village air with the sound and threat of fury.

The officer wore a breast plate and greaves. The setting sun sparkling and dancing upon his armour threw a giant shadow across the Square. The sombre dullness of sword belt, boots and harness seemed totally in tune with the general air of menace his followers bore. The long, dark, curled hair framed a cruel, coarse face bloated with strong drink, lacking any sign of kindness or compassion. The officer's dark, cold eyes flicked contemptuously over the poor dwellings of the villagers, lingered long on the Stone House as if weighing its military and strategic worth and then swung towards the church and the castle. If the officer's presence bespoke cruelty and menace the mighty pikemen drew gasps of fear from the villagers. The combined weight of each man's corselet, ridged iron helmet known as a 'combe-cap', sword, rations, kit, clothing and 16 foot pike with its massive iron head required a tall and powerful man to bear it. The pikemen were the mighty elite of the army and this group had been chosen for effect. Powerful, crude, brutal men they marched with arrogant contempt. The four musketeers at the rear of the column attracted as much interest but generated less fear than their predecessors. Somehow the swinging bandoliers, shouldered muskets and heavy swords seemed strangely less menacing than the cumbersome and obsolescent pikes.

Conscious of the effect they were having the marchers went straight to the castle entrance where they halted, swung about, shuffled and appeared as a military cordon around the entrance. Followed only by the musketeers Captain Young rode across the double arched bridge, through the archway of the gatehouse and up to the door. The clatter of his horse's hooves stopped abruptly to be replaced by the hollow thunder of his sword hilt on the main door of the castle. The sound of his hammering and the roar of his voice echoed across the evening air.

'Open in the name of the King and the Parliament. I take possession of this Careswell House to hold and safely keep it against all enemies of all people.'

The Widow Cradock had no choice but to obey.

Having drunk well of George Cradock's cherished store of wines the replete and slightly inebriated captain studied his orders.

'It is ordered that Captain Young shall forthwith repayre to Carswall House and safely keepe the same for the use of the Kinge and Parliament until he shall have order to the contrarie but he is to leave his horses behind at Stafford.

He is likewise to use Mrs. Cradock with all respect and not suffer any spoyle or waste made of her goods and he is permitted to send his errants and gain provision of victuals out of the Constablewick for the maintenance of his men which shall be abated out of their weekly pay.' [26]

The following morning the Parliamentary stamp was impressed more firmly upon the confused villagers. The Captain's constant references to 'King and Parliament' bewildered the simple country folk into uncertainty. The men were placed in billets around the castle. The parish was to provide 20 armed men to be stationed constantly at the Castle to assist in its defence against all enemies of the King and Parliament. Those members of the force created *'to keep the County quiet'* were ordered to attend forthwith, parading with such arms and accoutrements as they possessed. Carswall was to produce a weekly levy amounting to £4.13s.4d to pay the wages of the garrison provided for its protection.

The villagers listened to the bull-like tones of the Captain in stunned silence. The sum of money to be levied was beyond the comprehension of the majority of them. The poorest families in full employment received only about 20 pence each week, the skilled artisans could almost double that in good times whilst only the most successful of the farmers could boast a weekly income amounting to 15 shillings. The whole weekly income of the parish at this time was probably between £22 and £24, at a stroke the wealth of the village was to be reduced by roughly one fifth and the parish living through hard times!

Captain Young was deprived of his command some short time after his arrival. His general coarseness and indisputable affection for the bottle rendering him unfit for command, his replacement was Mr. James Creswall.

'Carswall House and Garrison'

'It is ordered by the Committee at Stafford that Mr. James Creswall shall take command at Carswall Hall and shall have 20 men constantly there with Armes of Knowne trust and fidelity to keepe the same for the use of the King and Parliament and that he and all the said men that he employes shall forthwith take the Protestation and that the said Mr. Creswall shall forthwith take in provision both of victuals and ammunition and shall cut and pull downe all trees and otherthings that may be anywise offensive to the same and shall also endeavour to do best that he can for the fortification and defence of it and see that there be constant scout maintaintion and that he shall receive nothing into the same for harbour that belongs to any papist delinquent or malignant nor take away any profit or any thing whatsoever that belongs to the Garrison at Stafford without order from thence and for the mayntenance of the said 20 men they do proportion £4.13s.4d out of the weekly pay of that constablewick provided that this shall not hinder anything that is arreare or behind of the said weekly pay which is to be forthwith payd to the Treasurer at Stafford also the remaynder over and above the said £4.13s.4d allowed as aforesaid and that Mr. Creswall during the time that he is employed in the said service shall be abated his weekly pay in regard of his paines there. It is ordered that Mrs. Cradock shall have towards the fortification of her house at Carswall liberty to take, fell, cut down and carrie away any timber or other materials from any papist delinquent or malignant'[26]

As Creswall's men went about their task of bringing the castle into a state of military preparedness the days shortened into autumn and woodsmoke from the burning timber seemed to hang everywhere. Gradually the impositions of the soldiery began to tell upon the villagers. As money ran short and life became increasingly less congenial with the hints of winter bitterness in the air, the villagers became increasingly restless. Theft, assault, rape and generally unruly behaviour became a commonplace as the less than genteel soldiery demonstrated that they were not as closely wedded to the precepts of Puritanism than their leaders believed. As local unrest increased, suspicions about Widow Cradock's allegiance began to harden particularly when she refused to avail herself of the right granted *'to take, fell, cut down and carry away any timber or other materials.'* The movement of military forces in the area as a whole seemed to merit careful thought on the part of the Committee at Stafford and gradually Carswall Hall seemed to assume a new significance. Control was transferred from Mr. James Creswall to an experienced military man, Captain Ashenhurst; the size of the garrison was doubled.

> *'Whereas Captayne Ashenhurst was appointed to be Governor of Carswall Hall for the King and Parliament. It is now ordered for the better in abling him to keepe the same that there shall be fourty soldiers constantly in the said garrison, viz: xxtie foote and xxtie horse besides the Captain, Lieutenant and two Corporals and that pay shall be provided for them according to theyr severall Qualities out of the weekly assessment of the Constablewick of Carswall: and that the arrears of the said weekly pay for the nine weeks last past shall be forthwith gathered and received in monies and provision at market prices for the better maintenance of the said Garison and payment of the soldiers and making of fortifications: And that the said Captain shall forthwith cause hay and oates for his present use to be fetched from Mr. Parker's of Weston Coyney and shall also have and receive from Trentham hall sixteen strikes of blendcorne and four strikes of wheate, And the weekly pay of the said Constablewick shall likewise be continued and payd to the said Captayne for the purpose aforesaid till further order to be taken therein.'* [26]

Things failed to improve. As the situation became more serious militarily so the increasing vulnerability of the Castle, which had never been designed as a stronghold, became more apparent.

> *'And the said Captaine shall have power to call for and command Teames of Horses for Carriages of Cales (coal) and of the said Hay and Corne and other necessaries as he shall have occasion: and likewise shall command bedding to be brought in and lent for the use of the said Garrison: and lastly that the said Captaine shall have power to call in to his assistance in time of danger such of the neighbourhood as he concieves will be faithfull to him: And the said Captaine is desired to have an espetiall care to prevent the carrying of salt or other provition to any of the Enemies Garrisons.'* [26]

It seems probable that the increased garrison contained either a large proportion of musketeers or some artillery for:

> *'It is ordered that Captain Ashenhurst have 20 pounds of powder and six skeans (skeins) of Match sent to Caveswell by his messenger.'* [26]

Things were not going well for the Puritan garrison commander for, having been empowered to collect outstanding monies,

> *'it is further ordered that the said Captaine shall apprehend all such persons, as he shall think fitt that have brought in theyr armes or horses to Mr. Sneyd or are in other respect delinquent and after he hath apprehended them to give information to them, the Committee here, of every such person that he apprehends and of what he can prove against them to the end they may undergo such censure as shall be imposed upon them by the said Committee.'* [26]

When such powers are necessary to contain a civilian population the value of the cause itself is rendered suspect. The next instruction must have come as no surprise to Captain Ashenhurst.

> *'That Carswell and Shugborough be also made unserviceable and the stores with the arms and provisions ther, to be drawne to this Garrison.'* [26]

All was clearly not well in the Parliamentary camp for later in the same month another order emerged from the Committee at Stafford.

'Whereas the severall Garisons of Painsley and Carswell were by order of 2nd March last past ordered by the Committee and Councell of Warre to be forthwith demolished and the Armes Forces and provisions there brought forthwith to this garrison at Stafford as by the same order appeareth yet nevertheless the same are not yet demolished nor the said order in any part performed by Major Ashenhurst or Captaine John Ashenhurst to whom the keeping of the said garrison hath been committed. It is now therefore ordered that warrants forthwith issue to the severall divisions and Townships that have been assigned to them for payment of theyr weekley pay for the mayntenance of the said Garisons commanding them to pay no more weekly pay to the said Garison or other of them but to pay the same to theyr Treasurer at Stafford or to such others as the same shall be assigned to by them. Major Ashenhurst and Captaine Ashenhurst shall forthwith make theyr accounts and pay to the Treasurer and Committee all such monies as they have received since the 2nd March last being the date of the order for demolishing the said Garison.'[26]

Whatever the reasons for the testy tone of that order and whatever the cause of the delay, by May 1644 the castle still stood and Captain Ashenhurst had been replaced by Colonel Chadwick. The defence of the castle appears to have been placed on a less formal footing for:

'Colonel Chadwick, Mr. Flacket, Mr. Campian, Mr. Ed. Kenel be desired with the rest of the well affected neighbours there, to keep and defend Careswal Castle until the removal of the enemy give opportunity for the demolishing the same and that soe many souldiers as will be maintained out of the weekli pay of the Constablewick of Careswall be allowed for the defence of that place.' [26]

In July 1644 the record shows.

'The Committee at Stafford understand there have been variances betwixt Colonell James Chadwicke and Captaine John Ashenhurst about the government of Carswall House which Colonell Chadwick saith he hath procured an order for from My Lords Generall Forasmuch as it appears to the said Committee that Colonell Chadwicke hath not a sufficient number of souldiers to defend that place: And that those souldiers that now secure it are Captaine Ashenhursts souldiers which Captaine is under Colonell John Bowyer who hath the command of the whole Hundred of Totmanslowe committed to him by the Generall and the pay thereof by them. This Committee according to his Lordships direction to them assigned to him. It is therefore by them ordered that for the present security of that place from the Enemy and the arayding contention Colonell John Bowyer be desired to take care to put souldiers into Carswall house to secure it untill the Lord Generall can be acquainted with it and shall further determine what shall be done concerning the keeping or demolishing that place. And that in the meane time Colonell Chadwick have all fair accommodation for himselfe and family in the house if he please to stay there with liberty if he please to go in and out at reasonable hours.' [26]

The difficult relationships between the members of the garrison and villagers were maintained into 1645 with the defenders being gradually reduced to desperation as their demands upon the impoverished and rebellious locals were increasingly ignored and the feuds between the Parliamentary field officers continued.

'Whereas it is informed that the Garison at Carswall is at a greate want both of provision of vituals and ammunition. It is ordered that the governor of the said Garison or in his absence his Cheife Officer shall forthwith collect three weekes pay within his asignation for the victualing of the said Garison: And the inhabitants within the space of *two months next shall be allowed them out of their weekly pay, otherwise they are to have it agayne: And Commissarie Flower is hereby ordered to deliver to Mr. Campian for the use of the said Garison 20 lb of powder and bullet proportionable but in regard to the scarcitie of match the governor is desired to make provisions for it elsewhere.'* [26]

That order was given in March 1645. During the summer of that year the King was present in the North Midlands with an army trying to break the Parliamentary control of the area. In one wide ranging march he led his troops from Cardiff north into Market Drayton, Ashley and Stone. The news that the King's army was so close was sufficient to frighten the unpopular, unhappy and impoverished troops into flight leaving the Castle intact. The King's army moved through Caverswall denuding the parish of everything edible, most things valuable and leaving it swept clean and embittered in a manner the Puritans had never quite managed. The vast fighting force moved away towards Uttoxeter, Tutbury and Lichfield pursuing a vision of glory that was soon to desert them. As the King's fortunes declined so did those of William Parker of Park Hall. Taken prisoner he was incarcerated at Stafford Castle where he was held until the Restoration in 1660 when he was released and his sequestered estates restored to him.

In 1655 Dorothy Cradock sold the estate to William Jolliffe and left the area to take up residence in the Puritan City of London taking with her the three daughters whose marital fates were to be later recorded upon the mural tablet in the Church.

One of a sequence of corbel heads in St. Peter's church dating from the mid seventeenth century. Could it depict one of the Cradock ladies or perhaps one of the Cradock men? It is difficult to certain about the gender.

1658 A.D.

MORE BITTER THAN DEATH

The gloom of Puritan England lay heavily upon Careswell.

Winter cold had seized the land in its savage claw. The harsh, brittle crust on the frozen earth of the autumn ploughing concealed the depth to which the frost had penetrated. The mill pond gleamed dully beneath the cold light of a gibbous moon, slender rivulets of powdery snow etching the inches thick ice coating its surface. Around the margins of the pond ice clad sedges rose sere and brittle, in a rusty circlet of icy death. Trees, naked, stark, and dead towered gaunt against the velvet, star flecked sky. The cold which lay upon the land had seized the bodies and the minds of men. In each slumbering hovel the cold lay upon with the shivering, fitful sleepers huddled for warmth beneath a mound of bedding. By night the cold sought a man's spirit, by day it racked his body until the whole world cringed beneath its questing breath. Beasts froze to the floor of stable and byre anchored in their frozen urine, starving slowly to death as the fodder stocks of a poor year were depleted by the continuing cold. To William Jolliffe shivering in the keen air of his Castle bedroom it seemed that the cold had been with them for as long as Cromwell's chilly grasp had been fastened round the throat of England.

All forms of play, recreation, smoking and the ornamentation of dress had long been forbidden. Even the traditional Wake or birthday of the Parish Church had been banned for such evening gatherings for feasting and merrymaking had a habit of becoming bawdy, rowdy, irreligious jollifications which sat uncomfortably upon the conscience of the good Puritan. The destruction of the maypole and the banning of the spring joys had been sad losses. The reduction of the Church holy days and festivals to interminable services rich in gloom, repression and high minded exhortation had been a serious deprivation but the extinction of those celebrations which had served to carry both the poor and the rich of the parish through the bitter winter nights and bleak winter days had brought a chilling sadness to the hearts of the villagers. Idleness in any form was anathema to the Puritans and they, unable to appreciate the need of both man and woman for relaxation and the warming pleasures of jovial company, had attempted to destroy that thread of joy upon which true faith and worship rests. The hearts and minds of the people of Careswell were ice-bound, their souls were dead and in the care of George Reeve a priest as idle, corrupt and absentee as any who has ever moulded the minds of the people of the parish.

The life of George Reeve had come close to making a mockery of the tenets of Puritanism. By those precepts adultery was punishable by death, ale-houses were subject to instant closure, swearing was an offence punishable by a fine selected as appropriate from a graduated scale. A duke giving public vent to an epithet could be fined 30s, a baron 20s and a squire 10s. The unfortunate but blasphemous common labourer escaped with a fine of 3s.4d. The superstitious indulgences called Church Wakes had been transmuted into monthly feast days. Christmas was damned as a time of carnal and sensual delights. Even walking abroad on the Sabbath save for the purpose of going to church was punishable. The baitable bears had been shot and the necks of the fighting cocks wrung. The whole county shivered under a lash of vicious punishments for petty offences, people crept in fear of the spying, prying zealot. All of this George Reeve knew full well and yet by professing Puritanism and preaching the word of its creed he held his place. By subterfuge, deceit and guile he had sought and acquired a modest income from two incumbencies one of which was Careswell a parish which, on this bleak winter's night could see no gleam of hope.

As the frost crisped the curtains of his chamber the 73 years old William Jolley or Jolliffe, that *'cunning miserable man to geet mony'*[27] shivered and turned to Anne, his 63 year old wife, for warmth. The villagers had often remarked upon the strange fates which had interwoven the life threads of the miserly, presbyterian from Leek and the generous, devoted woman from Gloucestershire whom he had married on the death of his first wife, Lady Mary Hastings daughter of the Earl of Huntingdon. For him the local people had few kind words but for his wife and her quietly given gifts, comforts and clothing the entire parish would speak.

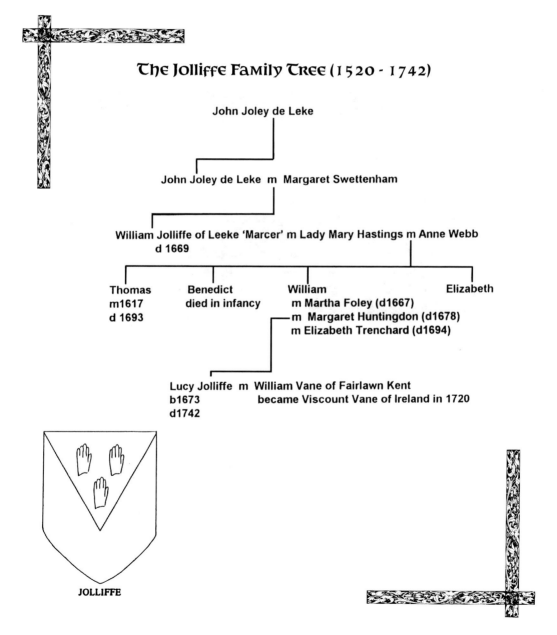

The Jolliffe Family Tree (1520 - 1742)

John Joley de Leke

John Joley de Leke m Margaret Swettenham

William Jolliffe of Leeke 'Marcer' m Lady Mary Hastings m Anne Webb
d 1669

Thomas	Benedict	William	Elizabeth
m1617	died in infancy	m Martha Foley (d1667)	
d 1693		m Margaret Huntingdon (d1678)	
		m Elizabeth Trenchard (d1694)	

Lucy Jolliffe m William Vane of Fairlawn Kent
b1673   became Viscount Vane of Ireland in 1720
d1742

JOLLIFFE

1660 A.D.

YOU SPEND ON YOUR DELIGHT

When the King came to his own again Careswell felt as if a perpetual, spiritual spring had settled upon the parish. Almost miraculously the celebrations seemed to set free the local love of jollity which had been stifled during the Commonwealth. Even old William Jolliffe who held that *'idleness was the nurse of all evil'* unbent from his presbyterian yoke far enough to concede that his villagers were:

'for the most part grown to be good husbands (farmers) and know how to improve their lands and to the uttermost as the farmer or country man'.

Fairs and Wakes were almost miraculously resurrected, fighting cocks appeared as if overnight and the Square thrilled once again to the sounds of maypole centred revelry and the measured rhythms of the morris dance.

Having never recovered from the death of his wife in April 1658 William Jolliffe moved to Leek. Of his family of three Sir William, Sir Thomas and Lady Elizabeth Jolliffe, his eldest son, Sir William, took over the residency of the castle and the management of the estate. Although a merchant with extensive interests in London he seems to have loved Careswell and brought to the castle in 1660 his first bride, Martha Foley, a sweet twenty-one year old who died in 1667 leaving a daughter Anne. By a strange coincidence William Jolliffe the younger chose as his second wife Mary Hastings, daughter of the eighth Earl of Huntingdon, a woman of 'strong and cultivated understanding and of exemplary conduct. [28]

Fate seems to have been consistently cruel to the tenants of the Castle for in December 1678 Mary died whilst visiting her family home, the castle at Ashby de la Zouch, leaving Lucy, a five year old daughter.

For a third time William Jolliffe took to himself a wife, this time a widow, Elizabeth Trenchard of Taunton and fate for a third time dealt him a cruel blow, his third wife died in London on 26th February 1694.

She was buried at Caverswall

'March Anno Domini 1694

Elizabeth Jolliffe the wife of William Jolliffe Esquire dyed at
London the 26th Day of February And was buried at Carswall the
ninth day of March following in Linen contrary to the ... two
and the forfeiture was paid one part of the five pounds to James
Corbit vicar informer and the other to the poor of Carswall.
Witnesses: Will Wassilbon, George Amore Wardin.' [28]

To protect the English wool trade it was required that corpses should be interred *'in woollen'* and a forfeiture paid if anyone infringed that statute. From the foregoing entry in the Parish Register it would seem that James Corbett, priest, had informed upon the Lord of the Manor.

THE JOLLIFFE FAMILY

It was a matrimonial link between the two families stretching back to the 1570s when George Cradock married Jane Jolley of Leek which led to the Jolliffe or Jolley family taking up residence in the castle.

The Jolliffe family was known in Leek as mercers before 1550. It is known that John Joley of Leeke married Margaret and that William who bought the castle was their son. William was born in 1584 and was serving as a Justice in 1654. It was his expertise as a merchant which generated the fortune which allowed him to purchase the castle.

Some dispute exists over the precise date upon which the Jolliffe family moved into the castle. The actual change of ownership is given in Plot's History of Staffordshire as 1655 but an article in the transactions of the North Staffs. Archaeological Society (XXX 1895/6) argues for 1650. What is certain is that the Hearth Tax for 1666 records the castle as having twenty standing hearths and being in the ownership of Wiliam Jolliffe.

William Jolliffe of Leeke or Carswall Castle was known to be 'Allwayes a pribyterian of the parliament party.'

William Jolliffe (senior) was known as a cunning, miserable man to geet money and a miserly presbyterian. The one remaining portrait of him does little to dispel the impression created by those words. He was also known to be an active member of the Parliamentary Committee.

It seems that William had two sons, William and Thomas. Thomas was the firstborn and responsible for the erection of a wall monument to his father who died in 1699. On that monument in Leek parish church William is described as a man of upright character and industry. His wife Anne is commended for her devotion and generosity to the poor.

His oldest son, now Sir William, first married Martha Foley who died in 1667. His second wife, Margaret Huntingdon, died in 1678 leaving a daughter, Lucy. Williams third wife, Elizabeth Trenchard of Taunton, died on 26th. February, 1694 and was buried in Carswall on 9th. March of that year. Her body was wrapped in linen which was against a law devised to protect the English wool trade and in consequence William was fined £5. Half of the fine went to the vicar who informed upon him.

Fate seems to have been ill disposed towards William Jolliffe for in addition to taking his three wives it also took his daughter, Anne, in 1693. In 27 years he lost four female members of his family.

William Jolliffe (Sen.)
'a cunning, miserable man
to geet mony'

(By courtesy of the Courtauld Institute
of Fine Art)

William Jolliffe (junior) appears to have loved Carswall although he spent relatively lengthy periods of time in London on business. During these trips he doubtless availed himself of the opportunity to keep himself abreast of new trends in farming. Books like John Levett's *'Orderinge of Bees'* may well have appeared in his library and served as the basis for many discussions with fellow farmers.

Through the parish raged a prolonged debate about the value of Carswall Common. The area between Roughcote, Hardiwick and Cookshill had been gradually shorn of trees and reduced to common land, a process which had been in hand since the days of Cafhere. The area served as pasture for the nondescript stock of the village during those months of the year when the rank grass was growing. It represented a precious and important part of the wealth of the village. Yet William Jolliffe and the brothers Browne could be heard claiming that *'one sheep in an enclosure was worth two on a Common'* and had withdrawn their own beasts to enclosed fields where their healthy appearance and the lush consequences of concentrated dunging could be seen by all. The health of their beasts testified to the fact that *'there are five rots in the open fields to one rot in enclosed land'*, whilst the passing traveller could not help but notice that the beasts roaming over Carswall Common were *'the Poore, the Blinde, Lame, Tired, Scabbed Mangie, Rotten and Murrainous'* [29]

Yet the villagers constantly rejected such arguments holding, with rural stubbornness to the view that the Commons belonged to all.

Potent as was the evidence that the Brownes could adduce the strength of the arguments of their opponents prevailed partly because the Brownes were content to protect their own interests and partly because death took a hand in the affairs of the parish.

John Browne died in 1665, William Jolliffe senior died four years later, whilst Ralph Browne died in 1670. George Parker of Park Hall had died in 1663 so depriving Weston Coyney of its leading citizen. He left a son, William, his wife, Bridget, and a second son George to carry on his family line. His neighbour, William Jolliffe left his Caverswall estate to his son William, a more sociable and practical man than his father.

Che Castle which passed to William Jolliffe (Junior)

An artist's impression based upon the drawing in Plot's 'A Natural History of Staffordshire' 1686.

Drawing by Francis Clare

1666 A.D.

THE MONEYS THAT SHOULD FEED US

The Hearth Tax Return for the Caverswall Constablewick records the existence of 59 stone hearths upon which tax was to be paid. Of that total 20 hearths were in the castle or, at least, were chargeable to *'Mr. William Jolliffe and his tenant'* leaving a total of 27 other persons with taxable fireplaces.

The record reads as follows:

Caverswall Constablewick	Hearths Chargeable
Mr. William Jolley and his tenant Thomas Harte	20
Mr. Thomas Parker	5
William Heath	1
George Brassington	3
William Cooper	1
William Tooth	5
Joane Walker	1
Thomas Kilford	3
Anne Heath	1
William Tooth	1
Robert Sale	1
Mr. Henry Haworth	5
Issabell Baddeley	I
John Watson	3
Mr. Ralph Browne	5
John Limmax	1
William Walter	1
Thomas Cookes	3
Ralph Fisher	2
Goodman Robinson	1
John Warriloe	2
Richard Wood	2
Mr. James Cressall	5
Widdow Hill	1
Roger Machin	1
Widdow Honde	1
Thomas Beech	1
Mrs. Eliza Warriloe	2

If the probable total of 20 hearths for the castle is accepted then it places that dwelling in the same social grouping as the great houses at Chartley, Ingestre and Madeley.

The overall distribution of hearths suggests that life had been kind to the people of Carswall. There may have been a vast gulf between the luxury of the castle and the solid comforts of the three and five hearth households. There was a similar gulf between the five hearth man and the truly poor but, overall, the lot of the people of Carswall had never been better. Even so, life, when measured against the standards of posterity was still

hard, devoid of comfort and something to be endured rather than savoured. Great chasms existed in the social awareness of the various groups, men looked to themselves and their own first and to their neighbours with either envy or relief.

The North Door of St. Peter's Church dates from this period of the history of the village. The door in the south aisle is dated 1673. This doorway with its round arch and hood mould is 17th century. The evidence suggests that the door has been adapted to fit the doorway. What was the link with the Sacheverell Family? Why the gift of a door?

The 1666 Hearth Tax Return also offers a useful guide to the size and nature of the parish.

Caverswall had 79 houses with hearths and 17 without, Weston Coyney boasted 60 houses with hearths and 10 without whilst Hulme boasted 30 with and seven without.

Overall Caverswall appears to have comprised 96 dwellings, Weston Coyney 70 and Hulme 37. If it is assumed that the average size of a family unit lay somewhere between three and five persons it is possible to hazard a guess at the relative sizes of the three settlements.

Village	Lower	Higher	Postulated
Caverswall	288	480	384
Weston Coyney	210	350	280
Hulme	111	185	148
Totals	609	1,015	822

The parish extended beyond the three main settlements and certainly included a number of isolated dwellings and a settlement around Adderley, some clustered hovels at Meer and some persons associated with Brookhouse and Simfield. Depending upon whether the isolated dwellings had hearths and were included in the figure for the nearest main settlement a population figure of not less than 650 and not more than 1,060 may be guessed at. Accordingly a median figure of about 830 or 850 would seem to be a not unreasonable estimate for the population of the parish in 1666.

1680 A.D.

THE FIELDS WHEREIN I STOOD

In 1674 Dr. Plot had announced his intention to make a journey through England and Wales *'to describe and investigate important features of cultural and antiquarian interest.'* As Keeper of the Ashmolean Museum and 'Professor of Chymystry' in the University of Oxford's Plot had conceived the project of covering the whole of England and Wales in a series of natural histories based upon a classical approach to the subject. His *'Natural History of Oxfordshire'* had been published in 1677.

In 1679 Plot had printed and circulated to the farmers and gentry of Staffordshire an *'enquiry'* or questionnaire asking about soil types, grains, farm implements, husbandry, minerals, plants, antiquities, natural and artificial curiosities. This enquiry, coupled with his reputation, had produced a stir of expectancy in the shire and now it was rumoured that the great man was coming to 'Carsa' to see things for himself.

The little group of riders arrived at Park Hall towards the end of what had been a long and thoroughly wet ride from Stafford. As they dismounted from their tired and mud-spattered horses William Parker and his wife Bridget came bustling out to greet them. Pride at having been chosen to receive the distinguished scholar from Oxford jostled with an anxious determination to offer their guests a sample of true Staffordshire hospitality.

Over the evening meal, whose centrepiece was a vast portion of beef crisped in the honey gold fat which betrayed the influence of the good grass of the midlands, the area and its features were explored in conversation. As copious draughts of warm 'buttered mum' began to take effect William Parker struggled to answer the learned doctor's questions about such diverse matters as soil types, farming practices, strange natural phenomena and the ways of the local people whilst trying to absorb the wealth of comment, anecdote and fact which seemed to flow through the scholar's discourse. Seldom had William Parker, the best educated man in the parish when William Jolliffe was not at home, felt himself to be on such uncertain intellectual ground.

Gradually the conversation began to follow more comprehensible paths. Questions from Dr. Plot about the vast bulk of sandstone rock which sheltered the Hall to the north-west and dominated the greensward which surrounded the moat encircled farmhouse allowed William Parker to explain their importance as a source of water pointing out how his moat and buildings were fed by one stream issuing therefrom whilst his mill and its pond were fed by another. Upon visiting the mill Dr. Plot was so impressed with the potency of the spring that he deemed it appropriate to record in his *'History'*, when he wrote the chapter entitled *'Of the Waters'*:

'There is one at Park Hall in the Parish of Caverswall belonging to the Worshipfull and most obliging Gent: William Parker Esq: which not only sends so full and uninterrupted a stream that it drives a Mill within less than bowshot but also makes such a noise in its exit that it can be heard at some distance without any difficulty.' [31]

Other wonders were yet to be disclosed to the worthy doctor for following his examination of the stream he was invited to explore the mill itself and in admiration for rural enterprise and ingenuity was able to record:

'At Mr. Parker's of Park Hall in the Parish of Caverswall I was showed an Oat Mill that husk't the Oats and winnowed them and then ground them to meal: the last mill

that ground them being not turned immediately by the water but by two wheels whereof one was fastened to the runner of the first Mill and the second to the runner of the grinding mill, a great rope interceding.' [31]

Of that rope Plot wrote:

'I was shown a rope that past between the runners of the Oat mill above mentioned made only of the pillings or rinds pulled off the pith of the juncus laeris panicula sparsa major or junis laevis vulgaris both of which it seems are candle-rushes, which, it seems, would not only last a year i.e. longer than one of hemp, but that it would not stretch as hempen ones doe which it seems is a great convenience in the working of such a mill.' [31]

They spoke of the coal exposures on and along the edges of Wetley Moor and Parker told of the *'footerills'* by which the coals burning in his hearth and in those of the castle were won. When asked about the hazards confronting those who tore the coals from the bowels of the earth he spoke of the acrid, stinging, choking smoke which came from the coal when fire was employed to soften the stone for the pick-axe. Several sorts of explosive damp were mentioned and by careful questioning the learned doctor identified them as 'globe damp', a ball shaped bubble of gas wrapped as if in a thick spider's web compounded of workmen's breath, sweat and smoke from the candles; 'fulminating damps which exploded when ignited by a candle; 'want of air' damp and smoaky' damp.

From the hazards of winning coal below ground the conversation moved to life in the farms and villages above ground. Mention was made of such wonderful marvels as the goose born with three legs; the lamb born with its rear legs joined together and which moved by dragging its thighs upon the ground. Reference was made to the longevity of the local people in particular the ages of the four men living at Cocknage whose combined years totalled 360 and the age of 127 years reputedly achieved by Ralph Leese of Totmanslow. From longevity the conversation turned to a discussion of the body and its imperfections. William Parker told of Richard Morfe a 'natural' or 'half-wit' who possessed *'a strange sagacity in distinguishing time'* being apparently well able to forecast such occurrences as eclipses of the sun and the moon. The same Richard Morfe was kept as a form of family pet or curiosity by the Fowler and Draycott families. Prefacing his story with a remark about the coincidence of names and an enquiry about the man's possible origins and antecedents Plot told Parker of one Brian Caveswell of Forton who was noted for the readiness with which he would chew ropes, blankets and sheets.

The candles flickered late into the night as Plot and Parker sat before the hearth, sipping their 'mum' and discoursing upon the curiosities of places and people. At length the warmth of the fire and the influences of their meal and subsequent drinking began to take effect, the conversation languished, heads nodded and sleep came. Outside the ragged rain clouds broke and scudded away before a stiffening breeze until the sky was studded with stars and a slender crescent moon hung low in the western sky.

On the following morning, escorted by William Parker the visitors rode eastwards trotting easily across the expanse of pasture land dotted with nibbling sheep and down towards the tree fringed marshy borders of the shallow and spreading River Blithe. Once through the ford with its pebble coated bed they followed in single file along the narrow track which curved among the scattered trees around the now dry millpond. Here Plot noted the characteristic local method of clearing trees. The tree bark was 'ringed' or stripped near ground level so killing the tree. The dead and naked timber was then allowed to stand until the wood was needed or an opportunity offered to fell it or the forces of nature took a hand so saving man's muscles the arduous task of felling with axe and saw.

In the Square they encountered the Vicar with whom Plot spoke at length about the spiritual health of the parish. James Corbett was a small, untidy man in worn and greasy clerical garb which bore, as did his hard and knotted hands, clear evidence of toil upon the land for, like his predecessors, he was a small farmer as well as a priest. Appearances can be deceptive for Corbett had a sharp intellect and a wealth of wordly wisdom born of curacies at Chapel Chorlton and among the potters in the village of Stoke. He also possessed a fund of human knowledge derived from more than twenty years in the parish. As he watched the verbal exchanges expand into clever debate William Parker reached the conclusion that the Vicar would be a useful prop for his own conversation that evening at dinner and seized upon a lull in the discourse to tender an invitation which was accepted by the priest with evident delight; he did not normally dine so well.

Beyond the church they studied the great open field sprawling away to the grazing lands beyond which fringed the forest edge to the southward. On the lower slopes of the higher ground to the east and here and there in the great field itself they noted the way in which smaller areas of arable and pasture had been enclosed in a haphazard fashion by the more enterprising yeomen whose holdings lay along the edge of the great swathe of common land which covered the nearly treeless high ground to the east and north-east of the village.

At the castle they met the widower, Sir William Jolliffe and his daughters, Anne, who was in her mid-20's and clearly discharging the duties of house-keeper in a firm and positive manner and Lucy, a spritely imp of seven years or so. Plot professed himself impressed by the castle and ever the shrewd businessman, made arrangements for his chosen artist, M. Burghers Esq., to produce an illustration of the castle which, he assured Sir William, would appear in his book with a suitable inscription, as would the family crest.

Impressed as he was with the castle, Plot never neglected the human interests of his readers and found himself unable to resist including the scurrilous addition to the inscription on the tomb of William de Careswell recording it as follows:

'Sir William of Caverswall here lye I Who built the Castle and made the pooles bye.'
'Sir. William of Caverswall here you lye Your Castle is down and your pooles are dry.' [31]

However, he went on to add
'as indeed they are, all but the deep moat about the castle in place whereof a fair house has since been built of squared stone not altogether unlike a castellated mansion the walls about it be flanked with hexagonal towers.' [31]

A horseshoe clinked proclaiming its looseness and the party turned aside to the smithy situated to the north of the Square just above the point at which a spring broke from the ground, its waters cutting a marshy rivulet down to the muddy remnants of the millpond. Whilst the smith set to his labours Dr. Plot examined the smithy in his usual manner and discovered yet another remarkable instance of rural ingenuity for in the Caverswall smithy he found:

'an engine in the smith's shop that managed a large sledge (hammer) to so great advantage that it frequently supplied the defect of a man ordinarily had (employed) elsewhere for that purpose, the sledge being set in an axis of wood from whence goes a rodd of iron fastened to a pallett that reaches out a little beyond the anvil which being drawn down by the foot of the smith who keeps time to it with his hand hammer is returned to it by two springs of holly that clasp the axis in a contary way.' [31]

During the repair Plot also noted some strangely barbed, forked pieces of iron and inquiring upon their use was told that they were fitted to the noses of hogs to prevent them rooting.

Dinner at Park Hall that evening was an occasion of some pleasure, the Doctor had gleaned much that was novel for his text, the Vicar enjoyed an unusually pleasing and stimulating debate whilst William and Bridget Parker were able to enjoy an evening as host and hostess watching guests and friends in jovial conclave.

Dr. Plot's *'Natural History of Staffordshire'* was published in 1686 and republished in 1973 by E. J. Morten of Didsbury. The references to Caverswall are taken from the 1686 edition.

Coal mining along the fringes of Wetley Moor has a long history, the monks of Hulton Abbey worked the measures below Werrington and Ash Bank during the Middle Ages. In 1772 Handley Hayes Colliery was in the charge of Solomon Wardle and Philip Johnson. In 1921 and 1926 local men, both amateur and professional miners, removed large quantities of coal in turbulent times which saw the death of the owner of a field just north of Ash Hall in a dispute about 'royalties'. Even today the shaft riddled surface of the moor presents a threat to the unwary walker. A contemporary proof of this mining tradition existed in the fields between Salter's Lane and Winterfield Lane where a private mine functioned until the early 1960s .

The type of small scale mining which existed near Winterfield
Lane until the early 1960s.

The site of the ford crossed by the travellers is easily identified as the point at which the bridge carries the road across the stream just below the Cricket Ground. William Parker's mill pond still exists but his house, sadly, has gone. The spring which provided the village blacksmith with water is now properly marked and set in the side of the highway close to the entrance to Yard Farm.

At the beginning of the 17th century Careswell had been home to some 70 - 75 families numbering in all about 250 souls. In 1700 that number had risen to something of the order of 117 families totalling about 468 persons. Weston Coyney appears to have increased from about 127 persons to about 265 whilst Hulme seems to have risen from about 97 to about 125 during the same period.

Such a pattern of expansion suggests that, on the whole, life had been relatively kind to the people of the parish. Family groups ranged in size from the widow with her single hearth making modest ends meet humbly living in a simple one or two roomed hovel to the lusty farmer housing a large brood of noisy and demanding youngsters in a substantial, black and white, timber framed house with, in rare cases, two storeys connected by a staircase.

In the main these families lived in or around the village area clustering around the Square and lining the sinuous path of High Street with a succession of narrow fronted dwellings often possessing a farm yard with access directly onto the street itself.

The presence of the farm, its yard and land was the dominant and integrating feature of the village landscape throughout the 17th century. The edges of the ancient forest had been pushed well back, its character had changed as the trees had been thinned and then cleared; its menace had been removed as grazing beasts drove back the undergrowth and revealed areas increasingly open to cultivation. Even so every villager was well aware of the presence of trees, the landscape still revealed far more evidence of tree cover than does the contemporary one of houses. The landscape was 'champion' but still well wooded. Yet the trees were subordinate to arable and pasture lands which themselves seemed to be the fertile soil from which the dwellings of the village sprang. The villages of Caverswall, Hulme, Weston Coyney, Werrington, Ash and Bucknall seemed to grow directly from the soil almost like strange fungi so close, intense and natural was the relationship between man and place. Each household had its own vegetable plot which merged almost without distinction into the sea of arable and pasture fields and strips which surrounded the village. Earth baulks, some fences and more hedges served to indicate changes of ownership where some enterprising yeoman had instituted the processes of consolidation and enclosure but even so the general impression was one of openness.

The land dominated labour and human activity but it did not reign supreme. By the latter third of the century some division of labour and local specialisation had begun to take place. In 1670 Caverswall boasted the smithy, Adderley had its potters, Werrington and Hulme had miners, quarrymen, stone workers and cottagers producing nails and small items of iron work whilst based upon Mr. Parker's pond and mill Weston Coyney could boast its corn and grain merchants.

Large houses of substantial character existed at Brookhouse, Ash Hall, Park Hall, Rough Cote Hall and Caverswall. Of these only the Stone House in Caverswall Square and the castle were of smooth ashlar construction the remainder were timber framed dwellings of a fairly common and uniform style. Perhaps the greater houses were not too dissimilar to Ford Green Hall.

Windmills probably broke the skyline at Meir Heath and Werrington as did smoke from the potters' kilns at Adderley and from the smelters and furnaces of the iron workers at Werrington and Meir Heath. The smoke from the primitive smelter at Meir Heath was a constant reminder of the way in which that smelter's voracious maw was helping the unceasing demands for building timber and cheap fuel to strip the parish and its surrounding landscape of trees.

By the final decade of the century the lines of movement through the parish had become established. The line of Salter's Lane and Green Lane could be traced through Roughcote and Cookshill, Caverswall and Forsbrook to its south-easterly junction with the lane which ran down the spine of the Pottery villages to Lane End where it splashed through the marsh at the Mere before striking out eastwards through the ford at Blithe Marsh and away through Draycott to Uttoxeter and London. The old priests' roads from the Abbey at Hulton to Croxden and from Dieulacress in Leek to Stone had been broadened into highways by farmers driving beasts to market, stockmen driving store cattle to pasture, dealers, itinerants and travellers moving about their normal occasions and carters and waggoners laboriously hauling turves, building stone, timber and agricultural produce about the parish. Necessities like salt from the Cheshire salt fields, rough pigs of iron for the blacksmiths and butter pots for the dairy farmers of the lush pasture lands of eastern and central Staffordshire all moved through the parish, most frequently by packhorse train.

Along these unmade tracks rutted hard and deep in dry or cold weather and ankle or axle deep in mire on wet days strode pedestrians, prowled vagabonds, pattered ponies, clattered horsemen or rumbled waggons in a variegated pattern of movement representing the life of the area. Each traveller in his own way sought a drier or firmer path until the trail became a ribbon of muddy turf and a potential morass of uncertain depth and variable width. Along the borders of that path flowed the carpet of grass, ferns, brambles, rank grasses and trees which marked the notional limits of the 'road'. A network of lesser paths, tracks and trails served to link places and localities possessing a common interest so that by gauging the nature of the track a man might learn much about the traffic it bore and its value to those who lived along it.

Throughout the century the area of cultivated land was extended, activity in the fields intensified, agricultural techniques improved and more stock, more dwellings, more movement, more intermarriage brought new faces into the villages and entered new names in the church registers. Despite outbreaks of cattle plague, crop failures, and stock diseases generally, the farming world seems to have been in good heart. The face and bodies of the villagers still bore evidence of dietary imbalance and the general consequences of uncleanliness. Yet better food, superior housing and gradually rising levels of awareness had produced a diminishing death rate, a much reduced level of infant mortality and brought a general air of well being to the parish which marked it out from the life styles of earlier generations. The villagers no longer feared that plague which in 1348/49 had wrought such havoc in the parish. Its relatively mild and infrequent occurrences had caused no concern for many years, apart from the savage outbreak in London 1665, as a dealer of death on the large scale the bubonic plague had virtually disappeared.

Better food, better housing, healthier lives and greater freedom of movement between communities led to increased opportunities for marriage, brought new blood into the parish and encouraged families to move more readily in search of employment.

A man could still rise by his own efforts or fail through his own indolence. Those families in the parish who had any aspirations to gentility tended by 1700 to eat with forks, most were well covered and warmly clad, albeit in rough and simple styles which had no pretentions to sartorial elegance. The better families had certainly heard of a device invented by Sir John Harrington and called a water closet which bade fair to resolve that most unhygienic of domestic problems if one had a convenient moat, river, stream or kennel into which the sewage could be channelled. On the other hand washing was still a novelty and unusual in the extreme unless the dirt encrusting the body became too objectionable to the body itself; powder, paint and perfume held a far higher place than soap and water even in the castle.

Whilst general domestic furniture in the form of tables, stools, benches, chairs, cupboards, tallboys and the like had improved; the bedroom, if it existed at all as a separate room, was still sparsely furnished, the wash-stand had not been invented and the jordan placed in a wall cupboard or under the bed was still the only certain indoor receptacle for bodily wastes. Clocks had developed apace after 1660, the bracket clock evolved from the latten (brass) clock which became popularly known as the lantern clock only to be replaced in its turn by a more elegant fitting with a long, decorative case to enclose the dangling weights; so the grandfather clock was born and in a fine walnut case, made its appearance in the castle. For the common people, however, time was still measured in hours of daylight, sabbath days and the rhythms of the farmer's year.

At the close of the century the true gentlemen of the parish found more comfort, relaxation and sheer pleasure in a long clay pipe, a jar of the finest Virginia leaf, a chair by the fire and a book upon the knee than ever their forefathers did at any level of society. Indeed it is a fair assumption that life at the close of the 17th century was good, for those in a position to savour its delights.

It is virtually certain that no one in the parish ever achieved the levels of indolence and arrogant affluence portrayed by Charles Cotton in his 'Epigram de Mons: Maynard'.

> 'Anthony feigns him sick of late
> Only to show how he at home
> Lies in a princely bed of state,
> And lived in a nobly furnished room ,
> Adorned with pictures of Vandike's,
> a pair of Chrystal Candlesticks,
> Rich carpets, quilts, the Devil and all
> Then you his careful Friends,
> if ever You wish to cure him of his fever
> Go Lodge him in the Hospital.'

For some life was indeed good although it should not be forgotten that only the '20 hearthmen' had relative luxury, the five '5 hearthmen' had some ease, the four '3 hearthmen' had a modicum of comfort but there remained 86 other dwellings in Caverswall in which life was bleak, hard and dirty to the point of squalor.

During his long ministry John Corbett was able to work steadily towards the reconciliation of reason and religion. At the close of the 17th century the people of Caverswall were better informed than ever before about the world in general. They sought explanations for aspects of the physical world which, they felt, needed explanation. As countryfolk they were patient and careful yet as human beings living in a simple and direct manner they were loath to wait upon the processes of observation and experiment in order to formulate a 'scientific' explanation. Vicar Corbett was not unaware of the impact of the 17th century and its 'Age of Reason' upon religious beliefs and accordingly he had worked steadily to play down the idea of miracles whilst acknowledging that they made good stories and attractive illustrations. He had tried to banish the concept of hell-fire, was often tempted to mock those whose religious views were intolerant and would oppose as unworthy representatives of the true Christ, those whose religious fervour bordered on fanaticism. In his sermons he struggled to argue the reasonable nature of the Christian ethic with God as an abstract essence and prime driving force.

It was during John Corbett's ministry that the church became a symbol of a new goodness which permeated the life and work of the village. His effectiveness was manifest in the way in which so many of the superstitious fears of his flock seemed to have been diluted into the more harmless forms of fortune divining.

It was held that witches were still abroad in the parish and present in the minds of his flock. Four times each year at Candlemass (2nd February), Lammas (Ist August), Hallowe'en (31st October) and May Day, threads of red material appeared on the doors of sheds, barns and byres to protect the contents from the witches who rode variously on brooms, forks and three legged horses to wreak havoc on what was known as 'the Witches Sabbath'. Above or on each house door appeared a branch of the rowan tree to fend off evil influences from the home and its family. No traveller would use the junctions at Cellarhead, Weston Coyney and Mere at night on those days for it was there that Hecate held sway with her evil black dogs each representing the souls and spirits of those who had died violent, unshriven deaths or by their own hands. More than one traveller delayed by the state of the highway and struggling to reach Caverswall and home on such a night approached those crossroads with fear, looking anxiously skywards, searching the tumbling clouds for the Devil's Hunt. As fear struck coldly into his heart he might well reverse his hat and cloak to confuse the assailing spirits. Then, with eyes shielded from all save the ground beneath his feet lest he see the evil conclave and so learn his own impending fate, he would hasten timorously across the dreaded spot.

Yet parish fears and priestly teaching were not so effective that witches were shunned. Indeed John Corbett knew of more than one household where witch bottles stood at the back of a shelf, hidden yet ready for use. When disaster struck and witchcraft was suspected the bottle was charged with urine, hair and nail clippings from the victim and thorns and pins to ensure agony. The mixture was then boiled over the fire at midnight in a locked house. If the blend was correct the ensuing agony would draw to the front door of the victim's house the witch responsible for the evil deed whereupon appropriate vengeance could be wreaked if the spell was not lifted.

Farmers would use a poultice of meal, salt, horsehair and bat's blood to cure a lame horse. Serious oaths were sworn on salt if no Bible happened to be available. New born babes received a tiny pinch of salt, placed upon the tongue, to prevent physical disorders spread by witchcraft from gaining access to the body whilst a whole saucerful was placed upon the chest of each corpse to ensure its safety from the attentions of the evil one. In this context Salter's Lane became the most sacred pathway in the parish, a haven and a place of pilgrimage for those beset by fears whilst the convoys of salt bearing packhorses were regarded as the harbingers of good, to meet one was an inestimable piece of good fortune.

Young girls would carefully hang a freshly washed chemise over a chair back, or bed rail or hang it from a peg in the wall on St. Mark's Eve (24th April) in the expectation that, should they wake on the stroke of midnight, they would see the likeness of their future husband coming to reverse it. Similar information could be gleaned by sleeping with yarrow, plucked from Salter's Lane or taken from the grave of a young man, beneath the pillow. An apple peeled in an unbroken strip was a sure sign of future matrimony whilst the peel, if thrown over the shoulder to land unbroken, would form the initial letter of the future husband's christian name.

Mature men and women had been known to seek divine guidance in the church porch at midnight by throwing the bones, watching for images on the surface of water contained in a wooden bowl or by breaking hen eggs. Candle flames, when set in the church porch, would gutter and burn dim and blue if death threatened the parish, such a phenomenon occurring at home spelt death in the family.

Bodily ailments of the lesser kinds could be cured by reciting suitable rhymes. Cramp, for instance, could be banished by reciting:

'There came three Angells out of the East
One brought fire and one brought frost
Out fire, in frost,
In the name of the Father, Son and Holy Ghost, Amen.
Cramp be thou faintless
As our Lady was Sinless
When She bore Jesus.'

Yet so hedged about were these practices with conditions and caveats that their failure could always be attributed to some inadequacy on the part of the person involved. They always worked...... if circumstances were right, when such was not the case then the entertainment provided by their pursuit was often sufficient pleasure and reassurance in its self.

Formidable as his enemy seemed Vicar Corbett was able to turn such beliefs to the service of his God. For forty years he had fought the good fight cheerfully arguing that the magical colour red was the symbol of Christ's Blood and so a most potent force for good. He blessed the fact that people would turn to the Church as the only place which could be safely visited at midnight and rejoiced that harmless diversions could bring simple comfort to his flock. The practice of studying the ground closely on dark nights was commended for, as everyone knew, the surfaces at the crossroads were pitted and broken, a danger to the unwary.

By such ploys and subterfuges John Corbett had fought to bear his people from the fears of darkness towards the light of the Church and after forty years the fruits of his ministry were clearly visible. The Church Festivals were enjoyed by all for the restraints and sourness of Puritanism had gone, driving before them the grosser excesses and liberties of their opponents. In this way the life of the village had come to focus itself upon the Christian Year. As in all such rural communities the frugality of Lent led to the joys of Easter, summer labour in the fields culminated in the joys of Harvest whilst the excited delights of Christmas seemed to lessen the glooms of winter. Such great landmarks were liberally interspersed with saints' days, holy days, 'Wakes' and 'Ales'. Particular family and village occasions like weddings, funerals, baptisms, churchings and the like served as lesser lights between the greater. Man lived close to the land and closer to his own nature, living and feeling such events with such unashamed intensity that faith became a potent cement in the social fabric of the parish.

Yet all was not idyllic, a vision of pastoral ease acted out against an idealised and benevolent backdrop. Winter cold still chilled the blood and chapped the face, autumn damps sought aching bones and creaking Joints, summer rains meant cold labour in clinging mud and the rank odour of damp, sweat soaked garments. Cold springs meant late harvests and low yields, poor crops meant empty bellies and crying children, dirt streaked and starving. Summer warmth brought flies seething around the damp ordure slowly baking in the sun, meant maggots in meat and cheese alike and spelt toil with sweating back and parching tongue. For the few life was good, for the many life was still hard, painful and full of strain.

NEW YEAR'S EVE 1700 A.D.

HEED OUR WARNINGS

John Corbett sat pondering his text. For forty years he had served his God and folk with humble dedication. He had helped the parish to recover from the tensions of Civil War and had marked its steady rise to prosperity. Unquestionably his flock were living better than ever before yet to his aging and perhaps jaundiced eyes things were not good. His parish, like his England, was rapidly dividing into two classes, rich and poor were moving further apart. For the rich life seemed to be becoming easier, more tempting and a prey to the insidious forces of evil. For the poor, life was growing harder, people were being trodden down into that mire in which vice and viciousness flourished. Would men never begin to think of others less fortunate than themselves? Would man ever raise his eyes from the counting table or the pain of toil and look around him?

Sadly he raised his quill and began to write, determined that his first sermon of the new century should have a message appropriate to the age. Unwittingly he began to pen a sermon which would have been acceptable to his predecessor John de Smallys, that other priest who had loved and served his native hearth and fellow man with deep and Christian love. Steadily his quill scratched its path recording his theme:

Proverbs 15 :17

> 'Better is a dinner of herbs where love is than a stalled ox and hatred therewith.'

Based on a contemporary drawing this picture depicts one of the problems John Corbett was seeking to address. The lonely old widow with only cats for company eking out a miserable existence was at once an image of poverty easily ignored and the potential target for suspicions of witchcraft

1703 A.D.

THE DAYS OF LACE RUFFLES, PERUKES AND BROCADES

The village was held fast in the grip of wedding fever. Lucy Jolliffe the thirty year old daughter of Sir William was to marry William Vane of Fairlawn, Member of Parliament. The village rejoiced in the news for Lucy had served as devoted house-keeper to her father for the past nine years since the death of her step-mother. The bloom of youth had left her cheeks and all who knew of her loving and devoted nature had begun to regret that so sweet a soul should devote her life to such a task. The trees themselves, decked in the rich hues produced by a warm, late summer and a sudden spell of clear, crisply cold weather, appeared to have caught the excitement in the air. The villagers had rallied round to help John Corbett cover the floor of the church with rushes freshly cut from the river bank and had decorated the church with autumn gifts. Around the churchyard local men

William Vane and Lucy Jolliffe
(By courtesy of Lord Barnard)

laboured to restore the low wall built to keep out straying stock so that the happy couple should feel no cares at evidence of neglect in the village which was to be their home.

The widower, Sir William Jolliffe and his daughter were determined that the wedding should be worthy of the family and had gradually driven the castle and so the village into a state of frenzied activity. For weeks people of all degrees had flowed into, out of and around the castle. In the kitchen recipe books were constantly open, preserved meats were prepared for the table, the wine cellar was constantly checked and replenished and rechecked until the cellarer began to feel that he knew every bottle by name. In upstairs rooms needles flashed, tongues clacked and ladies applied their skills to the making of some clothes and the embellishment of others to both grace the day and amaze the on-lookers.

From the church doorway to the castle the villagers had spread a path of rushes. The arched entrance to the castle grounds had been decorated with corn dollies, an art form which had its roots in a fertility rite older than the village itself. Beyond the archway stood the castle, candles gleaming from its windows as the soft grey gloom of an autumn evening crept across the sky slowly snuffing out the brittle warmth of a dying sun.

William Vane was a figure of splendour, clad in a large, elaborately coloured and pow-dered periwig, a loose pleated neck scarf with fringed ends hanging down fan-wise some six inches from the neck and a long, skirted coat of blue brocade pulled in tight at the waist, falling nearly to the knees and close buttoned to the chin, having rows of buttons down the front and being elaborately embroidered down the seams with gold lace. Around his waist he wore a wide silk sash with fringed ends. His breeches, cut moderately wide, were of the same material as his coat and were tied at his knee with a bunch of ribbons. His legs were clad in white stockings whilst his feet were encased in fine leather shoes with high scarlet heels and large, jewelled and enamelled buckles.

Mistress Vane was resplendent in a scarlet, satin gown and blue satin petticoat se-cured in a straight line just above the bosom. The puffed, elbow length sleeves were turned up with white and fastened with a bow of blue ribbon. Her face, naturally some-what angular was indifferently and overheavily made up, framed with carefully trained small curls known to the fashionable ladies of London as 'heartbreakers', upon her right cheek she wore a single, small heart shaped patch. In her hand she carried a small lace and cambric handkerchief matching the material of the large, repulsively snuff stained handkerchief secured to the breast of her husband's coat by an ornate, jewelled brooch.

Around them swirled the cream of North Staffordshire society, liberally sprinkled with acquaintances from further afield. The hubbub of conversation, almost drowning the music provided by the imported flautists and fiddlers, seemed to fill the great ban-queting hall with a layer of solid sound which smote upon the ear as fiercely as the swirl and flash of colours struck the eye. Bewigged gentlemen clad in the long coats favoured by the late King rubbed shoulders with more soberly clad members of rural society. Bare female necks and shoulders shone and flashed in a sea of jewel sparkling silks, velvets and brocades contrasting sharply with the more decorously clad but no less attractive local ladies.

Within the hall the guests were free to choose from a range of Spanish wines, burgundy, claret and sherry whilst outside the villagers toasted the bride and groom with vast quan-tities of 'mum', an ale brewed with local wheat instead of hops and its derivative 'buttered mum', a similar beverage warmed and enhanced with sugar and cinnamon. Supporting the vast and over-powering wedding meal which had begun at mid-day was a mighty array of beers, ales, wines, punches, possets and cordials including a thoroughly destruc-tive local brew called 'cock's ale' a great favourite of the local gentry.

'Take 10 gallons of ale and a large cock, the older the better, par boil the cock, skin him and stamp him in the stone mortar until the bones are broken. Put the cock into two quarts of sack to which add three pounds of raisins of the sun, stoned; some blades of mace and a few cloves. Put all of this into a canvas bag and a little before you find that the ale has done working put the ale and bag together into a vessel. In a week or nine days butter it up and leave for the same time to ripen as other ale.' [32]

For those who preferred something less lethal and more delicate coffee was available, there was even some talk among the knowledgeable ones present of a new and expensive drink called tea!

To absorb this vast ocean of fluids was a wealth of meats, pies, fish and birds all served in elaborate style with the exception of simple but tasty home cured hams and tongues. The dishes ranged from potted swan which consisted of swan minced with bacon and seasoned with butter, salt, cloves, mace and nutmeg all moistened with claret and butter the whole thing being baked in an earthenware jar; to the almost unbelievably large 'turienier' pie. The turienier pie was of an incredible size and content.

'Take a large china bowl and at the bottom lay some fresh butter, then get three or four beef steaks of the larger kind larded with bacon, then three or four veal steaks of a like size dipped in egg yoke. Over these steaks place a layer of forcemeat, then young pigeons, chickens and rabbits, sweetbreads, kidneys and coxcombs, sheeps' tongues and calves' tongues, whole yokes of hard boiled eggs, pistachio nuts, forcemeat balls, sliced lemon, barbaries and oysters.' [32]

This mixture was then seasoned with butter, salt, nutmeg, sweet herbs, more butter and a quart of thick gravy. The whole was then covered with a thick puff paste and subsequently baked for eight hours.

To sweeten the palate after the sequence of main dishes the guests could choose from a range of puddings, cakes, biscuits, lemon cheese cakes, almond cheese cakes, wigs, quinces, jellies and cheeses.

As the day wore into evening and evening became night liquor loosened tongues and widened the gulf between 'town' and 'country'. The rural gentry staggered and roared across the room bellowing coarse jokes in a broad local dialect. Their town cousins, equally inebriated, proclaimed indelicate advice in more refined and equally uncertain tones struggling to demonstrate that veneer of decency which was the product of wider experience and more constant practice.

Outside in the darkened village the villagers staggered off to bed replete and intoxicated, for once blissfully unaware of everything save an extended belly, a swimming head and a burning desire for bed even if bed were little more than a pallet of straw in an odorous hovel.

The Caverswall lands passed, with Lucy to William Vane. During the lifetime of their parents the young couple received a yearly allowance of £700 from Mr. Jolliffe and £500 from the less affluent Bernard Vane of Barnard Castle. As a gesture of affection, however, Baron Bernard granted to his daughter-in-law £100 a year 'pin-money', *'with which not husband nor any other shall have to do or intercede. '*

Sir William Jolliffe died in January 1711 and was buried in Caverswall churchyard; *'Guillemus, Jolliffe, Armiger, sepultus fuit'.* Upon his death Caverswall Castle passed to Lucy Vane. In 1720 her husband was elevated to an Irish peerage as Baron Dungannon and in 1734 was elected Knight for the County of Kent.

THE FIRST LORD VANE

In 1703 Lucy Jolliffe married William Vane of Fairlawn, Member of Parliament. The young couple received a yearly allowance of £700 from Lucy's father and £500 a year from Baron Barnard, the groom's father. In 1720 William Vane became Baron Dungannon.

A document dated 11th. November 1703 suggests that Lord Barnard also gave to Lucy a Personal allowance of £100 "with which not husband nor any other shall have to do."

A painting of the couple, made perhaps at the time of their betrothal, conveys an air of confident superiority. Their personal happiness was to be tarnished by the conduct of their son William Holles Vane, the second Lord Vane.

The young couple seem to have lived in the castle during the last years of the life of Sir William Jolliffe. Sir William died in January 1711 and was buried in Caverswall Church.

In June 1720 William Vane was created an Irish Peer and in 1734 was elected knight for the county of Kent. Sadly he died three days later.

Lucy, Viscountess Vane survived her husband for eight years most of which time was spent at Caverswall. She died on 27th. March, 1742.

In 1714 on 4th February their only son, William Holles Vane was born. Early in life he became noted for his cruel, unpredictable and irresponsible behaviour. From the time he entered Oxford University in October 1730 his behaviour caused his parents increasing anguish, the savagery of his nature matching well the *'thin, meagre, shivering creature, of low stature, little black eyes, a long nose, a sallow complexion and pitted with the pox'*. Three days after being elected Knight for the County of Kent William Vane died, some said of a broken heart, leaving his wife Lucy a widow after 31 years of a contented and happy marriage.

Lucy Viscountess Vane survived her husband for eight years dying on 27th March, 1742, at the age of 69 years. Throughout her declining years the behaviour of her son brought her nothing but anguish as the *'imbecile spendthrift'* dragged the family name through the mire and impoverished the estate.

Five years after entering Oxford University William Holles Vane, Viscount Vane, Baron Vane of Dungannon, in the fullness of time, heir to vast estates including Caverswall Castle married the lately widowed Lady Frances Hamilton. He was 21 years of age, a poor physical specimen, lacking in dress sense and heir to vast wealth. She had been married at 15, widowed at 18 and was, by her own claims, *'gifted with youth, exceptional beauty, an inborn love for pleasure, innocence and a sensitive affectionate heart'*. Contemporary opinion was more blunt, *'She is a very great whore and he a great fool'*.[33]   The ill-

William Holles Vane -
'the imbecile spendthrift'
(Courtesy of the Courtauld Institute of Fine Art)

Lady Frances Hamilton
'a very great whore'
(Courtesy of the Courtauld Institute of Fine Art)

advised and ill-starred marriage with the wealthy, besotted young fool who owned Caverswall Castle was a more fortunate prospect than the immoral, arrogant and selfish young widow had any right to expect. On her part at least the marriage was viciously calculated. The *'advantageous terms of settlement'* offered by the arrangement were sufficient to render her independent financially, whilst she held her husband in such scant regard that she was able to claim publicity:

'I considered myself as a person absolved of all matrimonial ties by the insignificance of Lord Vane who, though a nominal husband was, in fact a mere nonentity.' [34]

It would seem that both partners in the alliance were guilty of serious errors of judgement. Lord Vane had assumed that he was marrying a devoted, beautiful young widow whose tragic background added a sentimental lustre to the physical charm which she radiated. He discovered instead that he had taken a promiscuous vixen into his bed. Lady Frances had assumed that her beau manque was a simpleton possessing great wealth to be tapped at will and a provincial fop open to ready deceit. She found instead that he possessed the vicious tenacity of a starving rat.

The strife began at Caverswall Castle immediately after the wedding when Lady Lucy Vane welcomed her daughter-in-law to the castle and with a mother's instincts, sensed the truly rotten soul hidden beneath the shallow eyes.

In less than a year the newly weds were back in London and Lady Frances was seeking the physical delights which she claimed were denied her by her husband with an almost incredible degree of complaisance. A sequence of stormy domestic interludes including one period of incarceration at Caverswall Castle when she was confined in her husband's *'house far in the country where my husband kept me guarded by soldiers'* was interspersed by periods of openly adulterous association with other members of the nobility or men of the mercantile world. During such spells of flagrant immorality Lady Frances would flee with her paramour whereupon Lord Vane would hire men, place advertisements in the popular press of the day and hunt her down for all the world like a huntsman pursuing a fox. The vixen's covert became England and Western Europe, the staying power of the hunt became the depth of Lord Vane's purse and although the outcome was never in doubt the victory was always uncertain.

18th century society stood aghast and scandalised at the behaviour of the pair. Sympathy generally lay with Lord Vane, as early in the marriage as August 1736 Guthrie wrote:

'My Lord Vane rid several times post through this towne (Boulogne). He was in search of his wife and had 40 or 50 people riding over France in quest of her. I hear she run from him at Paris with one of the Shirleys, who carried her to Brussels ... I pity that poor unhappy Lord, if he lives a few years he will be a beggar. The only wise thing he could do would be to get his marriage annulled, put his estate into the hands of trustees and entail it to the next heirs.' [35]

In 1737 the Earl of Egmont recorded that:

'I read this day in the newspapers My Lord Vane's advertisement offering £100 reward to him that should discover his Lady who for some time had eloped from him. One would think he had lost some favourite spaniel bitch, for he describes her person very particularly even to the clothes she wears.' [36]

The prodigality of Lady Frances and the vast sums spent upon her pursuit by Lord William inevitably threw him into debt. On 15th May 1753 he leased the Castle at Caverswall for one year to the 'most noble James Duke of Hamilton', the indenture reads in part:

'witnesseth that for and in consideration of the sum of five shillings to him the said William Lord Viscount Vane hath bargained and sold unto the said James Duke of Hamilton and Thomas Duke of Leeds their Executors, Administrators and assigns ... all that Castle or Capital Mansion House called Caverswall Castle ... and all that Park or enclosed ground lying near the said Castle or Capital Mansion ...' [37]

Remembering that Lady Frances Vane was the widow of Lord William Hamilton and considering the peppercorn nature of the fee involved one is led to suspect that Lord Vane, that 'silly young man, half mad, half fool' was either soliciting help from James Duke of Hamilton or seeking to win the good opinions of his wife. The latter seems more probable for there is a view that, whatever the other faults of Lord Vane, he was never niggardly with money towards his wife, indeed he was criticized by his contemporaries for his unthinking generosity towards her.

This view is borne out by the Release deed relating to the previous indenture which is dated 15th May 1753, it reads:

'This indenture ... made the fifteenth day of May in the twenty- sixth year of the reign of our Sovereign Lord George the Second ... and in the year of our Lord one thousand seven hundred and fifty-three years. Between William Glanville of St. Clere in the County of Kent Esquire and John Jackson late of Cursitow Street but now of Great Queen Street in the County of Middlesex. Gentleman of the first part the Right Honourable William Lord Viscount Vane deceased of the second part and the most noble Thomas Duke of Leeds Knight of the Most Noble Order of the Garter of the third part. Whereas by Indentures of Lease and release bearing dates respecting the fifteenth and sixteenth day of May which was in the year of our Lord one thousand seven hundred and thirty-

five. The Release being quadrupartiti and made between the said William now Lord Viscount Vane. The Right Honourable Frances Lady Viscountess Vane his wife by her then name and description of the Honourable Frances Hamilton commonly called Lady William Hamilton widow and Relict of the Honourable William Hamilton Esquire deceased commonly called Lord William Hamilton brother to His Grace the most noble James Duke of Hamilton and Brandon, Knight of the most Ancient Order of the Thistle (also deceased)... The said James Duke of Hamilton and Brandon and the said Thomas Duke of Leeds and Frances Hawes of Purley Hall and Thomas Hawes of London Mercer. In consideration of a marriage then intended and which soon after took effect and was solemnized between the said William now Viscount Vane and Frances Hamilton now Lady Viscountess Vane and of the sum of six thousand pounds her marriage portion and for other considerations; in the said Indenture quadrupartiti mentioned... And also all that Castle or Capital Mansion House called Caverswall otherwise Caverswall Castle standing and being in Caverswall... in the said County of Stafford, And all that Park or inclosed ground lying near the said Castle... And all those several parcels of land meadow and pasture to the said Castle or Mansion House... together with all houses outhouses, barns coach houses, woods... Whatsoever to the said Castle... belonging. Now this indenture witnesseth... that the said Thomas Duke of Leeds hath bargained... and each of them doth bargain, sell a lien, release and confirm unto the said Thomas Duke of Leeds in his actual possession now being by virtue of a Bargain and Sale to him thereof made by the said William Glanville and John Jackson... to have and to hold the said manors.'[37]

Viscount Vane's generosity coupled with his prodigious expenditure upon enterprises designed to locate his errant wife served to empty his exchequer at a considerable speed. His wife appears to have had money to spend freely when they were together so adding to the drain upon her husband's purse. By 1759 he had sold the Caverswall estates whilst retaining a life interest in them, for £4,000 to the Lady Mary Countess of Stamford and mother of Booth Grey. He had also sold to the Duke of Newcastle his reversion of the vast Holles estate, also part of his inheritance. The financial resources of the husband and the physical charms of the wife were squandered and dissipated by a pair of fools who sought to ignore the harsh realities of life. Lady Frances Vane, used and discarded returned to her pathetically besotted spouse as a worn, raddled and aging beauty. With him she found security and in that security her old nature briefly flared. A last desperate round of costly parties was unable to restore her lost allure or retrieve her popularity among the shallow socialites who had taken her to their hearts some fifteen years before.

Lady Frances Vane died on 31st March 1788. Her husband outlived her by one year and five days.

THE SECOND LORD VANE

William Holles Vane was born 4th. February, 1713 and was enrolled as a student at Christ Church College, Oxford on 1st. October, 1730 where he earned an unenviable reputation for eccentricity and cruelty.

In his early years William Holles Vane earned the nickname of the imbecile spendthrift because of his cruel and unpredictable behaviour. After his marriage the behaviour of his wife, and his response to her adultery became a source of shame to his parents.

The second Lord Vane married Lady Frances Hamilton after she had been married at fifteen and widowed at eighteen. On her part the marriage was viewed in a cynical, financial manner and she took pride in the advantageous terms of the settlement since later she made no secret of the fact that she had been forced into marriage against her will by her family.

Individual portraits of William Holles, the second Lord Vane and his wife exist. They show two remarkable individuals and certainly not the persons described by Lady Frances.

She described herself as being gifted with youth, exceptional beauty, an inborn love of pleasure, innocence and a sensitive affectionate heart. She described her husband as a, thin, shivering, meagre creature, of low stature, little black eyes, a long nose, a sallow complexion and pitted with the pox. A nominal husband, a mere nonentity. Others, perhaps with less malice, referred to him as:- that silly young man, half mad half fool.

Lady Frances had married Sir William Hamilton at fifteen and widowed by his premature death, at eighteen. According to her account she had been assiduously courted by William Vane whom she did not love but agreed to marry after pressure from her family. Her brother-in-law James Duke of Hamilton and Brandon had acquired his title dishonourably having taken bribes to betray the Scots and prepare strategies favourable to the Court parties during debates about the nature of links between England and Scotland in 1705

In her autobiography she blamed her attitude to life upon her father 'I was the only child of a man of good fortune, who indulged me in my infancy with all the tenderness of paternal affection'. She wrote that in her early years she was carried to all places of public diversion, the court itself not excepted, and indulgence that flattered my love of pleasure, to which I was naturally addicted and encouraged those ideas of vanity and ambition .... I was lively and good natured, my imagination apt to run riot, my heart liberal and disinterested, though I was so obsessively attached to my opinions, that I could not well brook contradiction and in the whole of my disposition resembled that of Henry V. as described by Shakespeare....

The Earl of Egmont wrote in 1736 that Lady Frances was a daughter of one of the South Sea directors whom Parliament had forfeited in 1721 for cheating the public! She was also noted for having been the mistress of Lord Berkeley among many others. She was also reputed to be the authoress of The Memoirs of a Lady of Quality, described by a later writer as indecent and appears under the name of Lady Frail in Smollet's 'The Adventures of Peregrine Pickle'. The autobiography seems to have been written in an attempt to re-instate herself in society. A letter quoted in that work suggests that society did not warm to her explanation of her actions . . . . 'the world is apt to put the worst constructions upon everything. . . . .'

Her flight with a series of lovers and his pursuit of them across much of Europe at great expense to the Caverswall estate was one of the scandals of the day and in 1737 attracted from the Earl of Egmont the comment that, 'she is a very great whore and he a great fool . . . . . . if he lives a few years he will be a beggar.'

In 1759 he was forced to sell the Caverswall estate for £4,000.

In 1842 Charles Vane, Marquess of Londonderry, was one of the Lords castigated by Charles Dickens in an article in which he attacked those noble owners of coal mines who were content to keep women and children at work in conditions of indescribable degradation. At this time the Vane family owned extensive coal mines at Seaham in County Durham.

1700 - 1750 A.D.

WHICH WE NOW POSSESS

Apart from the gradual destruction of the personal fortunes of the Vanes the first five decades of the 18th century proved to be good ones for the parish. Despite occasional gales like that of 1703, the desiccative droughts of 1716, 1717 and 1719 when even the spring at Park Hall failed, the destructive droughts between 1740 and 1743 when many cattle died of heatstroke and the bitterly cruel winters between 1740 and 1745 the half century was, on the whole, blessed with excellent farming weather.

The parish was very much a place of villages and hamlets which seemed part of the soil from which they drew their living. The countryside was still a vast sea of open country in which the few yeoman-run farms and the great estates which had begun to plant hedges to mark their enclosed holdings seemed strangely alien. The great swathe of Caverswall Common ran from the slopes south-east of the church where 'Heath View' now stands, northwards in a great open belt of sheep nibbled and trampled turf to the slopes above and beyond Sheepwash. From this higher land the tree cover had been pushed back onto the steeper slopes, into the deepest parts of the valleys and up to the edges of the damper ground.

A belt of woodland, Caverswall Wood, clothed the western slopes of the Blithe, flowed over the high ground at Meir and away towards Longton where master potters were just beginning to plan the development of their tiny backyard ovens into proud new 'pot-banks'. At Weston Coyney the fine timbered home of the Parker family rose proudly above the vast fields which covered the whole of the area between Park Hall Hills, the marshes along the Blithe and the hillock north of Meir. To the west, at Adderley, lay another extensive island of cultivation in the thinly tree clad greenness which flowed away northwards over the flanks of the hills above Hulme where another island of cultivation interrupted its progress towards Wetley Moor.

Improved drainage, increased cultivation, an unceasing demand for timber and pasture coupled with individual initiative and energy had served to create a vast spread of 'champion' country, devoid of hedges and sprinkled with fine standard oaks in the drier parts and occasional small stands of birch or clumps of alder in the parts where dampness still prevailed.

In such a landscape it was difficult to conceive the existence of poverty, dirt and disease. At first sight the poet's picture of rustic life offers a vision of prosperity:

'Before the yellow barn I see
A beautiful variety
Of strutting cocks, advancing stout
And flirting empty chaff about
Hens, ducks and geese and all their brood
And turkeys gobbling for their food
While rustics thrash the wealthy floor
And tempt them all to crowd the door. '

The unweathered timbers of the barn suggest its recent origins and so imply expansion; the wealthy floor piled high with its great cash crop wheat and the implication of good living in the form of well fed poultry suggest prosperity.

For some in Caverswall the miller who dwelt :
'In a plain, pleasant cottage, conveniently neat with a mill and some meadows a freehold estate'
and who, on Sunday, was

'Bedecked in his homespun array
At church he's the loudest to chant or to pray
He sits to a dinner of plain English food
Though simple the pudding, his appetite's good.
At night when the priest and exciseman are gone
He quaffs at the alehouse with Roger and John
Then reels to his pillow and dreams of no ill;
No monarch more blest . . .'

offered both a fair image of the present and a hope for the future. For many other village dwellers however such prosperity was a slowly vanishing dream as the larger land holders gradually increased their estates pushing the most impoverished labourers still further down the social scale. For some in the parish the future offered naught save the prospect of unending, back-aching, sweat streaked labour beneath the warmth of Caverswall's summer sun or the prospect of hard graft and low pay in the dust and heat of the slowly expanding potteries. Such ordinary folk knew only too well the grim truth that *'there never lacks a job for Giles to do'*. Through the first half of the century and indeed until the end of the Napoleonic War in 1815 for a majority of the lesser folk agriculture, supported by their own endeavours, offered a living and provided modest opportunities to save a little of their hard earned funds although these were always vulnerable to bad weather and illness.

Some of the less industrious or more desperate turned to poaching and fell foul of the new game laws and their enforcers, the gamekeepers. Such unfortunates suffered for their hunger under a lash more grievous and more fearful than that with which their Norman predecessors had beaten their Saxon serfs.

Others discovered and capitalized upon their own special skills by providing a service or producing a product which could be bartered for kind or sold for cash. In this way there sprang up a slender network of cottage industries; weaving at Werrington, nailmaking at Cellarhead on the site opposite the ground now occupied by the Methodist Chapel, nailmaking again was practised at Salter's Lane Farm, stone quarrying at Washerwall, mining around Wetley Moor and the water mill at Malthouse were all, in some degree, a response to this challenge. For such artisans life was better than it might have been, they too rose above the truly poor.

As the gaps between social classes widened and new social strata began to emerge so the parish seemed to prosper. A new stone windmill appeared at Werrington in 1730. Stone tablets commemorating the lives of the leading citizens of the area appeared in the church. Such tablets refer not only to the leaders of parish society like Bridget Parker (1702), her husband William (1703) and George Parker (1716) but also to worthy and prosperous yeomen like William Smith (1709), John Bradbury (1705) and George Wood of Adderley Green (1722). As further evidence of prosperity two new church bells were added, one in 1743 inscribed 'Henry Bagley made me' and another, given by John Coyne and founded by Thomas Hadderley, in 1754. These bells alone would be sufficient testimony to the wealth of the parish but at roughly the same date a further proof appeared in the guise of a large, tithe barn built of stone blocks and standing along the south-eastern edge of the church-yard, directly adjacent to the open field. In this field stood the massive dove-cote which had, for generations, provided the occupants of the castle with a supply of fresh meat. The tithe barn dominated the field and in seeming to extend the bulk of the church was elequent testimony to the perceived need of the church to *'pull down its barns and build greater'.*

The period between 1700 and 1750 has well been called 'the Golden Age of the Peasant' and this was as true of Caverswall as elsewhere. Those men who had beasts would graze them upon the Common in spring and summer fattening them before the lean days of autumn and winter arrived. As the natural fodder crops were exhausted they had to choose between selling off the beast to show a cash profit and gambling on a mild winter during which sufficient fodder could be bought, earned or acquired to keep the beast alive for another breeding season. Increasingly a sequence of mild winters induced more and more men to gamble in this fashion and so expand their holdings. Sometimes by careful dealing and frugal living a villager might amass the £25 or £30 necessary to purchase an acre of good land and so progress from labourer to smallholder. Fresh meat appeared with increasing frequency upon the peasant's table replacing sour tasting joints hacked from the salt steeped carcases of aged, half starved oxen. Wheaten bread became the life staple of more than half the parish. Work existed for those who sought it and real wages climbed steadily. Those with special skills found ready markets for their talents. Home for most was still a modest cottage but increasingly it boasted a stone flag or quarry floor, sturdy furniture and bore withal, an air of neatness which bespoke a pride in possession and a consciousness of self.

At the top of the social scale the large landowners like the Parkers could concern themselves with improved techniques and debate the merits of Jethro Tull's book *'Horse Hoeing Husbandry'* which claimed that the use of ridge sowing, wide drilling and deep hoeing would permit land to be cropped repeatedly with the same crop and without the use of manures. A shallow philosophy which enjoyed but a brief vogue in Caverswall bringing a new and untypical, short-lived pattern of agricultural practice to the parish.

The villagers were kept constantly aware of the problems which faced people elsewhere in England. Between 1715 and 1723 alone the parish received 'Briefs' or letters from the Crown or some other Authority directing the collection of alms for certain purposes in order that aid might be given to parishes in need, on behalf of no fewer than thirty different counties in England and Wales. In addition support was solicited on behalf of one church in New York and one in Poland. Judging by the records the parishioners of Caverswall responded to pleas which were near to home and close to the heart.

In 1720 the records show that 15s.2d was collected on behalf of *'Sufferers by Thunder, Hail, etc: in Staffordshire'* when total damage was estimated at £4,163. Three years later to replace *'loss by fire'* amounting to £1,166 at Heartsease in Radnor County the parish raised just 9d. It is an interesting deduction from the former Brief that the intense drought of 1719 may well have culminated, characteristically for such conditions, in an explosion of thunder, hail and storm to such effect that the damage referred to in the Brief resulted.

Roads throughout the parish were still indifferent, Admiral John Leveson-Gower gave their measure when, after a coach journey through the area in mid-century, he observed that he *'would rather be in the Bay of Biscay in a storm than on one of the Dillhorne roads in a carriage'.* Lacking clearly defined limits to their extent such uneven tracks tended to sprawl on either side of the main line for *'travellers know no highwaies in the common fields'.* Each traveller sought carefully to avoid the wheel ruts of his predecessors whilst driven beasts trespassed as they would, often until a swathe of destruction had been wrought twenty yards on either side of the main path. Such behaviour did little to sweeten the dispositions of open field farmers in the parish who already agreed as little as the *'wasp doth with the bee'.* Open field farming was a constant invitation to plough up common headland, to move one of the flimsy markers, to turn and plough closer than was honest to a neighbour's holding and even to filch portions of a neighbour's crops during harvest time.

Despite a continuing sequence of good harvests, warm summers and benign rainfall the villagers were too mindful of the proximity of disaster to all forms of husbandry to believe that they were destined to prosper unchastened indefinitely. Even so the cattle plague of 1746 came as a savage and bitter shock to the parish, marking with brutal finality the end of the golden age.

St. Peter's Church as it was depicted in 1750
and as William Holles Vane 'The Imbecile' knew it.

1745 A.D.

EACH FOR HIS OWN LAND, DIED

1745 had been a year of anxiety. After a dry summer, autumn had come early, cold and wet. With it had arrived rumours of insurrection in Scotland.

By late November rumours were scudding through the parish to the effect that an army of Scots led by the Pretender to the throne, Charles Edward Stuart, was marching south on a line that would bring it through the parish if it was maintained without diversion. The parish throbbed with fearful excitement, thrilled by the prospect of seeing the handsome 'Bonnie Prince Charlie' at close quarters yet apprehensive of the consequences of being visited by an army of allegedly savage and brutal Highlanders who lacked every vestige of that precious nobility and decency possessed by their royal master.

On 3rd December 1745 word reached the village that the Highlanders were in Leek; rumours of murder, arson, rape and robbery swept across the county. Days of confusion were followed by a second definite report that the Highlanders had marched in triumph for Derby, were now retreating in disconsolate disarray and had re-entered Leek on Saturday, 7th December. Now the tales were different, the Scots were sadly disorganised, demoralised, shorn of bombast and discarding anything likely to encumber their rapid retreat northwards.

It was rumoured that so complete was the collapse of morale that the Jolliffe family, still noted for its parsimony, had eagerly taken charge of a small keg jettisoned by a retreating Scot in Leek market place hoping to find therein a quantity of the firey fluid known as 'uisebeatha'. The tippler's dismay became the miser's delight when it was realised that the keg contained not the golden liquid anticipated but a wealth of golden coin, apparently part of the paymaster's hoard. After a brief spasm of excitement occasioned by the arrival of a detachment of redcoats who had missed the road to Cheadle where their fellows lay under the Duke of Cumberland's command, the village settled down again to face the threat of what was proving to be a damp and humid winter.

A fragment of a letter dated 3rd December, 1745 and written by Mr. J. Comyn to Mr. William Clark, of Caverswall, near Stone, Staffordshire, offers an interesting sidelight on the passage of the Highlanders. It refers to the inability or reluctance of the villagers to pay their dues:

'. . . as well as the rest of the Kingdom but am much surprised my tenants be so faulty in their payments before they came near them for when you went they could have no just excuse and refusing their just debts without one is much in the Highland strain. However I hope these troubles will soon be at an end and shall then depend on your care and diligence to recover my arrears. We are not much afraid here of these Highland men but however they have much hurt the trade so that what with them and the disease among our cattle affairs are but now indifferent, but please God to grant the Duke success we shall soon be right again. The Pretender's youngest son is certainly taken.

I am

Your humble servant
J. Comyn [3]

Dec. 3rd 1745

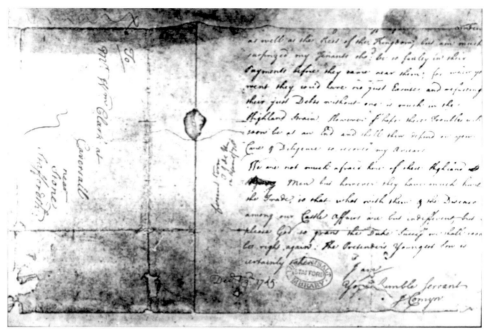

The fragment of a letter dated 1745

The real horror began just before Christmas. Three beasts turned out to graze on the impoverished fallows were found to have blisters on their tongues and lips. Around their udders and teats similar vesicles were discovered. Their obvious restlessness and physical discomfort betrayed the fact that their feet too were infected. In a matter of days the parish found itself in the savage grip of a cattle plague which had not been known in the area since 1724.

Reluctant to cast their wealth aside too readily many farmers hesitated to slaughter suspect beasts. By the time the symptoms had hardened into certainty other beasts were infected, some families had eaten contaminated beef and most had drunk tainted milk. Beasts were locked in barns and byres under the watchful gaze of youthful guards who were given strict instructions to keep the animals inside under all circumstances. Workmen were charged to wash their face and hands with vinegar. Outer garments were to be cleansed. When a beast was proclaimed to be indisputably sick everything it had touched was to be burnt. The walls of barns and byres were to be whitened and disinfected morning and evening for eight days with a mixture of herbs and vinegar. All mangers and water troughs were to be swilled and sweetened with vinegar in a suspension of sulphur

Yet all seemed to be in vain. Day after grey, damp day the stench of burning flesh, the reek of smouldering straw and the pungent odours of sulphur and vinegar lay over the parish. Palls of dirty grey smoke each marking the funeral pyre of a farmer's hopes rose throughout the parish. Adderley, Hulme, Weston Coyney, Ash and Caverswall all cowered in desperate, uncomprehending anger beneath their dread of the present and their fears for the future.

Spring and summer 1746 were lean seasons in Caverswall. The common lands carried few beasts, the small artisans found no market or their skills, the small farmer toiled to sow a crop which, God willing, might offer a yield sufficient to finance a beast to re-establish his herd; the greater farmers dipped into capital and knew hard times.

Somehow the parish rose from its depths of despair. In thanksgiving for the better times of the early 1750s a third bell was added in 1754. The steady enrichment of the church continued with the donation of a magnificent set of church plate by Sir Thomas Parker in 1760 .

THE CHURCH PLATE OF St. PETER'S CHURCH, CAVERSWALL

*O*ver the centuries church plate has served many purposes. It has been regarded variously as a store of wealth, a token of remembrance, proof of patronage, evidence of a willingness to dedicate and commit worldly wealth to God's service and as a means of adding dignity and lustre to divine service.

The church plate of St. Peter's appears to fall into three categories. The first comprises a chalice and paten of unknown origin. It is reasonable to assume that this earliest element of the church plate - a chalice and paten (a shallow dish upon which the bread is laid at celebrations of the Eucharist) was to facilitate the service of Holy Communion. The existence of 'on challes of silver with a paten(t) parcelgilte' - (one silver chalice and a partly gilded paten) - is revealed by an inventory of church property carried out during the reign of the sickly boy king Edward VI who reigned from 1547 to 1552. It seems possible that these items were donated by either the Montgomeries or, more probably, the Giffards. These two families occupied the castle between approximately 1480 and 1550.

The keystone of the collection is a complete matching set of plate which was the gift of Sir Thomas Parker, Lord Baron of the Exchequer in 1760. His daughter, Martha, became the wife of Sir John Jervis, Earl St. Vincent.

The set consists of a flagon, chalice, paten and alms dish in silver gilt and engraved with the Parker crest. The oldest items in the set appear to be the flagon and the alms dish: these are of similar hammered work. The alms dish bears the date 1628 and carries the initials T.T. presumably the identifying mark of the silversmith. The dish also bears an engraving which reads The Gift of The Lord Chief Baron Parker To The Parish Of Caverswall 1760. At the same date Samuel Wood of Adderley Green presented a silver collecting dish.

The third element in the collection consists of two more recent items, a small pyx or bread box given by Clarissa Veale in 1915 and a large brass tray given in 1906 by the Caverswall Mothers' Meeting in memory of Alice Bowers

*On display - The Church Plate of St. Peter's Church, Caverwall.
These items are deposited in the strong room of a local bank.*

1766 A.D.

THE MAINTENANCE OF THE PARSON

The Church Terrier for 1766 gives a fascinating insight into the agricultural activities of the parish. A 'Terrier' is a book or document recorded on parchment which describes the land and property in the possession of the church, the word is derived from 'terre' the French word for land. Such a record presents both a picture of the agricultural fabric of the parish and a clear statement of the hold the Church had upon the community of the day.

All that remains of the great tithe barn. The rough ashlar blocks at the foot of the wall appear to mark the foundations of the great tithe barn in which the parson stored his tithes.

The community to which the Terrier refers was dominated by the stone built church, tithe barn, castle and Stone House; around and yet apart from these dominant features straggled and huddled a clutter of poorer dwellings. Some were of shaped stone blocks with the beginnings of an enclosed yard and field patterns marking them out as the holding of a prosperous farmer. The great majority were simple, timber framed houses of modest quality, all were capped by a heavy thatch. Beyond the dwellings stretched the open countryside in a green, yellow, brown mosaic of work-a-day patterns flowing over the undulating landscape with effortless beauty. Scattered over the openness lay a sprinkle of farmhouses and private dwellings ranging from the Hall at Weston Coyney and Captain Parker's great farmhouse at Roughcote to the dwellings of the nailmakers at Cellarhead and the mills at Malthouse and Werrington. Within this fair field full of folk the life and work of the parish ebbed and flowed with the seasons, it was from the produce of that work that the parson drew his maintenance.

THE TERRIER OF THE CHURCH OR PARISH OF CAVERSWALL
(1766)

Imprimis belonging to the Vicar one mansion or dwelling housecontaining 2 Bays Item a Barn and Cowhouse containing 3 Bays together with one Garden and Fould Yard the backside a Croft commonly called the Moat Yard the Hill Croft the Barngorse and 3 pieces of Land called the Moor Edges about an Acre of Land at Hulme 3 daymath and half in the Town Meadows together with Common and Turbary upon the Heath Lands and Wastes The Church Yard together with Mortuarys according to the Statute Tithes as follows Imprimis all the Great Tithes of the Vicarage Glebe when occupied by the Vicar Hem Tithes hay in kind from the following Grounds Viz. All the Land belonging to Cookshill Hall All William Cooks Estate all the Land belonging to Captain Parkers Great House at Roughcote and the Land belonging to the Cockin All the land which was Inclosed or taken from Wetley moor the Demains of Westoncoyney Hall The Hill Croft and Hill Meadow belonging to Holehouse The Calverhay and Calverhay Meadows those pieces belonging to the Bankhouse All the Stacklow Calf Croft Oulder Doles Margerysich and twining Meadow Smithey Heath together with all the Living if converted into Meadowing or Mowed A piece of Ground in the possession of Wm Austin of the Rowitch called Cowops Copy likewise a piece of Land at Meer called Longdoles together with all manner of tithes of all the Glebe Land belongs to the Vicarage All the rest of the Old Meadow Land in Caverswall parish is coverd with or by Moduses which free it from paying of Tithe hay in kind Item the tithe or tenth of Apples pears plumbs Item for every Strike of Hemp seed sowd in the said parish one Shilling and for every Greater or lesser Quantity proportionable and for every peck of flax seed sow'd one shilling Item the Tithes or tenth of wool Lambs pigs Geese Item Tithes in kind of pottatoes parsnips carrots turnips and all manner of Roots Item the Custom is, the parishioner may take up two fleeces of wool two Lambs pigs or Geese and then the Vicar to take his Choice Item the Custom is if the fleeces of wool or number of lambs pigs or Geese Amount but to the number of seven the seventh is due to the Vicar if the parishioner hath above the number of seven and not seventeen then he shall pay to the Vicar one penny for each Lamb above the Number and if not seven one penny but if the number of fleeces of Wool or Lambs amount to seventeen then two fleeces of Wool or Lambs are due to the Vicar and after seventeen one at every ten Item the Custom is if the parishioner or parishioners shall sell any Sheep or Lambs or send them out of the parish at or after the first day of the Annunciation of the Bd, Virgin St. Mary that then the parishioner so selling or putting out of the parish as afforesaid shall account recken and pay to the Vicar for the same in kind in as full manner as if the said Sheep or Lamb sold or sent out of the parish before the said feast day of the Annunciation of the Bd, Virgin St. Mary the sum of one penny to be paid to the said Vicar Item for every Sheep layd, out only to Winter within the said parish one penny the Custom is if the Number of pigs or Geese shall amount to the number of seven the seventh is due to the Vicar as in Case Afforesaid Concerning Wool and Lambs Item there is due and payable for every Milkin Cow the sum of one penny and for every Calf one halfpenny for every Colt twopence for every Cast of Bees one penny for every hive of Bees killed to take the honey twopence Item tithe Herbage according to the Statute Item at the feast of Easter then is due for every house or Cottage and Garden the Sum of twopence for every person which is above the age of 15 years whether Communicating or not twopence Item tithe of Eggs According to Custom y', is to say for every hen turkey or Duck or other hen three Eggs for every Turkey or other Cock or Drake two Eggs Item

Surplice fees as follows a Modus upon every Christening for Churching the Woman the Sum of one shilling upon publishing Bans of Marriage one Shilling upon every Marriage by Bans published one Shilling and six pence upon every Marriage by License five shillings Item every parishioner man or Woman if Married in another Parish is Accountable to the Vicar according to the before rates Item upon every Corpse Burried one Shilling the Custom is if any parishioner goes out or Foreigner comes into the parish to be baptized Churched or Burried then the Vicar is to be paid double the fees above Specified Item if any Minister shall come to preach any Wedding or funeral Sermon that then the party requesting the same shall pay to the Vicar ten Shillings for his Licence Item There is due to Vicar fifty Shillings Per Annum for Preaching two Sermons one on the 13th of Decr. and the other on the 24th June being an annual Bounty Left by Mr. Ralph and Mr. John Brown of Cookshill and the Meer Item there is due to the Vicar Yearly twenty Shillings for preaching two Sermons one on the 25th March and the other on the 29th September being an annual benefaction left by Mrs. Bridgett Parker of Park Hall Item One seat Room in the 4th form on the North side of the Isle of the Church from the uper End doth belong to the Vicarage Item it is Lawful for the Vicar of the same Vicarage aforesaid his servants or any other person or Persons Authorized by him to have free Ingress Egress and Regress into any house Cottage Close or Ground pasture or Meadow at all and every time and times in the Year to view take or carry away all manner of Tithes Dues and Duties with any manner of Wain Cart Waggon Oxen Horses or any other Carriage or Carriages Whatsoever or to order Spread Cast and Dry any tithe hay or Grass in as free and ample manner as the Owners of the same pieces may or can do for the Residue without any let suit trouble or Molestation interruption or disturbance whatsoever

This is a true Copy of the Terrier of the Parish of Caverswall 1766

Samuel Willott Vicar
John Woolfe
Joseph Steel
Churchwardens

Reduced to simple terms the Terrier states that Reverend Samuel Willott, Vicar, had:

(i)   The right to graze his beasts on the common lands and waste land and the right to cut peat from the same.

(ii) A tenth of the hay taken from some 17 different areas of land.

(iii) A tenth of all apples, pears and plums.

(iv) A payment of 1/- for every strike (measure) of Hempseed sown in the parish and a pro rata sum for the remainder.

(v)   A payment of 1/- for every peck of flax sown.

(vi) A tenth of all wool, lambs, pigs and geese.

(vii) A tenth (in kind) of potatoes, parsnips, carrots, turnips and all other root crops.

(viii) The right to select from all save the two best fleeces, lambs, pigs or geese when taking his tenth.

(ix) The right to claim one penny for every item or creature above seven and below seventeen in number. At seventeen the Vicar could take two items or creatures or units and thereafter one for every ten.

(x) The right to curb attempts to sell out of the parish before the day of reckoning by claiming the value as at that day, on the sale.

(xi) The right to receive one penny for every sheep wintered in the parish, one penny for every cow in milk, one half penny for every calf. Two pence for every colt, one penny for every cast (swarm) of bees, two pence for every crop of honey taken by destroying the bees.

(xii) The right to a poll tax of two pence whether communicant or not, if over the age of 15 years, the tax to be taken at Easter.

(xiii) A tenth of all eggs with three eggs for each hen bird and two for each cock.

(xiv) The right to free access and passage for himself and his servants at any time in order to check, count and carry away his due portion.

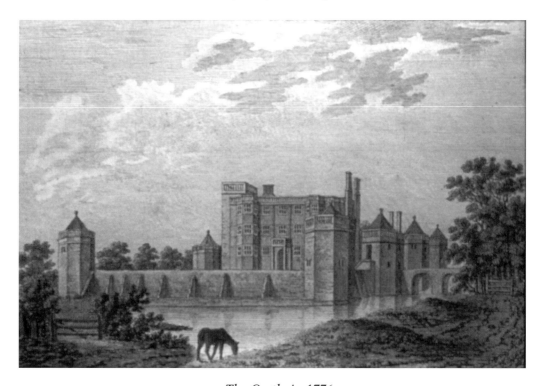

The Castle in 1776

As if such exactions were not enough by themselves nature began to take a hand, gradually life became less pleasant. Almost imperceptibly the summers had become cooler and wetter than they had been during the early decades of the century. Winter began to start in autumn and finish in late spring, snowfalls seemed to be heavier and more frequent.

1767 had died muffled beneath heavy snowfalls which mantled the entire parish in a smothering blanket of snow. The new year was born into a world whitened by snow and hardened by frosts. The intense cold brought the parish almost to a standstill. Water in the chamber pots beneath the beds in the castle and the fine timbered farmhouses froze solid. Cold chilled the poor people to the marrow, numbing fingers, chapping lips and rendering sore, red, running nostrils. Meat froze so hard it could not be spitted; horses in particular succumbed to an epidemic of distemper which killed some and broke the wind of others; birds died in large numbers victims of cold and starvation. So the pattern was set for the years which followed. Summer rains delayed harvests, summer storms flattened the standing crops, cold wet autumns and winters delayed ploughing; black, sodden springs delayed planting. Only the grass grew well, only the cattle flourished.

Inevitably the gulf between the social classes widened. The greater families had enough wealth and sufficient other interests to soften the hammer blows of a sequence of bad harvests but even their resources were stretched to breaking point as the trend continued. The lesser families had no such financial cushion and more than one local man in the desperation of hunger began to look towards Lane End where the manufacturers of pottery were seeking labourers for their newly established 'pot banks'. Those who were free tended to drift away townwards exchanging the clean poverty of the countryside for the increasingly squalid degradation of the towns. Lacking skilled, manual dexterity such men found themselves relegated to menial and laborious tasks discharged in unwholesome surroundings. So, by its presence, the town which offered so much and delivered so little began to shape and destroy the life of the parish.

1772 A.D.

DUE ENQUIRY CONCERNING THEM

On the 10th April, 1772, the Bishop of Lichfield wrote to the minister of the parish of Caverswall 'being desirous to obtain as particular a Knowledge as I can of the state of my Diocese'. Samuel Willott, Vicar of Caverswall, was in ill-health when the inquiry arrived, before he could complete and return it he was summoned to his maker. His successor Joseph Saunders was formally installed in 1773 and found answering the questions posed by his Bishop an invaluable introduction to his new living.

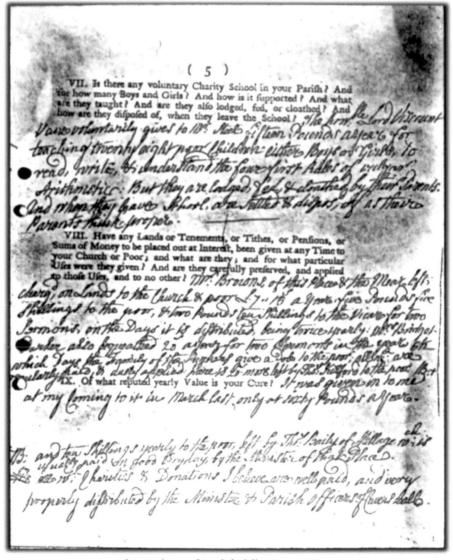

The Bishop of Lichfield's Survey 1772

The completed document serves as a useful 'snapshot' of the ecclesiastical parish as it was early in 1773. Eager to impress his Bishop, Joseph Saunders strove to complete his report honestly whilst slanting some of his answers in such a way that the Bishop could not help but notice his readiness to serve.

To the Minifter of the Parifh of Caverswall SIR,

BEING defirous to obtain as particular a Knowledge as I can of the State of my Diocefe, in order to qualify myfelf for being more ufeful, I fend you the following Queftions; under which, if you pleafe, after making due Inquiry concerning them, to write the proper Anfers, to fign them with your Name, and tranfmit or deliver them to me, as foon as you are able with Convenience, you will greatly affift and oblige.

Your Loving Brother

Ecclefhall, April 10, 1772 B. LICH. and COV.

(i) *What is the Extent of your Parifh? What Villages or Hamlets, and what Number of Houfes doth it comprehend? And what Families of Note are there in it?*
The extent of our Parish from North to South is four miles; the circumference, I judge to be upwards of sixteen: there are three Villages in it viz, Caverswall, Weston Coyney, and Hulme; the Number of Houses are about 130: And the only Families of Note are, Lord Vane of Caverswall Castle, and Thomas Parker Esq of Park Hall.

(ii) *Are there any Papifts in your Parifh, and how many, and of what Rank? Have any Perfons been lately perverted to Popery, and by whom, and by what Means; and how many, and who are they? Is there any Place in your Parifh, in which they affemble for Worfhip; and where is it? Doth any Popifh Prieft refide in your Parifh, or refort in it; and by what Name doth he go? Is there any Popifh School kep in your Parifh? Hath any Conformation or Vifitation been lately held in your Parifh by any Popifh Bifhop; and by whom, and when; and how often Is that done*
I have not heard, neither do I know of any of thefe Matters.

(iii) *Are there, in your Parifh, any Quakers, Prefbyterlans, Independents, Anabaptifts, Methodifts, or Moravians. And how many of each Sect, and of what Rank? Have they One or more Meeting-houfes in your Parifh, and are they duly licenfed? What are the Names of their Teachers, and are they qualified according to Law? Is their Number leffened or increafed of late Years, and by what Means?*
There are only two Quakers: Four Metgs: We have some few who go to hear the Methodists at Times, but they have no Meeting Houfe in our Parish; and I have obfervd, of late that some of thefe have been at Church, both at Morning and Evening Services. I know of no other Sect either Prefbyterians, Independents and: Befides.

(iv) *Do you conftantly refide upon your Cure, and in the Houfe belonging to it? If not, where and at what Diftance; and how long in each Year are you abfent; and what is the Reafon for fuch Abfence? And have you a licenfed Curate refiding in the Parifh, or at what Diftance from it; and who is he? And doth he ferve any other, and what Cure? And what Salary do you allow him? And is he in Deacons or Priefts' Orders?*
I do refide upon my Cure, and defign so to do. I have no Curate nor shall have, so long as it shall pleafe God to enable me to do my Duty. I live at prefent in Part of a

Houfe in Caverswall, near to the Church: But defign to go into the Vicarage House next Spring; tho it be such a poor one, that believe none of my Predeccfsors ever lived in it; It is inhabited by a Tenant at prefent.

(v) Is publick Service duly performed twice every Lord's Day in your Church, and one Sermon preached? If not, what is the Reafon? And on what Days befides are Prayers read there. Is there any Chapel in your Parifh; and at what Diftance frorn your Church; and how often are there Prayers and Sermons in it? How often, and at what Times do you cathechife in your Church? Do your Parifhioners duly fend their Children and Servants, who have not learned their Catechifm, to be inftructed by you? And do you either expound it to thern youfelf, or make ufe of fome printed Expofition; and what i it? Are there any Perfons, who frequent publick Worfhip, an are not baptized? And whence doth this proceed? How often is the Sacrament of the Lord's Supper adminiftered? And how many ufually receive it each Time?
Service is duly performed twice every Lord's Day and one Sermon preachd,and prayers read every Holy Day besides We have no Chapels. The ufual Time of Catechifing is in Lent but I find it will be more convenient after Eafter when the Days are longer: A greater Number may then be had - to whom I expound our Church Catechism in a plain and practical manner according to the beft of my Abilities. There are none, I know of, who frequent public Worfhip and are not bap-tised The Sacram': of the Lord's Supper if adminiftered one Day at Christmas, three Days at Eafter, on Whitsunday, and at Michelmas, and the ufual number of Com-municants each Time are from twenty to forty and upwards.

(vi) Is there any Free School, Hofpital, or Alms-houfe, in your Parifh? And for how many, and what sort of Perfons? And who was the Founder; and who are the Governours, and what are the Revenues of it? And are they carefully prefervcd, and employed as they ought? And are the Statutes and Ordinances made concerning it well obferved?
We have none in our parish.

(vii)Is there any voluntary Charity School in your Parifh? And for how many Boys and Girls? And how is it fupported? And what are they taught? And are they alfo lodged, fed, or cloathed? And how are they difpofed of, when they leave the School?
The hon^ble Lord Viscount Vane voluntary gives to Mr: Heel fifteen Pounds a year for teaching twenty eight poor children either Boys or Girls, to read, write, and under stand the four first Rules of vulgar Arithmetic: But they are lodged, fed, and cloathed by their Parents. And when they leave School, are settled and disposd, of as their Parents think proper.

(viii) Have any Lands or Tenements, or Tithes, or Penfions, or Sums of Money to be placed out at Intereft, been given at any Time to your Church or Poor; and what are they and for what particular Ufes were they given? And are they carefully preferved, and applied to thofe Ufes, and to no other?
Mr: Browne, of this place and the Mear left chargd, on Lands to the Church and poor £7 15s 0d a year, five Pounds five shillings to the poor, and two pounds ten shillings to the Vicar for two Sermons, on the Days it is diftributed, being twice yearly: Mrs: Bridget Parker also bequeathed 20s a year for two sermons in the year on which Days the Family of the Parkers give a Dole to the poor; allms are regularly paid, and duly applied: there is 20s more left by Thos Kilford to the poor and ten Shillings yearly to the poor, left by Thos Baily of Millage the 10s is usually paid on good

Fryday by the Minister of that Place. Allms Charities and Donations I believe are well paid, and very properly diftributed by the Minister and Parish Of ficers of Caverswall.

(ix) *Of what reputed yearly Value is your Cure?*
It was given in to me at my coming to it in March last, only at sixty Pounds a year.

(x) *By whom, and to what Ufes, is the Money given at the Offertory difpofed of?*
It is given to the poor in the Parish, particularly to those who communicate, by the Minister and Churchwardens.

(xi) *Is there any other Matter, relating to your Parifh, of which it may be proper to give me Information? And what is it?*
I know of nothing material at prefent: But as I think it my Duty at all Times to give my Diocefan the beft Information I am able, in Regard to the Church of England and its Laws and Conftitution, so I shall efteem it a peculiar Honour and Happinefs to have my good Lord Bishop of Lichfield and Coventry's Advice and Afsistance when any Thing extraordinary happens in the Parish of Caverswall: The Cure of which was given by your Lordships Inftitution and Committees, to your Lordship's most dutiful and faithful humble serv[t]:

Joseph Saunders, Vicar[39]

What Vicar Saunders was not required to record was the rate at which the landscape of the parish was changing. Hedgerows were creeping rapidly across the parish creating the hedge and field landscape familiar to modern eyes. So rapidly was this progressing that by 1811 only Caverswall Common and the higher untilled areas like Park Hall Hills and Wetley Moor remained unhedged. The disappearance of trees save where they had been incorporated in hedgelines or clustered as spindling, second growth in untilled localities, had forced man to use local stone for building and so, within easy stone hauling distance of Wetley Moor, the houses were built of the characteristic massive, dark blocks of mill-stone grit to form small square, solid dwellings standing hard against the soft verdure of the fields and hedges. Elsewhere the timber framed dwellings were beginning to show their age. As they decayed brickwork was used, initially to fill the spaces between the elements of the timber frame and later for the entire building.

Three metalled turnpikes had stamped their stony faces upon the parish; like ribbons of stone the roads ran from Lane End through Meir to Blythe Marsh, from Stone through Meir, Weston Coyney and Cellarhead to Leek and from Shelton through Bucknall and up over Ash Bank to Cellarhead. At certain crucial locations stood their custodians, the size-able but squat toll houses built of millstone grit and equipped with tiny toll windows peering in each direction along the line of the turnpike whose edges were fringed with hedgerows and trees. So commonplace had the passage of vehicles along these roads become that the rumble of wheels elicited no more interest than idle curiosity and no comment beyond a casual exchange of pleasantries. Only the occasional Mail Coach with its gleaming scarlet paintwork, brightly polished metal fitments and pounding horses whose approach was proclaimed by stentorian blasts upon the guard's *'yard of tin'* re-tained sufficient excitement and glamour to attract excited watchers and admiring com-ment.

Toll gates are known to have existed at Forsbrook, Meir, Meir Heath, Longton, Weston

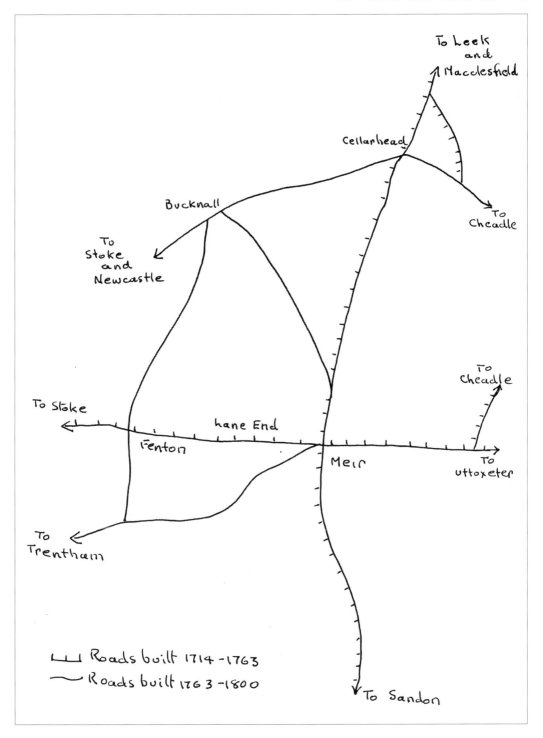

To Leek
and
Macclesfield

Cellarhead

To
Cheadle

Bucknall

To
Stoke
and
Newcastle

To
Cheadle

To Stoke

Lane End

Fenton

Meir

To
Uttoxeter

To
Trentham

⊔⊔ Roads built 1714 -1763
〜 Roads built 1763 -1800

To Sandon

A map to show Turnpike roads in the vicinity of Caverswall

Coyney, Withystakes, Bucknall, Blakely Lane and Heath House. Only one good example now remains within the parish, that at Withystakes. This building boasts a small porch on the west side with tiny observation windows in each of the other walls and carries a name plate proclaiming it to be 'Toll Bar Cottage'. The toll house at Weston Coyney stood roughly where the garden in front of the house beside the Weston Coyney Spar Shop now is. The Spar Shop was established on the site once occupied by the Coalville Filling Station which was built when the toll house was demolished in the early 1960s.

Among the commoner crops of the day were cabbages which were used generally as fodder crops. Fed to milking cattle they were reckoned to enhance the milk yield. When used to supplement the poor fodder available to grazing sheep they were cut and carted to the grazing ground where they were scattered about the field. Potatoes were beginning to assume an importance above subsistence level. The fields between and around Caverswall and Dilhorne were particularly noted for two things, the excellence of their yields of wheat and barley and their massive crops of potatoes *'which essentially contribute to the comfortable support of many thousand manufacturers in Mr. Wedgwood's beehive of commercial industry, the Potteries'*. So important had this urban market become that only the dampest grounds between Hulme and Werrington were left permanently in grass. Everywhere else in the parish, on the heavier grounds particularly around Caverswall and Hulme the farmers had adopted a six crop rotation of fallow, wheat, clover, oats, beans and barley. Occasionally turnips shared the bean field as form of fallow. This pattern of cultivation appeared as a checkerboard array of colours and forms upon the landscape. If the weather was not always kind and yields low the farmer lost little for the expanding urban market always had money for food and in hard times higher prices simply meant higher profits for the producer. Good times, gluts and low prices suddenly lost their attraction for the farmer.

For the poorer families of the parish life seems to have been built around a regime in which the head of the house entered paid employment as a labourer whilst his spouse raised potatoes.

'Give a cottager in the Moorlands (Werrington - Dilhorne - Caverswall) with a wife and 10 or 12 children a cow and a rood or two of potatoe ground and you make him a happy man. He goes to his daily labour, earns money to purchase clothing etc: for his large family; the younger children collect dung and soil from the public roads for the improvement of the potatoe ground and the industrious dame with her stouter children, keep the ground clear and attend to get in the potatoe harvest, the chief support of their long family in about nine months of the year.' [40]

Was reality ever as idyllic as that extract implies?

At Handley Hayes Colliery the coalmasters, Solomon Wardle and Philip Johnson, were paying Is.Od. a day for boring, Is.4d. a day for stone getting, banksmen were paid Is.4d. a day, bottomers received 10d a day whilst sinking was rewarded at rates varying between 2s.6d and 6s.0d a yard. Coal sold at 4s.0d a stack.

On the western slopes of Park Hall Hills lay Ford Hayes Farm, just one of the scatter of isolated holdings which helped to break the sweep of open country. There in 1772 was born, Hugh Bourne the carpenter and builder whose simple, fervent faith was to become the foundation stone upon which Primitive Methodism was to be built. A present reminder of his life and work is the Primitive Methodist Chapel just south of Cellarhead crossroads. This building was erected in faith and sited squarely beside the old bull baiting pit or ring as a direct challenge to Satan and his works. It was sold in January 2000.

The stone base and the ring to which the bull or bear was tethered was removed during road widening and is now in the museum at Shugborough.

At intervals the measured throb of the side drum and the lilting squeal of the fife were heard in the parish as red-coated recruiting sergeants and their musicians toured the country seeking recruits for the 64th Regiment of Foot. This county regiment had been formed in 1758 and had seen action during the capture of Guadeloupe in 1759. More than one local man woke with a blinding hangover to find himself clutching *'the King's shilling'* and faced with a life of military service. Others volunteered and among this number were the two worthies from 'Werynton' who served throughout the American War of Independence and returned home, defeated, some time after 1776 bringing with them the seeds of the cotton plant which flourishes to this day on Wetley Moor. Return they may have done but the cotton plant is no more than the Cotton Grass (Eriophorum Angustifolium) whose bobbing white curls are such an attractive feature of Wetley Moor.

Death continued to walk the parish. Death by violence was not unknown and tales about the ruthless and vicious dwellers around Ash, Werrington and the fringes of Wetley Moor were rife. Death by accident in the mines and quarries was accepted as a hazard of employment. Death by sickness had always been a feature of rural life when prayer and local remedies failed to cure. Death under the hoofs of a horse or upon the horns of a bull was always a risk to the farmworker as were the myriad prospects of injury through some other form of misadventure. Death at the hands of Time came to all. When, in 1772 Edward Coyney of Weston Coyney died his family arranged for the placement of a tablet which may be seen on the north side of the nave high up near the chancel arch. This tablet together with windows dating from the 14th and 15th centuries constitute the sum of the monuments to what seems to have been one of the leading and most turbulent of the local families.

Throughout the latter decades of the 18th century the Castle seems to have been occupied by lessees. The prodigality of *'the imbecile'* spendthrift caused Lord Vane to sell it to Lady Mary, Countess of Stamford for £4,000 in 1759. From her it passed to her son Booth Grey, who acquired full title to the Castle and its estates when Lord Vane's retained life interest lapsed with his death in 1789. Booth Grey seems to have spent little time in residence at the Castle and lived and died a bachelor. Ownership of the Castle by Booth Grey ceased during the period 1810/11 when the estate was sold through lawyers one of whom was Walter Hill Coyney.

A property inquisition carried out on 10th March 1783 records:

Staffordshire to wit - An Inquisition indented taken at the dwelling house of Samuel Martin victualler situate and being in the Parish of Caverswall in the County of Stafford on the tenth day of March in the twenty third year of the reign of our Sovereign Lord George the Third by the Grace . . . and in the year of our Lord one thousand seven hundred and eighty three before me Richard Gildast Esq: Sheriff for the County of Stafford . . . by virtue of the writ of our Sovereign Lord the King to me the said Sheriff directed and delivered and to this Inquisition annexed upon the oaths of John Bradbury Richard Steel James Ball William Walters William Gilbert William Adams Philip James Samuel Martin Sampson Martin William Spooner William James and William Walters good and lawful men of my County who being impanelled sworn and charged to inquire of several things in the said writ specified upon their oath say that William Vane late of London Esquire Lord Viscount Vane in the Kingdom of Ireland in the said writ named had in my said County on Monday the Feast of the Apostles Saint Simon and Saint Jude in the twenty third year of the reign of our said Lord the King on which day he was outlawed in London at the suit of Henry Reddington and William Reddington in a plea of tresspass on the case to the damage of the said Henry and William Reddington of Five Hundred Pounds as in the said writ is mentioned and on the day of the taking of this Inquisition hath in my said county of the several goods and chattels particularly mentioned and specified in a certain Schedule to the Inquisition annexed which said goods and chattels are now being in a certain Mansion House called . . . Caverswall Castle in the Parish of Caverswall . . . and in the outplaces and outbuildings thereto belonging. And which the said goods and chattels the Jurors on their oath do extend and appraise at the sum of One hundred and sixty-three pounds three shillings and sixpence according to the due value thereof. And the Jurors . . . say that the said William Vane in the said writ named on the said Monday the Feast of the Apostles . . . had and at the time of taking this Inquisition hath in my County the several lands and tenements herein after particularly mentioned that is to say A capital messuage or mansion house called Caverswall Castle with divers lands thereto belonging called the Park and the Wood with the appurtenances lying and being in the Parish of Caverswall containing the whole by estimation One hundred and ten acres now in the occupation of the said William Vane and of yearly value of Fifty pounds One other messuage and one hundred other acres of land with the appurtenances in the parish of Caverswall . . . in the occupation of Thomas Pratt of the yearly value of ninety pounds. One other messuage and one hundred and five other acres of land with the appurtenances in the parish of Caverswall in the occupation of Joseph Steel of the yearly value of one hundred pounds.

		Yearly Income
40 acres (Caverswall)	Samuel Scragg	£28
35 acres (Caverswall)	ThomasElkin	£25
15 acres (Caverswall)	William Nickson	£10
130 acres (p. Leek)	Samuel Sleigh	£100
50 acres (p. Leek)	Johnson	£30
30 acres (p. Leek)	Godwin	£24
7 acres (p. Leek)	Hugh Sleigh	£7
40 acres (p. Cheddleton)	Philip Turner	£25
20 acres (p. Cheddleton)	RichardGodwin	£15
10 acres (p. Cheddleton)	JohnHolling	20s

Of all which said estates the said William Vane is seized of an estate for his life but whether there are any and what mortgage charges incumbrances on the said premises or any of them the Jurors . . . know not. And which said several lands and tenements before mentioned the Jurors . . . do extend and appraise at the several values . . . amounting in the whole to the sum of Five hundred and five pounds according to the true values thereof which said goods and chattels lands and tenements before mentioned I the said Sheriff on the day of taking this Inquisition have taken into the hand of our said Lord the King by the extent and appraisement aforesaid. And the Jurors . . . further say that the said William Vane on the said Monday . . . or at any time of taking the Inquisition hath any other or more goods or chattels lands and tenements in my said County . . . which can be extended appraised or taken into the hands of our Lord the King . . .'[41]

Clearly six years before his death Lord Vane was in serious financial difficulties .

In 1804 Booth Grey leased the Castle and estates to Sir Thomas Lowten for one year. The attested copy of the indenture reads as follows:

'This indenture made the twenty second day of March in the forty fourth year of the reign of our Sovereign Lord George the Third by the Grace of God of the United Kingdom of Great Britain and Ireland King, Defender of the Faith and so forth and in the year of Our Lord one Thousand eight hundred and four between Booth Grey of Nether Knutsford in the county of Chester Esquire first and only son and Heir at Law of the Honorable in

... of the one part and Thomas Lowten of the Middle Temple London Esquire of the other witnesseth that for and in consideration of the sum of five shillings of lawful money of the United Kingdom of Great Britain and Ireland as used in England to the said Booth Grey party as hereto in hand paid by the said Thomas Lowten at or before the sealing and delivery hereof the receipt whereof is hereby acknowledged and for divers other good causes and considerations him hereunto a moving He the said Booth Grey party hereto hath bargained and sold and by there present Doth bargain and sell unto the said Thomas Lowten . . . All that the Manor or Lordship of Westwood . . . being in the Parish of Leek in the County of Stafford and also all that Castle or capital Mansion House called Caverswall Castle with the Courts, Gardens, Motes, Woods, Outbuildings and appurtenances situate standing and being in Caverswall in the said County of Stafford and now in occupation or possession of the said Booth Grey party hereto containing together by admeasurement thirty nine acres one rood and twenty nine perches ore thereabouts be the same more or less . . .' [42]

This rather strained wording may well explain why, in 1809 Thomas Lowten found himself involved in a legal wrangle over rights with a certain George Leycester Esquire who claimed:

'. . . the Castle of Caverswall with all belonging to it park manore, woods, watermills, one windmill, fourteen dovehouses, forty gardens, 600 acres of land, 300 acres of meadow, 500 acres of pasture, 200 acres of woods, 100 acres of furge and heath, 100 acres of rushes, 100 acres of moor, 100 acres of land covered with water.' [42]

The Court decided in favour of Thomas Lowten.

Toll bar cottage - the small window was used by the keeper of the toll gate to check upon the people seeking to pass before he ventured out.

1783 A.D.

WHAT'S THAT SO BLACK AGIN' THE SUN?

Some three months after the completion of the Property Inquisition of 1783 a frightening event occurred. On 20th June 1783 the sky gradually darkened from the north-east. Creeping across the sky from above and beyond the skyline at Wetley Moor and Windycote came an eerie grey-blue pall. Labourers easing their aching backs, looked up expecting to see storm clouds and saw instead what appeared to be a featureless shroud easing southwards without break or diffusion. As it passed before the sun the cloud seemed briefly to resemble a thick November mist slowly stealing the sun's glare and its summer warmth, leaving naught but a pale orb hanging idly behind the thickening cerement. As the pall passed over blotting out the hot blue of the June sky it seemed to thicken and darken until in the vicinity of the sun a strange, unearthly rust-coloured hue appeared which persisted and deepened as the cloud passed on.

The sun set that day in a bloody glare which threw malevolent rays and shadows across a darkened and strangely silent parish. Men prayed that night with a strange fervour, for when the moon rose it shone with a frail, blue light. Despite the apparent cooling of the sun when the cloud first passed its face the night seemed to be strangely airless and oppressive. The morning that followed was similarly torrid. Day followed sultry day. Each morning the blood red sun rose behind its shroud chasing before it the feeble blue moon. Each evening it sank into a sea of blood and dark shadows leaving man and beast gasping and afraid.

By day even the innermost rooms of the Castle seemed to glow with a weird copper hue which enhanced the soft browns of the stone in Castle, Church, Tithe Barn and Stone House until the buildings themselves seemed wrapped in a soft red halo. Flies finding the air to their liking seethed and twisted in clouds, driving horses frantic and causing cattle to gallop aimlessly tails awry. So intense was the warmth that milk curdled almost as it was drawn from the cow, hens lay sprawled in the dust, flapping and shuffling languidly trying to still the ticks which itched in their feathers. Meat seemed to putrefy almost overnight. Labourers gasping for breath noticed that added to the sweat streaked grime of toil was a new and darker dust. Gradually the dust began to coat grass, bushes, leaves, hay ricks, even the surface of standing water until cattle became reluctant to eat or drink.

Women whispered and muttered that Lady Vane's evil immorality had brought the curse of the Lord upon her village. Men looked up and wondered about their own misdeeds. For more than a month the parish cringed under the red sky and the strange blue moon until, as gradually as it had come, the pall moved away heedless as ever of the motion of the winds.

In the early summer of 1783 the Icelandic volcano called Laki exploded into one of the greatest eruptions of historic times throwing a mass of fine volcanic dust high into the atmosphere. It was that dust which produced a 'blue moon' over much of western Europe and so terrified the people of Caverswall.

Shortly thereafter the cloying warmth having proved too much for his 88 year old constitution Sir Thomas Parker fell ill and although he rallied with the invigorating crispness of a cold autumn his condition continued to give cause for alarm. Courageously he fought his way into the New Year but at last nature triumphed and he slid almost without protest into the deepest sleep of death.

1784 A.D.

DUST AND DUST OF ASHES CLOSE

The black clad hearse, its sable horses and the sombrely dressed, sad visaged attendants stood motionless in the dust of the Square. A fitful wind stirred the dust around the fetlocks of the horses and ruffled the plumes of their head gear.

The village lay stunned and silent for whilst Lord Vane was still its supreme authority and Booth Grey was notionally the tenant of the Castle Sir Thomas had long been regarded as the only true country gentleman in the parish. He loved his land and its people; he respected his neighbours, employees and tenants, he had long cared for and lived in the parish, had shouldered its burdens and advised its people and now was going to his long home.

Within the church sorrow lay darkly upon the congregation. Dressed in the garb of woe family mourners occupied the family pews, behind them sat, stood or knelt almost the whole parish. Each man, woman or child bearing some emblem of grief upon arm or hat.

The candles flickered in the breeze which forced its way in stirring the foetid air into life. Before the altar steps lay the gleaming coffin, coldly inert to those who had known the zestful life of Sir Thomas who, well into his 88th year had remained alert and active.

As he rose in the pulpit Joseph Saunders cast his eyes over the congregation and reflected that seldom could a parish priest have faced such a diverse gathering at such a solemn moment. He glanced down at his notes based on a sermon delivered some years earlier by the Reverend Doctor Isaac Watts and began to speak, his words falling into the silent church like stones dropping into a well.

'On this solemn and mournful occasion we pay sad and pious respect to the memory of Sir Thomas Parker a worthy and gallant gentleman and an excellent Christian who lately departed this life in a good old age.

Let us not fix our eyes upon death, dust and the grave but upon those upper and brighter regions into which the path of the soul of our departed friend may be traced. That leads us to consider and remember the communion we have with those blessed spirits in heaven of which the apostle says we in the gospel state are come 'to Mount Zion, to the heavenly Jerusalem, to the innumerable company of angels and to the spirits of just men made perfect'.

The spirit of Sir Thomas Parker our patron and benefactor is rendered just because his sins were forgiven through the death and righteousness of Jesus Christ for it is written that 'by the obedience of one shall many be made righteous'.

Righteousness comes to the nature of the soul through the spirit of grace for holy writ tells is of 'the new man, which is created after the image of God, in righteousness and true happiness' The life of Sir Thomas Parker was righteous and conformable to the will of God as revealed in His word and so we may be certain that the spirit which departed from the mortal clay which was its earthly home has found its way to heaven and the perfection thereof.

In its most sublime and absolute sense perfection belongs only to God for He is the sum and centre of all perfection for ever. The perfect soul on earth is advanced far above its fellows in knowledge, Christianity and all charitable deeds. So it was with the deceased for he stood above all men in charitable Christian love and wordly wisdom whilst he lived and now by his death has achieved a far more exalted degree of those same virtues. The perfectly exalted soul increases in knowledge without falling into error, stands high in holiness without falling into sin and enjoys constant peace and joy without sorrow and unease. So it was with Sir Thomas. Let us rejoice that in its exultant perfection his soul stands before God our Lord and Saviour in all His exalted glories and rejoices with joy and unspeakable superior glory sharing a perfection of knowledge, holiness and Joy.

Let us rejoice that he no longer knows the ignorance which besets and pains our earthly souls.

Let us rejoice that his noble spirit has cast off its cottage of clay and has fled the painful, dust darkened ignorance of our lives to enter the halcyon lands of eternal light.

Let us rejoice that he no longer has to praise his Saviour with the feeble fluttering paeans of praise and the poor hallelujahs played upon discordant strings that serve to proclaim our praise.

Let us rejoice that his soul has travelled the dark passage over which hangs the shadow of earthly death to enter that world of sublime joy and perfect praise with sacred delight and rapture.

Let us rejoice that we are met to honour the memory of an uncommon Christian. There are some among us who believe the soul of man to be his blood, his breath or some sort of vital flarne or refined air or vapour or a composition or motion of fluids and solids in the animal body. They believe that this principle dies when the animal flesh dies and returns to life when the body is raised from the grave. I would say unto them 'How can that be so for the new principle cannot be the old principle after such an experience and re-creation'. Indeed why should the new principle be punished for the sins of the old which ceased to exist at death?

There are those who hold that the soul but sleeps when the body dies. Yet to do this requires the soul to be material, to have something of solidity and density since mere emptiness or space cannot sleep and serve as a repository of the material soul.

No, the soul of man is a conscious and active principle, subsisting by itself and made in the image of God. It remains the same and unchanged being whether it be contained m the animal body or set free by death which is itself but the pathway to that divine perfection which is the just soul's reward.

Sir Thomas Parker was a man of justice, virtue, courage, love and generosity, His soul and its goodness showed clearly in his life and through every act that it was worthy of the Lord who gave it and to whom it has unhesitatingly and most surely returned to become elevated to the sublime, divine perfection of God's grace which we who mourn on earth shall never enjoy whilst we remain separated by that thing called life from the God who made us.

Let us therefore kneel and give thanks for the life of Sir Thomas. Let us rejoice that he is free of earthly shackles and even now stands before the throne of Grace.

Above all let us rejoice in his life and works, revere his memory and copy his glorious example for it was surely to lead us forward to a greater good that his life was lived.

Amen!'

As the mourners left the church the villagers, old and young, male and female alike pushed, jostled and scurried to gain a clear view of the hero of the day for, although all felt deep and genuine grief at the death of Sir Thomas, none could resist the proud curiosity engendered by the presence of Martha Parker and her husband of only a year, Commander John Jervis, who, as captain of the 'Foudroyant' had earned respect as a fine seaman and rigid disciplinarian and had won renown by capturing a French warship off

Brest in the year of his marriage. Now Member of Parliament for Launceston he had travelled to his family home at Meaford and thence to his wife's home at Park Hall to attend the funeral. The gaping villagers were not to know that in 10 years time that same sailor would be removing the French from Martinique and Guadeloupe and that in 1797, at Cape St. Vincent, aided by Captain Nelson, he would deal a crushing blow to the combined French and Spanish fleets. It was sufficient that, in their midst, was a man whose name was known throughout England.

THE JERVIS FAMILY

The connection between the family of Sir John Jervis, Earl St. Vincent and Caverswall is slender. Its principal manifestation is the white marble figure of a kneeling young woman in the round, situated in the chancel. It is a memorial to Martha, the Countess St. Vincent and was sculpted by Sir Francis Legatt Chantrey.

Martha was the daughter of Sir Thomas Parker of Park Hall who became a judge and later Lord Chief Baron of the Exchequer and a Privy Counsellor. The memorial was erected in 1818 to her memory by her husband Sir John Jervis. Martha married Sir John Jervis of Meaford in 1783 the year after he was knighted by King George III following his capture of the 'Pegase' a French 74 in a naval war which had not been markedly successful up to that point. John Jervis had entered the navy in January, 1749 and was promoted lieutenant in 1755. He was present at the capture of Quebec and became captain of the 'Scorpion' in 1759. In 1760 he was promoted to the rank of post captain, (post signified captain of a sixth rate or larger vessel) and commanded the Alarm (32 guns) in the Mediterranean.

On 14th. February, 1797, he commanded the British Fleet which defeated a Spanish fleet in the Battle of Cape St. Vincent. It was Jervis who laid the foundations of Nelson's band of brothers by the way in which he treated his captains. Among those serving under him on that occasion were Nelson (in the Captain), Foley (Britannia), Saumarez (Orion), Collingwood (Excellent),and Trowbridge (Culloden) : Jervis was in the Victory whose captain was Calder.

Sir John Jervis died in 1832 and was buried in the grounds of St. Michael's Church, Stone.

*Chantrey's memorial
to Martha,
Countess St. Vincent*

Fate had not finished with the Parkers. In 1791, after a prolonged dry spell, the ageing timbers of the old hall caught fire. Valiantly as the servants strove they could not check the swirling rush of the flames which had gained a firm hold in the faulty stonework of the kitchen chimney. The massive timbers of the framework seemed to be alight from within as bucket after bucket was borne, brimming with slimy water, from the moat and hurled into the raging furnace which the old house had become. As the flames penetrated the brickwork and wattle filling of the walls clouds of black smoke rose and swirled into the darkening sky. The fierce glare called help from Caverswall, the smoke attracted assistance from Hulme and Adderley but to no avail. When at last the roof fell in with a hollow roar and a towering pillar of sparks a halt was called and smoke grimed, heat seared men and women sank exhausted to the ground watching the fire wear itself out in a fury of destruction.

The family moved into temporary quarters at Rough Cote Hall and debated the next course of action. The decision was easily made, a new house would be built, away from the site of the former, looking east and south across the open country below Park Hall Hills. It was to be of the latest design and style, of brick-built construction and to have a magnificent lake and island set before its main entrance. The water for the lake would come from that potent spring which had so impressed the learned Doctor Plot some 100 years earlier.

Park Hall as it was rebuilt after the fire of 1791

So the parish acquired its first major building since the reconstruction of the Castle by Mathew Cradock. The use of brick was an innovation which attracted much admiration when its reddish hues were offset by white Doric pillars and lintels. So impressive was the brick house that within 10 years two other important brick-built buildings, Bank House Farm and Dove House Farm, had been erected. Bank House took its name from the steepness of its site, Dove House, enshrined in its designation the former use of its location for it was on that same spot that the massive dove-cotes, which had fed the people of the castle since the earliest days, had stood.

Bank House Farm

1811 AD

IN LITTLE PARCELS LITTLE MINDS TO PLEASE

To Reverend William Eddowes the Year of Our Lord 1811 seemed to be a singularly inauspicious one for the parish of Caverswall. True the census return for that year would show that the population of his parish had risen since the first ever national census of 1801 from 756 persons to 900: every parish priest welcomed the prospect of an expanding flock. True that the vaguely asinine and indisputably coarse antics of his predecessor Reverend St. George Bowles who had raised and served as Commandant of, the Caverswall Moorland Volunteers had come to an end with his untimely death, charitably attributed to the frantic plunging of a frightened horse. True that, with the great victory at Trafalgar, the prospect of invasion by Napoleon had disappeared and that in consequence the pseudo-warlike fellowship of the volunteers had become diluted into the more Christian ethic of the Caverswall Mens' Friendly Society. True that the prosperity which initially and invariably accompanies wars had brought a significant increase in parochial wealth and had tempted the farmers to push cultivation to its limits so bringing to the parish an air of intensive industry that it had never known.

Yet, as he rode slowly from the new house at Park Hall down the rutted trail to Caverswall, he felt in his bones that all was not well with his parish.

Many of the younger men had been lured away to or pressed into the war with Napoleon. As the war effort had bled dry the pockets of the nation, prices had risen bringing prosperity to those with food to sell. Wheat prices stood at 151 shillings a quarter bringing profit only to the farmer and the corn factor whilst poverty threatened the villager. Three bad harvests in a row, the result of cold, damp summers had served to empty barns and deplete stockyards. The ever ravenous, expanding pottery towns were eagerly devouring whatever supplies of foodstuff the parish could produce again bringing prosperity to the farmer but a crippling dearth to his labourer. No longer could the yeoman purchase directly from the farmer the milk, eggs, butter, cheese and meat necessary for his table or even the swill and waste so necessary to his pig. Now the farmer sold direct to the town based wholesaler leaving the villagers no choice but to purchase rather less from the profit seeking retailer.

Even the once great Caverswall estate, now somewhat dilapidated after a period of indifferent management at the hands of the absentee Booth Grey, had been placed on the market at a ludicrous price. Rumour and speculation about intending, future owners was rife, with whispered reports that a group of Benedictine Nuns was the leading contender. That at least, reflected William Eddowes, was correct, for that very day at Park Hall he had spoken with Mr. Walter Hill Coyney a Catholic lawyer who was acting on behalf of the nuns who had put up the requisite £4,000 to purchase the castle. Thomas Parker of Park Hall was employing the same lawyer to purchase, on his behalf, Dove House Farm as an extension of the Park Hall Estate.

News of the sale of the castle had arrived almost simultaneously with the news that the Enclosure Act for the last unenclosed areas of the parish had received parliamentary assent so marking the end of the last great expanse of common waste in the parish. The not so hated hedgerows marking the end of the labourer's common grazing rights had already divided most of the parish into *'little parcels little minds to please'.*

It seemed to William Eddowes that the world was changing so rapidly that a man knew not which way to turn in search of order and stability. Not least was he troubled at the prospect of having within his parish a powerful Catholic community. Compassion for those who had suffered the terrors of the Revolution in France or who had been forced to flee from their home in Ghent before the anti-clerical spirit of the revolutionary regime was one thing and a wholly worthy, Christian thing at that, but to have ensconced in an Anglican parish a community of Catholic nuns was another and very different thing.

To the 15 Benedictine Nuns and their confessor who arrived in Caverswall in the spring of 1811 the year seemed full of naught but hope and certainty. In 1794 they had fled from the turmoil and tumult of the Revolutionary Wars, leaving their mother house in Ghent to find a sanctuary in England. The tiny nucleus had increased in number and expanded its educational activities to such an extent that its first home in Preston had become inadequate. To the Sisters the purchase of Caverswall Castle seemed to promise hope, safety and security for their devoted labours. For a purchase price of £4,000 and a further sum of £500 necessary to make good defective glazing, woodwork and fittings the Sisters had acquired a new, attractive and secluded home. The necessary repairs were undertaken by *'the reliable Mr. Jefferies'*, a *'master joiner of Stone'*.

THE HOWITT FAMILY

Mary Howitt was born, Mary Botham, at Coleford in the Forest of Dean in Gloucestershire in 1799. She married William Howitt in 1821 and bore him twelve children.

Her father was a lawyer and strict Quaker who practised in Uttoxeter and during the years 1810 and 1811 acted for the lessee, a Mr. Tidesmore, during the purchase of the castle by a community of Benedictine nuns. The story at this point becomes a little confused. Mary Howitt is confident that the nuns were to purchase the castle for themselves . Robert Plant in his History of Cheadle states that the castle was bought by Walter Hill Coyney and leased to the nuns. Other evidence suggests that Walter Hill Coyney acted for the nuns. It is possible to fashion an account which embraces all three options. The question of how Tidesmore who held a short lease rather than title to the property came to be the vendor is one which also arises.

Mary visited the castle and played with the children of the Tidesmore family whilst her father discussed the sale of the property with Mr. Tidesmore. In her autobiography, 'My Own Story' she tells how she travelled from Uttoxeter in a gig torn with doubts about the impending arrival of papists about whom she knew nothing but "Bloody Mary, the faggot and the rack." She convinced herself that since the nuns were Catholics fleeing from Napoleon and not papists there could be no harm in them.

She reported that, on their arrival they were greeted by about twenty dogs and a rosy-faced, good-tempered farmer who proved to be the father of six boys and four girls. Two of the boys were attending the daily school whilst the others were in a school at a distance. She writes of the vastness and singularity of the building, the lovely garden, the paved court, the drawbridge and the moat. A moment of darkness creeps in when she recounts how the infant George Tidesmore was drowned in the moat. His epitaph is recorded,

Weep not for me my parents dear
I am not dead but sleeping here
A living flower that shall expand
Its beauty in the heavenly land

She also mentions a poor idiot who lived in a cottage by the gate into the churchyard. She described him as a doleful object who sat on a chair in the sun chewing straws. Finally she tells how they climbed out onto the lead covered roof of the castle and carved the outline of their feet into the lead before picking and eating cherries from the trees in the garden.

She became a well regarded writer of childrens' stories and poems including 'Buttercups and Daisies', 'September', 'A Spring Song', and 'The Seagull' in *The Book of a Thousand Poems*. Her best known poem is probably 'The Spider and the Fly'. 'Will you walk into my parlour ? said the spider to the fly. . . . . .'

The castle circa 1820
(By courtesy of Miss L.C. Walters)

By 1812 attendance at the Masses celebrated in the small chapel in the Castle had risen to such a level that it was apparent that a new Chapel was needed. Between the house and the eastern turrent flanking the northern side of the gate lay an area of level ground. Beyond the moat stood a line of slowly decaying stables, it was an easy task to demolish the stables and to re-use the stone to provide a Chapel sufficient for the needs of all who wished to attend the services. The work of the school prospered. As the only boarding school, possibly in the whole of the Midlands area, for the daughters of wealthy, upper class Catholic families its fame spread rapidly. For a fee of 30 guineas per annum the young ladies received board, lodging, instruction in the Catholic faith and an education embracing *'English, French, Writing, Arithmetic, History, Geography, the use of the globes and plain and ornamental works'*. Music and dancing were taught by *'the most approved masters'* whilst drawing was taught by *'the ladies of the house duly qualified'*.

Pupils arrived, possessing as basic requirements, two pairs of sheets, six hand towels, four table napkins, a knife, a fork and a silver spoon. For general wear the young ladies were required to provide a dress *'of striped cotton printed for the purpose'* or one of white muslin which was to serve as a *'better dress'*. The villagers strained curious eyes through the trees eager for a glimpse of the sombrely clad Sisters and their young charges.

By 1817 the roll of the school had risen to some 30 pupils and Pitt was able to record:
'Their discipline is sufficiently strict; the pupils wear a uniform of buff-coloured cotton; they are not suffered to ramble beyond the bounds of the gravel walk which surrounds the moat and two or three small fields; they walk two and two like other boarding school girls and in their half hour's exercise along the walks in the garden are required as a religious duty, to utter their Ave Marias and Paternosters in a low voice.' [40]

Of the Sisters he wrote:
'The nuns themselves may be termed the Black Ladies. Their dress is entirely sable, with a long, thick veil thrown over the right shoulder. Their demeanour is grave and they generally walk with a book in their hands; their countenances are pleasing and pensive; and if a man approach them, they turn away as if they feared the imputation of vanity.'

For all their sober and secluded pursuit of virtue the nuns were never able to feel wholly free. Bitter and black memories of the Dissolution and of the rabid anti-Catholicism of the 17th century still lingered. Local people suspected the apparently flourishing prosperity of the secretive Sisters. Rumours about improper and unnatural activities began to circulate, fostered to a large extent by villagers who resented the energy with which the nuns sought to persuade them to change faith. Hostility towards the nuns intensified. Eventually the combination of local hostility and economic pressures forced the nuns to move. They moved in 1853, to a large country house at Oulton near Stone. Their final act before departure was to demolish their precious Chapel to prevent its use for secular purposes. As their lingering contribution to the landscape they left behind the small cemetery which contained the remains of those nuns who had perished whilst at Caverswall

That cemetery may be seen below the boundary wall at the west end of the churchyard. The rectangular fields resulting from the final stages of the enclosures may be seen near Gable Cottages and Heath View.

1825 A.D.

BENEATH THE JOYOUS SMILES OF HEAVEN

The fictitious prosperity of the war years had vanished almost overnight with the victory at Waterloo. The first intimation of the changes to come had been noticed when those who had marched, or stumbled in a bleeding or drink befuddled press, away to the wars returned and began to search for work. Wages tumbled and farmers found themselves as buyers in a market packed with eager hands seeking employment. Then prices began to slide, farmers who in 1812 had been selling wheat at 152/- per quarter found themselves able to command nothing better than a humble 55/- per quarter not withstanding the demands of the voracious pottery towns. Thinking hard about the costs of production, particularly his labour costs and the diminishing levels of profit to be won each farmer made his own decisions about the use of his lands. First to go out of laborious cultivation were the damp, heavy soiled, low yielding fields around the fringes of Wetley Moor where yields had seldom been anything better than modest. Those lands were followed into permanent damp pasture by the lands of the valley floor between Hulme, Boltongate, Foxearth and Cellarhead. The tide of agricultural activity which had flowed to the limits of profitable cultivation during the war years was ebbing fast by 1825.

Yet that ebb tide left in its wake some undeniable benefits. The parish could show clear signs of prosperity. Fields had been hedged and drained, arable land had been won from heath, fern, marsh grass and stony waste. New, improved roads ran through the parish; a scatter of new brick-built buildings including the proud farms at Bank House and Dove House as well as the more modest but improved stone block dwellings at Washerwall

Fields enclosed by Act of Parliament in the early 19th. century tended to be narrow and rectangular in shape, this one on the left of Blythe Bridge Road contrasts with the older fields opposite

spoke of better living conditions for more people. New commercial and economic ties had been established between the parish and the pottery industry at Lane End, Hanley and Stoke. These links assumed tangible, albeit transient existence in the small, weekly market days and more spectacularly in the two great fairs held at Cellarhead on 5th May and 5th November each year when town and country met to transact their mutual and separate businesses against a background of relaxation, entertainment and abandon.

The site at Cellarhead was chosen for several reasons. The area between the present crossroads and Withystakes was open, flattish land grazed clear by successive generations of sheep and cattle, and, as part of the moorland waste not in the clear ownership of any individual It lay at the junction of two main routes and so could be easily reached by turnpike from Meir, Stoke, Leek and Cheadle. It was set sufficiently near the towns to attract a range of would-be purchasers and small scale artisans with artifacts to sell and yet sufficiently deep in the country to attract farmers with produce to sell and labourers seeking new or renewed employment. Such labourers would arrive at the fair with a straw token set in hat band or bonnet ribbon to indicate their quest for work. Would-be employer and employee would gauge each other carefully, if chance offered seek *'characters'* on each other from those present then, if the omens still seemed propitious, would bargain over wage rates and conditions of service. When agreement had been reached hands were spat upon, clasped and the deal made, the straw token was discarded and a hiring fee paid by the employer. The employee was then free to spend that sum and any savings he might have, should he, or she, so desire, as a fairing before he or she reported for work at the appointed hour. To help separate such employees from their bounty a variety of entertainments and corruptions were provided

Tents selling foodstuffs and strong waters blossomed around the site. Scattered around and beyond them were the carts, waggons and occasional coaches of the more affluent employers or vendors, the handcarts and barrows of the tinkers, sellers of gee-gaws and trinkets and those small men whose stock in trade was the dainty skill rather than the item of bulky produce. Beyond them again clustered or wandered the livestock offered for sale by farmers and gypsies each of whom viewed the other with deep suspicion. More than most it was the gypsy who brought colour and excitement to the fairs. Members of that *'quiet, pilfering, unprotected race'* would arrive as if by magic their gaudy vardoes clustering a little apart from the throng, their curs yapping, snarling and fighting over scraps of food until they disturbed the Romany's stock in trade, his horses, and they in turn became restless, stamping and whinnying, tossing their heads in fear. The strangely demure yet fierce eyed, dark-skinned women told fortunes, sold herbal cures, purveyed spells, charms, philtres, potions and love tokens with a furtive intensity that contrasted sharply with the noisy oratory of their husbands. Eagerly and vociferously the male gypsies proclaimed the virtues of their horses, denying and disguising defects extolling their qualities, health and stamina and offering all sorts of assurances that the beasts were sound in wind and limb. The itinerant fiddler could seldom outplay the babble of voices, the lilting cries of the vendors or the swelling tumult of savage voices around the bull ring. As the day wore on and an increasing number of business arrangements were completed the urgent restraint of trade gave way to the abandonment of ale encouraged jollity. Drunken brawls flourished briefly in a tumult of alcoholic uncertainty and died as suddenly as they had started. In the bull-ring the hard earth floor lost its covering of grass in a welter of tearing feet, broken carcasses and scarlet foam. Dogs were tossed. gored and destroyed by a rangy, raw boned, long-horned bull whose fang torn hide, dog savaged muzzle and rolling eye proclaimed him an experienced protagonist of that degrading sport. The blood lust seemed to infect even the human observers as they pushed and seethed around the blood stained ferocity in the ring. Money changed hands in wagers of all kinds.

All that remains of the bull baiting ring at Cellarhead

Foot races both pre-arranged and impromptu attracted much interest as did the other forms of physical contest many of which were closely related to the basic skills of the farm and the countryside.

Prize fights conducted under the traditional code of the bare knuckle ring drew large crowds who seemed impervious to the boring, protracted savagery of the inconclusive early rounds of most fights.

As evening came the proceedings sank into a satiated stupor, returning merrymakers, traders, vendors, farmers, labourers, children, beasts and waggons thronged the roads, choked the lanes and trailed across the moor until all that remained were the ale tents, the vardoes and the flickering camp fires of the gypsies.

The bull-ring lay between the present sites of the Hope and Anchor and the Primitive Methodist Chapel and was finally destroyed, earlier road works having taken its western side, when the car park was extended. The niggardly habits of the chief seller of ales, a female miser of formidable quality earned her the nickname of 'sell'er yed', so gradually to go to 'sell her yed' for ale came to mean going to the fair and ultimately gave its name to the location. The ale tents were replaced by stone block and later brick-built ale houses which acted as way stations for travellers along the turnpikes seeking rest for themselves and their horses after the long slow haul up to the crossroads from all directions.

Until as late as 1905 the crossroads at Cellarhead could boast four substantial inns. The existing pair the Hope and Anchor and the Bowling Green (originally The Spotted Cow) were matched by the Red Lion, opposite the Bowling Green and the Royal Oak. These hostelries did not depend solely upon the two great spring and autumn horse and cattle fairs or upon the casual travellers for every Monday a lesser market or fair was held at Cellarhead when the more immediate needs of the local people for the smaller necessities of life and work could be met.

In and around Caverswall life must have pursued a steady, even and quiet course. The Benedictine nuns in their sable habits produced a quietening effect on the village. The steady expansion of the pottery towns enticed the more ambitious young people away and yet the population continued to grow. In 1821 the population had risen to 1,082 souls and by 1825 the population had just exceeded 1,100. The village plan was set firmly upon the landscape. The old mill pond had disappeared, its site having silted up and been fenced into arable fields although the poorly drained nature of the site made tillage difficult.

A cluster of dwellings had appeared around the road junction at Little Weston where an enterprising tavern keeper had realised that money might be made from those waiting whilst the watermill below Cookshill did its work of grinding bones to powder for the pottery manufacturers of Lane End.

The absence of educational opportunities within the expanding parish was a cause of some concern. A number of semi-literate ladies were ready to offer a modicum of rudimentary instruction in return for modest cash payments from their pupils but their efforts could in no way replace the opportunities available in a school.

On the 13th July, 1825, Thomas Howe Parker of Park Hall, The Right Honourable Edward Jervis, Viscount St. Vincent, Walter Hill Coyney of Weston Coyney, William Wingfield Yates of Weston Coyney, James Aspinall of Bank, Thomas Mackenzie Doctor of Physics of Newcastle-under-Lyme, William Baker of Fenton, Thomas Hawley of Lane End, Edward Lockhard Hubbard of Moor Villa, Caverswall, and the Reverend Ralph Sneyd Vicar of Caverswall came together and for the sum of £10 of *'lawful money'* purchased a site measuring one rood 14 perches in a close belonging to Thomas Howe Parker but occupied by one William Bradbury upon which a *'School House hath lately been erected by public subscription'.* The school house was to be used *'as a National School for the instruction of the children of poor persons resident within the said Parish of Caverswall'...'provided that it always be a standing and irrevocable rule that all the children who attend the said Caverswall National School be required to attend divine worship regularly in the established church'.*

The site in question was that occupied by the present St. Peter's Church of England (Aided) School. In 1825 it lay, as it still does, at the angle of roads converging onto The Dams but was surrounded on all sides by open fields. The early days of St. Peter's School were typical of the education being offered in church schools throughout the land. The teacher, not always a schoolmaster in these early days, was barely more literate than the pupils. Sand trays were commonly used to enable those who were learning to write to practice their letter shapes without waste. Arithmetic was taught in a similar manner. As standards of proficiency rose the pupils graduated to slates and reading cards the latter being cards printed in bold type in such a way that expenditure upon books for individual reading could be avoided.

Throughout the early history of the school standards were abysmally low, instruction was given in a mechanical style which matched well the evolving age of the machine.

An aerial view of the school as it was in 1976. The original buildings are on the right with the Master's House clearly visible as an integral part of the building. To the left of the playground is the Horsa unit which had to be demolished when it became unsafe.

Dreary indoctrination in the catechism and the bible combined with unceasing emphasis upon one's God given place in society served as an almost indigestible repast for the poor children of the parish.

Much emphasis was laid upon memory work and each day the piping, rhythmic chant of children at study floated across the fields.

'Two pints will make one quart,
Four quarts one gallon strong
Some drink too little, some too much
To drink too much is wrong.
Eight gallons one firkin make,
Of liquor thats called ale:
Nine gallons one firkin of beer
Whether 'tis mild or stale.
With gallons fifty-four
A hogshead I can fill
But I hope never shall drink much
Drink much whoever will.'

A child was taught his letters by their shapes. First came the straight line shapes, H. T. E, these were followed by the shapes based upon angles, A, V, N. and finally the shapes based on circles or curves were taught.

Such laborious calligraphy and pedestrian indoctrination did little to carry even the most able pupils to a point at which Mr. Walkingame's 'Tutor's Assistant' (1825) would be comprehensible.

MULTIPLICATION

'Begin with that Figure which stands in the Unit's Place of the Multiplier and with it multiply the first Figure in the Unit's place of the multiplicand. Set down the Units and carry the Tens in Mind, till you have multiplied the next figure in the Multiplicand by the same figure in the Multiplier; to the product of which add the Tens you kept in Mind, setting down the Units; and proceed as before, till the whole line is multiplied. When the Multiplier is more than 12 and less than 20, multiply by the Unit Figure in the Multiplier adding to the Product the back Figure to that you multiplied.'

Within and around the village the farms presented certain characteristic features. Although there was a considerable variation in size many were inconvenient and tended, due to the processes of enclosure, consolidation and expansion, to be elongated with the buildings clustered at one end of the holding. In Caverswall village the farm buildings of Dove House Farm lay adjacent to the church but the farm lands sprawled away south and west. At the other end of the village Bank House Farm's holdings stretched away eastwards.

Similarly the farms whose yards fronted on High Street and Blythe Bridge Road had lands which extended eastwards in elongated units rising up the slope to the east of the village and spreading out onto the slightly more level ground at the summit of the rise.

Dove House Farm reflects many of the characteristics of the village farms of the period 1820 to 1840. The house stands looking proudly out across the farm lands. Behind it, arranged in a crude square designed to offer shelter from the raw northerly and easterly winds stand the farm buildings which comprise brick-built barns for storing and threshing corn, stables and a yard for the horses. Missing from the present buildings are the open wooden sheds in which the carts and waggons were sheltered and the abysmal, ramshackle, clutter of cattle sheds wherein, during the winter months, beasts subsisted on near starvation diets. Sanitation in such units was non-existent and a liquified mass of manure and urine, richly diluted by rain water was allowed to swill across the yard and into a convenient pond or ditch. In a hot summer, until the foetid mass had dried into a repulsive yellow green crust, the stench was hideous. In winter when bitter cold reduced the liquid mass to tinted ice and the crisp air searched the depths of the lungs the odour was almost unnoticed but between the extremes of sun-baked summer and winter cold the whole farm, the whole village was bathed in a gentle, fruity redolence.

Dove House Farm. Built on the site of the massive dove cote which once served the castle the farm house stands as proud and confident today as it did when it was first built.

In general the roads were few and bad, away from the metalled surfaces of the turnpikes the surfaces of the lanes ranged from hard, rutted tracks to miry sloughs changing with the seasons. Where hedges fringed such lanes they tended to be overblown, straggling, spindly things of value only as an indication of extent or ownership offering little or no value as a shelter-belt.

Although efforts had been made to improve drainage generally very little real success had attended drainage schemes once the excess of surface water had been removed. Cylindrical, clay, land drain pipes did not begin to appear until the late 1840s. Fields were tilled with heavy wooden ploughs laboriously pulled by five horses or six oxen and attended by teams of men and boys. Since the technique of ploughing was still essentially that of their medieval predecessors the same tendency to produce ridge and furrow topography in the fields persisted. This explains the gentle undulations apparent in many of the fields within the parish.

Harvesting was still a matter of hard, grafting, endless labour. Corn fell before the rhythmic sweep of the gleaming scythe blade. Behind the scyther followed a gatherer, a binder, a stooker and a raker. Such a team led by a good scytheman could clear two acres a day. Threshing was done with a flail on the floor of the threshing barn, the chaff was blown away by means of a draught created by a hand turned wheel, the grain was shovelled in small quantities into a hopper from whence it ran down a screen or riddle separating the seeds from the larger grain. The wheat was then piled and 'thrown' to separate the heavier grain from the 'tail'. To remove any residual chaff a large 'fanning' basket was employed. Finally the corn was measured and bagged in four-bushel sacks ready for market. Within the dust and sweat of the threshing barn a dust laden gloom prevailed; through a suitable door or shutter the progression of the sun's rays over notches cut in the woodwork measured the passage of time towards lunch and dinner break until darkness put an end to the labours of the day.

CAVERSWALL IN 1840

1840 A.D.

PARTNERS IN THE TOIL

The general form of the area around mid 19th century Caverswall is depicted clearly on a map dated 1840. Apart from trees incorporated in hedgerows the forest cover had been reduced to four main locations and four small copses, everywhere else had been enclosed, hedged and parcelled into fields of various sizes. The major concentration of housing was within the village proper, a second cluster of buildings had developed around the Auctioneer's Arms at Little Weston and a scatter of dwellings had sprung up along the line of the Uttoxeter turnpike. In the main the dwellings along the Uttoxeter Road were farms whose characteristically rectangular holdings stretched away from the road in field patterns whose shapes proclaim their genesis. Away from the villages and ignoring the earthen surfaces of the byroads and lanes the landscape was almost exactly as it is today. Trees have come and gone, hedgerows have thickened and changed their character and composition, the generally higher standard of contemporary husbandry has imparted a neater appearance to the countryside but, such minor reservations apart, the landscape in 1840 was, as it is today. Life was cast fairly and firmly in the general round common to rural England in the fourth decade of the 19th. century.

The huge feather-like snowflakes of a raw, dark, grey January evening drove withering, winnowing and weaving through the chill air, whipped on by a raw north-easter. Within the Red House, so called from its brick-built shell, countrymen clustered round the fire and the bar finding physical warmth in companionship and comforting communication in the discussion of country matters. The price of grain, the problems of foddering stock, the damage being done by the prolonged hard frosts and the hardships being suffered on account of the prolonged bitter weather vied with the talk of bankruptcies and politics gleaned from an aged news sheet and prophecies culled from *'Old Moore's Almanac'*. The cheerful fire, the dancing candlelight and a warmth of good fellowship bespoke an air of comfort within and gentle reward at the end of a laborious day. Perhaps it was in such surroundings that scurrilous slanders about the doings of the nuns in the castle were first fashioned.

Overnight the swirling snow which had been whipped and twisted by the wind into smoothly shaped ice sculptures froze into crispness wrapping the village in a cold, pristine shroud. Before dawn, in the soft velvet brightness of a cloud free sky the village began to wake. An early labourer crunched and cursed his cold path through the ankle deep snow marking a stark path across the square to the great threshing barn at Dove House. Soon his prints were crossed by others as the milkers and fodderers ploughed to their charges. The milkers chaffed stiff fingers and bent to their tasks, finding some slight comfort in the steaming body odours of the cattle. The fodderers tugged at hay ricks with pitchforks tossing forks full of their precious store to the hungry beasts. Wrapped in cold the fields, farm implements and buildings lay listless and still. Only around the farm doors was there life and activity as the yard stock clustered in the expectation of domestic bounty. At the edge of the Dove House yard a boy clanked a pump, gushing water swirled into a rime encrusted trough and the released, milked and fed stock surged to drink. Their breath and body heat as they pushed around the trough created a fine white mist which shrouded the sweating, pumping lad in a strangely ethereal nimbus. In the wood-yard an axe rang sharp on timber as kindling was gathered for the needs of the day.

In the village square, throbbing with life, children revelled in the snow, more than one forgetting the urgency of his mother-set errand in the pleasures of winter sport. In the trees around the castle a swarm of starlings chattered, cackled and whistled, swirling up like dark snowflakes and settling again to rest, their unceasing quest for food dependent upon the chance exposure of soil or grass. Around the castle, muffled black against the raw cold the Benedictine Nuns moved, gliding like dark spectres over the snow, their secluded life-style and earnest advocacy of their faith fuelling hostility, rumour, suspicion and innuendo. On the western side of the village the vicarage stood foursquare against the sky, isolated, proud and confident as befitted the powerful role of the church within the community.

The Old Vicarage, Caverswall. This building was demolished during the 1960s and replaced by a modern building situated in Vicarage Crescent.

The afternoon sun had produced a slight thaw which set again into ice with the onset of evening crusting each building with a miniature palisade of icicles. As the sky darkened into night snow was kicked from boots at cottage doorways, implements and working garb cleaned, shaken free from snow and placed in suitable readiness for the morrow. Those who had worked away from the village and who earlier had trudged outward cursing their lot returned more blithely bearing the profits of their task. The odd, snared rabbit, perhaps a trapped and possibly poached, pheasant or wood pigeon and the inevitable bundle of kindling which will be stacked to dry ready for the morrow. Singing kettles, steaming pots and savoury pans marked the end of a weary day.

The meal over, the family gathered round the fire. Chat, anecdote and banter flowed freely as expert fingers made, did and mended. A bedraggled song bird, perhaps taken by liming moved about a home-made cage, candlelight flickered on the gleaming fire-irons arranged for show rather than use around the hearth. As always on such occasions the conversation was laced with a sequence of cautionary anecdotes about boys drowned through skating on ice too thin to bear their weight, about the murder at Dead Man's Grave, about the dangers and destructiveness of strong waters; about the fairies, spirits and sprites which sparkled, sly and mischievous around houses, wooded glades and secluded dells when humans were absent and so on and on until bedtime approached and the children tense with fear would climb, with guttering candle, into their crowded bed. In this way the morality of the age and the mores of the village were transmitted to succeeding generations.

Caverswall Castle at about the date that Sir Joseph Percival Radcliffe took up residence.

The thaw of February began slowly with thatch appearing through the snow, ice underfoot turning slowly to slush and then to mud and the air filling with the sparkling brittleness of spring bird-song. Freed from the sense of winter's hold the villagers moved briskly and cheerfully about their tasks, little knots of gossiping women gathered and dispersed around the square adding a pattern of changing forms to the routine of life in the village. Beyond the village the wildlife of the countryside responded to the increasing warmth and day length. Fox, hedgehog and badger began to prepare for the serious business of breeding. Stoat and weasel became increasingly quarrelsome as if the warmth of spring had rekindled the venom in their natures. In the hedgerows the soft traces of green, the swelling buds and the glad yellow of the early primrose all spoke of warmth to come.

With spring the tempo of life in the parish quickened. The hedger worked steadily, chopping, trimming, filling gaps in such a way that the woody stems were interwoven to form a lattice over which the green foliage could spread to produce a stock proof barrier. The ditcher toiled in mud and water clearing choked watercourses, repairing frost damaged banks and draining the small ponds which had developed on the waterlogged soils.

Ploughboy and sower worked in sequence over the damp, clinging soils in the time honoured rhythm and sequence of the land. In some strange way the sowers, plodding over
the fields, arms swinging to scatter the precious seed seemed to embody the essence of
spring hope and rural labour.

With April's later warmth began the profusion of blossoms and colour which were so
much a feature of the parish in spring. Cowslips yellow, daisies white, violets purple and
primroses clustered in a brightness which spoke truly of spring. The gentle, soft green
foliage which, at first, had enhanced the delicate tracery of the hedgerows and trees had
hardened into a larger, stronger, deeper growth of green sufficiently dense to hide the
variety of nests and their precious eggs from the eyes of all save the most assiduous of
lads. Amid the fervour of life the call of the first cuckoo, the eager twittering of the swal-
lows and finally the screaming, wheeling swifts proclaimed that summer had come.

The joys and warmth of summer brought a new dimension to Caverswall. The air above
and around the village seemed to ache with bird song and hum with insect life. In almost
every patch of grass a grasshopper sawed merrily attracting the eager eyes and clutching
hands of the children as they swarmed around the village, chasing insects, each other and
loose bouncing balls, chasing through and round the churchyard, playing hide and seek
among the tombstones or shouting to make the echoes ring. Eagerly they swarmed the
lanes marvelling at the carpets of bluebells, the whiteness of lilies of the valley, astonished
by the starkly powerful crimson of the corn poppies, gazing in awe at the pimpernel
which mysteriously could respond to changes in the weather and mark the approach of
evening so that the village youngsters named them 'go to beds' and explored the validity
of the folklore which surrounded so many of the plants.

In the fields the herd boy tended the slowly grazing kine with a wary indolence, trusting
the lush pastures to hold them but knowing that he would feel the weight of his master's
hand if, through his neglect, they grazed into the growing corn crops. In the hayfields the
rhythmic swish of the scythes and the near silent application of the sweat streaked teams
of labourers bespoke the unrelenting toil of harvest. In the fallows the ploughman, his
sweating skin and garb dust caked moved up and down the furrows. Beyond the fields on
the edge of the more open grazing lands the shepherds busied themselves at the sheep
wash, thrusting in their charges to clean the stained fleeces before confining the bleating,
clustering creatures in the dipping pens to await the attention of the shearers with their
hand clippers and tar pots. To slake the thirst of the shearers and to clear from their
mouths the rank stench of sheep 'the maister' invariably sent down quantities of ale or
frumity which was swallowed at necessary intervals during the course of the day's labour.

Through high summer the parish was rich in the warm, teasing scents of the countryside. Pollen heavy air, enriched with the lingering scent of hay and the odours of the
hedgerows seemed as warm as it was heady beneath Caverswall's sun of summer. Beneath
the warmth of the summer's sun only the visitations of the tithemen, overseen by Reverend Alexander Goode brought a note of displeasure to the life of the village. Carts piled
high with sun dried hay rumbled steadily between field and farm to the almost unceasing accompaniment of chatter, bawdy commentary and snatches of song. Equally steadily
between farm and field rode a boy, usually mounted on some favourite horse too old and
tired for work but too cherished to slaughter, laden with panniers of food, bottles of ale
and the other necessities of life which would be consumed by the toilers who sought the
scant shelter of favoured spots. During such breaks, as the unshackled horses snuffled in
their nose-bags and angrily swished their tails at the nagging flies, many of the prelimi-
naries of courtship were conducted for this was one occasion when men and women were
thrown together in toil and could share each others company whilst rejoicing in the
pleasures of the open air at harvest time.

As the hay makers cleared each field and moved on, the shepherd with his scrawny, naked flocks moved in. The pink nibbling sheep found plenty left for their regalement and by fertilising the ground with their droppings discharged a function which had been theirs in the village for something more than seven hundred years.

Occasionally word would come that a herd of cattle was being driven through to market and the children would dash eagerly to the turnpike or the by-ways to watch the bovine tide flow past. Should the herd in question have originated from Scotland then even the men would stop work to gaze at the huge, oddly garbed, petticoat wearing herdsmen who carried great blankets over one shoulder and wore strange flattened bonnets.

Such excitements were relatively scarce however in the Caverswall of 1840. Day usually followed laborious day in an unrelenting pattern of labour from dawn till dusk. Each evening brought a tiring day to a cool and welcome close. Gradually as the sky lost its brilliance and the sun sank behind Park Hall Hills the heavy scent laden dew of summer would bring a cooling dampness to the air. Throughout the parish the people would turn homewards through the damp coolness with a sense of relief, anxious to be free of the superstitious threats of darkness heralded by the early hunting owl, betokened by the alert, long eared hares poised like familiars in the fields and presaged by the strange log-like 'churn-owl' or night jar which flitted spectrally over the backs of ruminating cattle and it was alleged, sucked the milk from their udders. The ploughboy who carelessly allowed a gate to slam on such tense evenings would glance over his shoulder in fear and hurry homewards fearful lest his unwarranted noise had stirred some slumbering mischief. Above the square, round the farms and over the castle swept and dipped bats, those other harbingers of malice, their high pitched squeaks audible only to the ears of the young. Milkmaids bore the last of the steaming pails carried on yokes across their shoulders from the byre to the dairy before tripping homeward across the square and past the smithy where the village boys played, scrabbled and hovered listening to the man-talk of their sires. Last preparations for the morning were hastily made as the fast fading light brought the labours of the day to a close. Around the Red House lounged the farmers and their men, eager to slake the day's thirst with strong ale and relax in good company before the cool of the evening turned to the damp chill of night and drove all indoors.

As the year progressed into August the corn fields ripened from luscious green into the sturdy tan of healthy ripe corn. Grey bearded barley, golden brown corn, the whitish green stubble of the hay fields and the lush green of grass and root crops served to cast a patchwork quilt of colour around the village. When the corn was ripe and urgent harvest pressed, the entire village seemed to die, everyone was urged to the fields to gather the village's most precious cash crop. Even the youngest toddlers were expected to do something towards the harvest although that something generally degenerated into tears and fretfulness as the sun scorched arms, the stubble pricked legs and the unremitting movement about the field induced weariness. As the corn harvest drew towards its close and the fruit trees began to yield their ripened treasures the vicar's tithemen again appeared checking, measuring, prying, collecting, until the villagers began to mutter that the new harvest hymn about 'all being safely gathered in' must have been written by a priest for priests.

Eager youths scoured the hedgerows for nuts, blackberries, hips and the other fleeting natural gifts that brought variety, briefly, to the cottager's table. The damp grey mists, early and late brought a chill to the air which lingered on by night and day. To keep the chill from their bodies the women and children gathered elderberries from which elderberry wine was pressed to yield a warming, soothing cordial. As the leaves changed colour and fell coating the village square and the lanes with a blanket of damp, heavy colour the morning mists lengthened into fog which shrouded the village and its unceasing round.

Somewhere in the foggy distance a hedger chopped and laid, shaping the summer growth into next year's barrier. Village girls muffled against the damp hastened about their business seeking vainly to keep cloak and skirt hem free from mud. Along the hedge-rows and through the small copses shuffled the older residents of the village seeking sticks, sodden and brittle which might be dried into kindling for winter evenings. Flocks of wood pigeons, starlings and finches decked fields, trees and hedges with a pattern of eager industry each feeding against the raw winter days ahead. As if to match their avine industry the threshers flailed away on the floors of the threshing barns each as intent upon completing his allotted task as the birds were upon gleaning sustenance from the land.

Slowly the village slid towards the end of the year and the onset of another winter. Such might have been the even, unhurried round of life in the parish of Caverswall during the 1840s.

There were interruptions to that ordered regime. The Chartist Riots of 1842 began in Hanley on 15th August and found fertile soil among the miners who, at that time, had been on strike for some weeks. To the miners were added a number of dissident pottery workers who had felt the increasing weight of the exactions pressed upon them by their employers. A substantial number of textile workers from Leek also joined in the disturbance. Wages had been pushed to low levels, the hours of labour extended virtually throughout the hours of daylight. That money was to be made from pottery manufacture there was no doubt for on every hand could be seen visible evidence of small potters grown great in the shape of their burgeoning new houses and increasingly luxurious life style. Among such men the egalitarian appeal of Chartism found eager recruits and the idealistic principles became inflammatory oratory. Stern and prompt action by dragoons under the command of Captain Powys broke up the revolt and soon disgruntled fugitives were streaming away from the disturbance looking for an easier prey. A group of this type moved up Ash Bank resolved to wreak vengeance on one such small man grown great, Job Meigh of Ash Hall.

During their unruly march up Ash Bank it rained hard. In normal times such a down-pour would have dampened the ardour of all save the most ardent revolutionary, but, inflamed by strong waters and hot words the mob surged on towards the new Hall which was being built to the south of the original site. Job Meigh was a man of resource and courage. Warned of the approach of the rioters he hastily gathered as many hats, cloaks and coats as he could and arranged them conspicuously as if they were drying, having been worn by recent arrivals. When the Chartists arrived Meigh was waiting for them having made sure that a half open door and uncurtained windows would favour prying eyes. An argument ensued in which Meigh refuted the demands of the mob with in-stances of his own generosity towards his workforce. Claim and counter-claim, challenge and rebuttal, allegation and refutation flowed to and fro in a noisy torrent. Gradually Meigh's confidence in the face of what were apparently such vast odds gave one of the more sober spirits food for thought. Looking into the window towards which Meigh had been manoeuvring them he spotted the outdoor raiment apparently drying.

The erstwhile Chartist paused, 'Hey lads, owd up, hay's got the bliddy militia in theer. Ay's trying tu trick us' . The mob paused, its resolution broke, its solidarity crumbled and away it began to drift slowly and then with increasing rapidity as rain drops once more began to blow over Ash Bank.

The pains of the late 1840s were accentuated by the potato blight of 1845. The villagers of Caverswall and Dilhorne were not to know that it was part of a vast blanket of pesti-lence which had settled over western Europe stretching through potato fields from the west of Ireland to eastern Poland. All they knew was that gradually the thick green foliage started to yellow, then to blacken and curl until it collapsed in a dry crumbling powder. Day after day farmers looked to their perishing crops and blamed the 'close' weather. Those who tried to lift what tubers might have formed below the decaying greenery found small, browning shells filled with a slimy, noisome substance. There were many empty bellies in the parish during 1845 and in the succeeding year. More than one family looked again at the developing urban area at East Vale and began to wonder about seeking a livelihood in the thriving pottery industry. The original Ash Hall which had decayed in the years prior to 1840 was demolished in 1843 when the new Ash Hall was completed.

1793 - 1849

RICHARD PLUNKETT
THE BACKBONE OF THE ARMY IS
THE NON-COMMISSIONED MAN

One *of the most interesting tombstones in the churchyard is that of Richard Plunkett. Richard Plunkett seems to have been born in the Parish of Castlebar in the County of Mayo towards the end of the eighteenth century. His date of birth is not recorded, a tentative date of 1793 seems reasonable.*

His military career is recorded in outline on his tombstone and in some detail in his service record.

3rd. April, 1807	*Enlisted under age as a drummer 101st. Foot.*	
1807 - 1812	*Still under age West Indies*	*Service in the West*
1812 - 1816	*Promoted Corporal West Indies.*	*Indies; active service*
1816 - 1818	*Reduced to Private West Indies.*	*against the French.*
14th. January, 1817	*Discharged.*	
18th. March, 1817	*Re-enlisted, 8th. Regiment of Foot.*	
25th. February, 1818	*Promoted Corporal.*	
1st. June, 1818	*Reduced to rank of Private*	*Service in the*
30th. August 1818	*Promoted Corporal.*	*Mediterranean on*
11th. October, 1819	*Reduced to Private*	*garrison duty.*
25th. September, 1820	*Promoted Corporal.*	
11th November, 1824	*Promoted Sergeant.*	
25th May, 1826	*Reduced to Private.*	*Service in North*
25th. March, 1828	*Promoted Corporal*	*America at Halifax,*
22nd. August 1831	*Promoted Sergeant*	*Nova Scotia.*
9th. September, 1831	*Reduced to Private.*	
10th. February 1832	*Promoted Corporal.*	

9th. November, 1833   Promoted Sergeant.

25th. October, 1843   Discharged after 36 years 279 days service.

Of his character and conduct the record has this to say :-

His conduct and character have been excellent although having been twice tried by court martial viz. by a Regimental Court Martial at Santa Maria in the Mediterranean on the 10th. October 1819, and by a Regimental Court Martial at Fort Charles, Halifax, Nova Scotia on the 8th. September, 1831. On the first occasion he was convicted of drunkenness and using disgusting language to an officer and on the second of drinking in company with a convict and a file of the guard and being in a state of intoxication.

The record contains the following breakdown of his service.

Total recorded service 36 years and 279 days.

In America   7 years and 300 days.

In West Indies   13 years and 25 days.

In Mediterranean   6 years and 182 days.

He was discharged in 1843 in consequence of the length of service and on grounds of disability since the record states :-

His disability has been contracted in and by the Service and does not appear to have arisen from vice or intemperance

W. Gardener, Surgeon 8th Regiment of Foot.

Although no specific disability is recorded this opinion was confirmed by the Principal Medical Officer at Chatham on 13th. November, 1843.

I am of the opinion that he is unfit for service and likely to be permanently disqualified from military service and I approve the opinion of the surgeon.

J.M.R.Smithson. P.M.O.

His final discharge was dated the 28th. November, 1843 and gives a description of him as he was at that date.

Age   49 years 10 months.
Height   5ft. 6 3/4 ins.
Hair   Brown.
Eyes   Grey.
Complexion   Fresh.
Trade   Labourer.
Marks and scars, whether on face or other parts of the body :- None .

His appearance in Caverswall is something of a mystery. He came to Caverswall as a married man with Eliza his teenage daughter and his wife, Charlotte. It is just possible that, after his military service, he found employment among the navigators or navvies who were working on the canals in the area. This is unlikely since the key canal works were completed well before his demobilisation. More probably he may have been engaged as a labourer working on the railways. The Derby to Manchester line which passed through Uttoxeter and near Froghall and Leek, was opened in 1849. The Uttoxeter to Stoke line was opened in 1848 and passed through Blythe Bridge.

An alternative theory holds that he may have been seeking employment with Lord Vane whose Irish estates included extensive tracts of land in Western Ireland. He could not have known of the changing fortunes of the Vanes but equally one must wonder how he could have known of the family link bearing in mind that he was aged about ten years when he left home in 1807.

His military career will produce a wry smile among those with experience of service with the colours. Clearly he was a man of some worth and personality. His demotion from corporal to private in 1816 whilst serving in the West Indies may have been a consequence of the reduced demand for soldiers following the end of the Napoleonic Wars. His re-enlistment in March, 1817 suggests that he found life in civvy street unfulfilling or perhaps unrewarding, the release of large numbers of soldiers and sailors from military service would have glutted the labour market. Thereafter his problems seem to have been drink related - what an entertaining story seems to be hidden behind the cold, military phraseology 'drinking in company with a convict and a file of the guard and being in a state of intoxication'. Whatever the true story it is encouraging to think that, in 1832 when it would seem that he married upon his return to England and was promoted to corporal, that his wife had sufficient influence to ensure that thereafter he conducted himself with propriety. Perhaps there is another story hidden behind the fact that his wife's name appears on both faces of the tombstone.

In a village as isolated and insular as Caverswall then was he must have been something of a character. His tales of military life may well have bored drinkers at the Red House or the Green Man but his associated anecdotes about life in foreign parts must have been the source of constant amazement among the villagers. He would no doubt have recited such experiences as the practice of catching fireflies and securing sufficient of them in a jam jar to provide a light for reading in his tent at night. Tales of flying fish, the practice of making broth from the hind legs and thighs of bullfrogs - called 'crapo' by the French, giant snakes like the boa-constrictor which doubtless grew in length and strength with the passage of time, tyrannical military discipline, snowball fights with sour oranges and the sharp practices of the paymaster and quartermaster must have enlivened many long winter evenings.

His discharge on the grounds of disability which had not arisen from vice or intemperance was apparently a device for obtaining his full release with his pension rights unimpaired. His death six years after his release suggests that service life had taken its toll although, at age 55 years, he had lived beyond the normal life expectancy of most labourers and peasants of the day and it could be argued that, for all the hardships, the decent accommodation and regular food offered by army life helped to ensure his health and well-being. Richard Plunkett died in 1849, his daughter Eliza died, unmarried, on 10th. April, 1852 and his wife Charlotte on 15th. February, 1860.

The tombstone of Sergeant Richard Plunkett and his wife in Caverswall churchyard

Richard Plunkett's tombstone, now almost illegible, lies near the road on the eastern side of the churchyard. The map of the Manor of Caverswall dated 1840 may be viewed in the County Record Office at Stafford. The Benedictine Nuns who inhabited the Castle between 1811 and 1850 left behind a small burial ground which lies to the west of and below the present churchyard. It was here that members of the order were buried until the Sisters moved away in 1850.

It was during the first half of the 19th century that the so-called Consall Plateway was constructed. Its purpose was to make possible the ready transportation of lime and lime-stone from the lime burning kilns at Consall Forge to the expanding industrial area of Longton. The track extended for a distance of some seven and a half miles from the lime kilns of the Cauldon Canal to a point in Weston Coyney Road near the Weston Coyney Arms. At intervals along its route evidence of its existence can still be seen in the shape of either embankments or cuttings or by the presence of stone sleepers often incorporated in walls or used as gateposts. The extension between Bolton Gate and the Weston Coyney Arms has now been almost completely obliterated by overbuilding.

Sleepers from the Consall Plateway appear in strange places and serve a variety purposes

In some ways the 1850s marked the end of what might be termed 'rural Caverswall'. The last impressive monuments to members of the landed gentry appeared in church in 1855 and 1856. The former date saw the appearance of the memorial to Martha, Countess St. Vincent whilst in the following year there appeared the tribute to Thomas Hawe Parker.

Between 1853 and 1855 a rich timber merchant from Liverpool called Holmes purchased the castle as a country residence but within a very short space of time had lost interest in the building, so depriving the village of a leading family until Sir Joseph Percival Radcliffe purchased it possibly in 1861 but probably somewhat before that date.

The Directory for 1851 43 summarises the more important facets of the area.

Caverswall parish included part of Cellarhead, Meir with its 'few scattered houses', Weston Coyney, Hulme, Adderley and Wherrington.

The parish boasted three families of gentle stock each with their own 'seat', the Coyneys of Weston Coyney Hall, the Parkers of Park Hall and the Walklates of Adderley House.

Opportunities for worship existed at the castle where the Benedictine Nuns assisted by Reverend William Jones provided catholic services, at St. Peter's Church where the absentee Anglican priest Reverend Alexander Goode, allowed Reverend Francis Leigh BA to discharge the duties of a living worth £240, at Wherrington where the New Connexion Methodists had a chapel or at the Wesleyan Chapel in Caverswall.

The school was in the care of one Thomas Rothwell who numbered among his charges 20 scholars who were taught free.

In the Caverswall, Cookshill and Meir areas the following leading citizens are reported:

CAVERSWALL

Foster, Miss Ann, abbess, Castle
Bullock, Samuel, victualler, Red House
Goode, Rev. Alex., vicar, (abroad)

Jones, Rev. Wm., (Catholic), Castle
Lakin, Thomas, butcher and victualler,
    Green Man
    (situated in The Green at Cookshill)
Leigh, Rev. Francis BA, curate, Vicarage
Read, Alfred, police officer
Rothwell, Thomas, schoolmaster
Sargent, Wm., grocer and draper
Thorley, Wm., wheelwright

Farmers
Boulton, Ralph
Bradbury, Wm.
Burgess, Mrs.
Burgess, Peter
Burgess, Wm. T.
Fielding, Thos.
Keen, George
Nicklin, James

Shoemakers
Abberley, Thomas
Miller, Thomas (parish clerk)
Oram, Wm.

Tailors
Austin, Stephen
Hulme, Joseph
Wood, Benj.

COOKSHILL

Lees, George, blacksmith
Mosley, George, corn miller
Slinn, John, blacksmith

Farmers
Barlow, Thos.
Heath, Rt., Hall
Hughes, Jos.
Marson, Wm.
Mosley, Geo.
Phillips, Wm., and also butcher

MEIR

Barns, Wm., victualler, Kings Arms
Heath, Thomas, joiner
Walters, John, butcher and cattle dealer
Whiston, Joseph, attorney's clerk

Farmers
Bailey, Ann
Ball, Timothy
Fallows, Thos.
Glover, James
Shaw, John

On the other side of the parish a significantly different pattern of occupations was recorded. The difference between the wholly rural eastern half of the parish and the slowly developing industrial character of the western portion emerges clearly:

WESTON COYNEY

Buckley, John, corn miller
Coyney, Chas., Weston-Coyney Hall
Hicks, Richard, guano merchant, Fox Earth
Keen, Geo, butler Park Hall
Broster, Mrs. Ann, housekeeper Park Hall
Slinn, George, blacksmith
Walklate, Mrs. Eliz., Adderley House

Beerhouses
Bentley, Wm.
Lees, Jno.

Farmers
Beardmore, Thos.
Bradbury, Jos.
Brookes, John
Hassall, Danl.
Heath, Wm.
Payser, Jonathon
Walters, Auty, cattle dealer, Blith House
Wardle, John

ADDERLEY GREEN

Pye, Thomas, coal master
Sturrup & Pye, coal masters

Inns and Taverns
Robinson, Samuel, Bird in Hand
Simcox, Jph., Waggon and Horses

Farmers
Forrister, Geo.

Shopkeepers
Daniel, Geo.

HULME

Bull, Wm., blacksmith
Walker, John, farrier, etc.

Inns and Taverns
Hurst, Wm., Coyney's Arms

Farmers
Davis, Joseph, and also butcher
Finney, John
Heath, Geo.
Shaw, Arty
Shaw, Jas & Spn.
Shaw, Ralph
Smith, John

Wain, Mrs.
Walklate, Thos.
Wright, Thos.

WHERRINGTON

Cooper, Samuel, schoolmaster
Prince, John, tailor
Reeves, Thomas, joiner, etc.

Inns and Taverns
Clarkson, L., Red Cow, and also butcher
Greatbach, Mk., Wind Mill, and also miller

Farmers
Lees, Gabriel

Shopkeepers
Downes, John
Greatbach, Mk.
Lees, John

CELLAR HEAD

Inns and Taverns
Heath, Thomas, Hope and Anchor

Shopkeepers
Shenton, Thos.

1858 A.D.

A PRELIMINARY INQUIRY

The fluctuations in agricultural prices, the impact of the potato blight, the extension of farm holdings to the exclusion of the smaller yeoman, the growth of a wholesale, retail dimension in traditional farming patterns, increasing population, a growing need for cash rather than kind and the lure of the expanding industries in Longton served to attract people into the western sector of the parish.

From 1801 when the population was a mere 756 to 1861 when it totalled 3,046, the population level at first rose steadily and then climbed abruptly from its 1851 total of 1,581 to almost double that in the next 10 years. The secret was not hard to find, it lay in the expanding urban area of East Vale.

The living standards of these parishioners may be deduced from the record of the Inquiry undertaken by Alfred L. Dickens Esq: C.E. Superintending Inspector under the auspices of the Public Health Act 1848. The Inquiry opened at 12 noon on 3rd March, 1858, in the Terrace Hotel, East Vale.

In 1801 the whole parish had contained just 756 souls. By 1851 that number had risen to 1,581; seven years later a further 1,300 persons had become concentrated into a dark, damp warren of just eight streets, Anchor Street, Melbourne Street, Cope Street, Howard Street, Railway Terrace East, Railway Terrace West, Ford Street and Palmer Street situated in the western corner of the parish.

The houses were serviced by 'decent privies' but had no regular system of sewage disposal. Piped water was available in all houses at a minimum charge of 6s.0d per dwelling, the water rate represented '5 per cent of the rack rent'. Foul drains emptied either into an open brook draining southwards towards Trentham or into a large open pond from which Messrs. Bridgewood drew essential water for their industrial and manufacturing processes.

The burial ground associated with the Longton parish church was deemed to be too small for the number of claims being made upon it. Between 1851 and 1857 the mortality rate within the parish stood at 30.5 deaths per 1,000 of the population and was held to be 'very high indeed'. 'Sickness' was a commonplace but the main killer was identified as 'fever'.

Over the whole sorry area lay a choking pall of heavy smoke which made personal cleanliness a nonsense and coated walls, windows, woodwork and thoroughfares with a soot-stained veneer.

After a prolonged inquiry, the petition to establish a new health district was approved and Caverswall lost its squalid industrial appendage.

1841 - 1901

WE LOOSE WILD TONGUES   ROBERT WILLIAMS BUCHANAN

Robert Williams Buchanan was born in Caverswall in 1841 and died in London in June 1901. His second name was taken from his mother's maiden name.

Chambers Biographical Dictionary contains the following entry:

'Born in Caverswall, Staffordshire he was educated at Glasgow High School and Glasgow University where his closest friend was David Gray with whom he set out for London in 1860. They found life hard in London and success came too late for Gray. Buchanan is noted for his attacks in The Spectator on Algernon Charles Swinburne and the Pre-Raphaelites under the pseudonym Thomas Maitland in an article entitled The Fleshly School of Poetry (1871).

London Poems was his first real success. He also wrote plays and novels'.

The entry is not quite correct. The two friends did intend to set out together and agreed the time and date but neglected to confirm from which of Glasgow's two stations they would leave. They travelled independently and lived impecuniously and apart for some time before a chance meeting enabled them to move into the same lodgings. In his account of the meeting Buchanan recounts how Gray described his own accommodation as *'A cold, cheerless, bedroom, nothing but a blanket to cover me. For Gods sake get me out of it...'* Gray died in 1861, probably of tuberculosis.

His work and talents were praised by Buchanan in 'David Gray and other Essays' published in 1868.

The story of Robert Williams Buchanan begins in 1840 when his father to be, Robert Buchanan, a journeyman tailor from Ayr left his trade and began to follow Robert Owen the founder of the Grand National Consolidated Trade Union. Owen was in Stoke - on - Trent during 1839 and 1840 sowing political seeds some of which were to flourish in the Chartist

Margaret Williams, the mother of Robert Williams Buchanan

Chartist riots of 1842, it was then that Robert met and married Margaret Williams. He was a free thinking, socially aware advocate of organised labour, she was the daughter of a local solicitor noted for his socialist inclinations and a willingness to support the under-privileged.

The wedding took place before a Registrar in the presence of Robert Owen. It was a civil ceremony conducted without the benefit of clergy a fact which later allowed Robert (Junior) to write that *'I was born - if not in the odour of sanctity, at least in the full and increasing daylight of the New Moral World'.* A sister born some twelve years later died in infancy leaving Robert as an only child to be idolised by his mother, a relationship which he strongly reciprocated.

At some point after Robert's birth his father became a reporter on the The Sun newspaper and opened a small newsvendor's. His mother, deeply embued with the socialist leanings of her father and committed to the free-thinking philosophies of the age was less confident when her husband put them in to practise. Angered by his numerous affairs she left home and took up residence in a community at Ham Green in Surrey. This liberated community was managed by William Oldham whose eccentricities included a preference for damp sheets over dry ones, a vegetarian diet consisting principally of raw cabbage and the rejection of salt and tea. Within the community all stimulants were banned as were indulgences of the flesh. As a married woman Mrs. Buchanan was not permitted to achieve full membership and shortly afterwards moved to a similar but more congenial community established in Hampshire by Robert Owen. Queenwood which flourished between 1839 and 1845 was a community of people who believed in the principle of association. Essentially it was a commune of voluntary vegetarians. Supporters described it as a happy and innocent community; detractors held it to be an immoral association. There is no record to show whether young Robert accompanied her on these excursions.

Robert (Senior) prospered and moved to London where the family moved in social circles which were predominantly socialist and intellectual. Here young Robert started school and later, writing of this time, stated that hunger had forced him to capture and eat snails from the garden because he found the vegetarian diet so unsatisfying. In 1851 the family moved to Glasgow when Robert (Sen.) became editor of the Glasgow Sentinel. There his son's schooling was conducted by day in a small school where he learnt some Latin and mathematics and in the evenings and at weekends by his parents and their friends with whom he read and discussed secular journals. During this phase of his life Robert (Jnr.) became an agnostic but he was never an atheist and in 1896 wrote that he had never lost the forlorn and perhaps foolish faith of my childhood, the faith in personal immortality, a supreme God or Good and in the Life after Death.

His family continued to prosper and Robert was sent next to boarding school on the Island of Bute. There he encountered *'an excess of Sabbatarianism,'* began to write poems, suffered intense bouts of home-sickness and survived the pangs of calf love for a farmer's daughter, Rebecca,

> *'O were she mine, with countless gems I'd deck her*
> *and give my all to beautiful Rebecca'*

Life on the island began to pall and having failed to persuade his parents to take him away set about getting himself expelled. His determination seems to have been fuelled in part by the failure of a second crush, this time upon a girl met at a school dance. she was nine, he was twelve and Rebecca was forgotten. When the girl's parents left the area taking with them his youthful Juliet he resolved to leave and applied himself vigorously to the business of getting expelled. At one stage his efforts to achieve expulsion involved the acquistion of a defective pistol.

Back home and aged fifteen he was having articles published in Glasgow newspapers not owned by his father and working diligently at his studies. When he moved to Glasgow University he read Latin and Greek but devoted an increasing amount of time to the theatre and enjoyed keeping company with actors and actresses. Of this period in his life he wrote :

'Morals had they none, or none to boast of; they tippled, they swaggered, they ran after petticoats and petticoats ran after them but the spirit of the savage old literature ran in their veins like blood'

How much of this was adolescent braggadocio remembered in age and how much a figment of the unworldly, dreamlike ephemeralism which coloured his approach to contemporary society in which he constantly sought a perpetual cloudland can only be a matter of conjecture.

The inevitable blow fell in 1859. Driven by continuing prosperity his father extended his business ventures well beyond his successful printing and newspaper interests. As a master printer owning three papers, the Glasgow Sentinel, the Glasgow Times and the Penny Post he was a man of substance. When he began to speculate in areas where his skills and knowledge were inadequate he over-reached himself, disaster struck and he was declared bankrupt. Scottish methods were abrupt and ruthless, the family was dispossessed and cast out onto the streets.

Robert (Jun.) resolved to try his literary luck in London. After eighteen years of comfortable living as a spoilt child in the lap of a prosperous family he had a tremendous self belief and was certain that fortune would favour his bold stroke. He left Glasgow Central station on 5th. May, 1860, with all the savings he could muster and a large stock of excel-

lent clothes. Almost inevitably the naive youth lost his ticket and his money, the railway authorities impounded his luggage and he found himself virtually penniless and alone in London. He took lodgings of a very doubtful kind and began to seek work as a writer and reviewer. In this way he made sufficient money to keep himself alive.

It was at this time he claimed to have witnessed a suicide committed by a fellow lodger. The man entered his room and asked Buchanan to free a tight button on his collar using a cut-throat razor. Buchanan did so whereupon the man returned to his own room and cut his throat with the same razor.

Perhaps this was one of the first urban myths for both Charles Dickens and Rudyard Kipling reported events of a similar nature experienced during their early years.

Robert Williams Buchanan
as a young man

His parents followed him to London and took a small house in Kentish Town. Robert moved back under the parental roof and began to write in earnest. His first significant success as a dramatist came with his adaptation of a lurid story, Crohoore of the Billhook which was staged at the Standard Theatre under the title 'Rathboys'. This stage play earned for Buchanan the sum of £20.

Within a year his circumstances had improved to the point at which he was able to marry. He chose a young girl, Mary Jay, still in her teens who proved to be 'afflicted by one of those painful internal maladies which are the death of health and domestic happiness and she often suffered tortures'. Mary Jay had a younger sister Harriet, who was adopted by the Buchanans some three or four years after their marriage. Harriet became a close companion of the married couple and remained with Buchanan after the death of his wife, Mary.

Mary Buchanan, the wife of Robert

Gradually Buchanan worked his way into the fringes of literary society. His letters and journals report meetings with such people as Thomas Love Peacock, George Eliot, Robert Browning and Dante Gabrielle Rossetti. His prose works attracted modest critical praise and many of his poems were well received.

Unfortunately his approach to his audience was an arrogant one based upon total self belief. He described his collection of poems 'New Rome - Ballads and poems of our Empire' (1898) as 'an attack on our civilisation in the name of humanity' and went on to observe 'such poems are not wanted by the public but they say what I believe'.

The 1860s were a prolific period for Buchanan during which he published several volumes of poetry, wrote a number of reviews and plays and articles on literary themes. Despite the generous sums he received for much of his work he was improvident and never achieved financial security. At one stage he was reduced to undertaking national tours during which he read from his own works to paying audiences in an attempt to raise money both in terms of an immediate cash return and in an effort to boost sales of his work.

During this period he spent a month or so in the village of Etretat in Normandy. The

An extract from what is possibly his best poem in which he imagines the soul of Judas Iscariot wandering through eternity seeking salvation

The Ballad of Judas Iscariot

Black was the earth by night,
And black was the sky;
Black, black were the broken clouds,
Though the red Moon went by.

'Twas the soul of Judas Iscariot
So grim, and gaunt, and grey,
Raised the body of Judas Iscariot
And carried it away.

And as he bare it from the field
Its touch was cold as ice,
And the ivory teeth within the jaw
Rattled aloud, like dice.

As the soul of Judas Iscariot
Carried its load with pain,
The Eye of Heaven, like a lanthorn's eye,
Opened and shut again.

60 verses later

'Twas the Bridegroom stood at the open door,
And beckon'd, smiling sweet;
'Twas the soul of Judas Iscariot
Stole in, and fell at his feet.

area provided much of the basic material for his romantic novel *'Shadow of the Sword'* (1871). In 1866 following the death of his father the family moved to Scotland settling in The White House on the Hill at Oban. Here his unworldly trust caused him to fall prey to a group of *'cowboy'* builders whom he recruited to add a wing to the house.

The contractor, one Angus Maclean occupied himself in abstruse meditation, coming two or three times to the spot, dreamily chewing stalks of grass and measuring imaginary walls with a rule. A carpenter was promised but did not appear, when a week had passed he was promised first thing in the morning. Donald Mactavish appeared three days later, smoked half a dozen pipes and sawed a board. His assistant was a lazy boy who *'came and went to sleep in the half finished room.'* Mactavish was a man who liked a wee drap, who was often unwell, who would not work if it were showery *'lest he caught cold,'* and who, when present, would often adjourn to the hillside and play his pipes. A plasterer came assessed the job and promised immediate action . . . . . *'upon his return from Mull!'*

Despite these problems he found some strength in the isolation of the area which seemed to please his melancholic spirit and he produced several volumes of poems and three prose pieces one of which was entitled *'The Land of Lorne'* (1871).

Of this piece the literary critic of The 'Athenaeum wrote' :

'. . . the tourist will find a pleasant companion and apt counsellor in the writer who, without boring them with the useful details of a guidebook, tells his readers what to seek or avoid and what characters to regard with suspicion at every stage of their journeying. . . . . the volumes contain not a little that will irritate snobs and stir many a Scottish laird with wrathful indignation at the insolence of the writer who presumes to censure worshipful landowners and teach a princess her duty'.

The princess in question was Princess Louise newly wedded wife of the Marquis of Lorne. 'Snobs' at the time the review was written, meant all who look up to those perceived as being of gentle birth or higher social status. The main thrust of the entire review is that the author should have given more thought to the market place before launching such a broadside of political philosophy. This inability to put himself in the place of the reader and to see the world as others might see it proved to be his downfall time after time.

In 1870 whilst detached from the literary world through his residence at Oban he read a volume of poems written by Rossetti which had been well received in the literary world. Buchanan had become obsessed with past criticisms, offended by modest or poor reviews and resentful of what he perceived as gratuitous insults which rankled increasingly with the passage of time. He was angered by a critical review by Swinburne of work by his erstwhile friend David Gray. Driven by a belief that his talent was so vastly superior and wholly confident that his own moral standpoint was unimpeachably correct he launched a savage and scathing attack upon what he called *'The Fleshly School of Poetry.'*

He wrote under the pseudonym Thomas Maitland; the article was published in the 'Contemporary Review.'

His essay opened with a withering criticism of those ladies who enjoyed reading the poems of Rossetti expressing the view that they were *'either very obtuse or very, very naughty.'* He described Rossetti's painting as *'the work of an artist who conceives unpleasantly and draws ill.'* Of Rossetti's writing Buchanan observed that *'Rossetti is not as glibly imitative as Morris nor as transcendentally superficial as Swinburne.'* In his attack upon the sonnets of Rossetti he described the lovers depicted in the poems as *'invariably snakelike in their eternal wriggling, lipping, munching, slavering and biting'* and goes on to express the belief that this must be the complete epitome of the art of love as practised by this group of poets. There is much more in a similar or more scathing vein. In one vast broadside he angered the leading literary figures of the day, antagonised those who read their works, offended those who published them and destroyed the position of those who might have supported a more reasoned commentary. Despite the fact that he was thirty years of age when the essay was written it reads like the frustrated outpourings of a repressed, confused, arrogant, unworldly and insensitive adolescent.

The subsequent furore rivalled in its bitterness and ruthlessness any internal feud between sects in any narrow field of human endeavour. Defenders of Rossetti and the Pre-Raphaelites described Buchanan as *'a disguised assassin guilty of stabbing a brother artist in the back and then hiding his head in darkness.'* In public Rossetti was more restrained simply referring to Buchanan as *'a minstrel in mufti.'* However, there is little doubt that the attack added to Rossetti's tendency to melancholic depression, and caused him to further abuse both whisky and chloral (a compound of chlorine and alcohol used to treat depression) and led to a breakdown in his health. Buchanan claimed to have the support of leading public figures including Cardinal Manning, Tennyson and Robert Browning but none spoke publicly in his defence.

Two extracts from Buchanan's attack upon 'The Fleshly School of Poetry'
unable to confine himself to a genuine criticism of the style on literary
grounds he damaged his own case by writing in this vein

There is nothing indecent in the human Leg itself; on the contrary, it is a most beautiful and useful member. Nor is it necessarily indecent to show the Leg, as some ladies do upon the stage, without in the least shocking our propriety.

The Leg disease, is subtle, secret, diabolical. It relies not merely on its own intrinsic attractions, but on its atrocious suggestions. It becomes a spectre, a portent, a mania. Turn your eyes to the English stage. Shakespeare is demolished and lies buried under the hecatombs of Leg! Open the last new poem. Its title will possibly be this, or similar to this - "Leg is enough." Walk along the streets. The shop-windows teem with Leg. Enter a music-hall - Leg again, and (O tempora! O mores!) the Can-Can. Jack enjoys it down Wapping way just as Jones does in the Canterbury Hall.

The inevitable consequence of this rash outburst was that he was ostracised by literary society and was reduced to getting his work published either anonymously or through the use of a pseudonym. Straitened financial circumstances followed. Convincing himself that the climate of Scotland did not suit him he sold his yacht, relinquished his shooting rights and moved to an isolated cottage called Rossport Lodge in the wilds of Connemara. In a letter written to William Canton he observes *'We have no gardens here. My lodge is a little place in the centre of a bog surrounded by huts even wilder than those you paint. . . . . . . I came here for economy and just now calculating up I find that it costs me as much as London though we only live in a tiny cottage.'* Whilst here Buchanan corrected the proofs of *'Shadow of the Sword'* and *'Queen of Connaught.'*

In 1880 his wife fell dangerously ill with cancer and died in November of that year. In the years which followed he produced a steady stream of novels and plays, written in haste as pot-boilers to generate income. In 1884 he went to America having contracted to write a play for the managers of the Union Square Theatre in New York. The play was not written and he offered instead a melodrama entitled Alone in London. The offer was refused and Buchanan chose to produce it himself, with some success, at the Chestnut Street Theatre in Philadelphia. During this visit to America he met Walt Whitman living *'in . . . lonely lodgings, ... old, worn, weary and weather-beaten.'* They drank brackish tea and feasted on custard pie for Whitman was simple in his tastes and very poor.

Buchanan's health and his theatrical ventures failed and he returned to England where he turned his hand to play writing. The pinnacle of his career as a playwright came with the success of *'Stormbeater'* based on his earlier novel *'God and the Man.'* This was followed by *'Lady Clare'* which ran for one hundred nights at the Globe Theatre and the London success of a work that he loved least of all *'Alone in London.'* Unwisely he had sold the rights to this play and was forced to watch as others prospered.

Through these successful years he developed a passion for horse racing. An acquaintance, Henry Murray, wrote of him, *'He (Buchanan) believed that Man is a gambler by nature and predestination . . . . and that the artist is the biggest gambler of all for he stakes his brains against public stupidity. Whenever he had a little money he never rested until he had ventured it in some kind of speculation and whatever that speculation might be, he never by chance came off an eventual winner. If he took a theatre he invariably lost by hundreds and sometimes by thousands and that too on the very plays which founded the fortunes of others.'* Buchanan's marked lack of affection for *'Alone in London'* reflects upon his judgement in so far as he sold the rights for a song only to watch it clear £10,000 profit for its purchasers in less than ten years.

Buchanan's inability to manage money pursued him to the turf. His reputation for generosity was reported to be widely known *'among tipsters, runners, gypsies, nigger minstrels, correct card sellers and other poor helots of the turf among whom he liberally scattered silver.'* On one occasion at Lingfield he was in need of £1,000 to save his show *'Butterfly'* from failure and himself from bankruptcy. Resolved to wager £100 at 20 to 1 on Theseus he became so heavily engaged in the social scene that he forgot to place the bet. Theseus won and Buchanan missed the chance to win £2,000. On a happier occasion he was rumoured to be the only man to have good money on both Cypria (66-1) and Red Eyes (5-1) when they dead heated in the Cesarewitch of 1893.

His mother died in 1894 prompting him to write a poem entitled *'Dedication'* which ended with the words ;-

> ' . . . O my dearest and best
> sleep in peace! till thy son
> creepeth down to thy breast'

From this blow he never really recovered although he continued to write and even ventured into the realm of publishing. Again financial losses resulted.

On the morning of 5th. January, 1899 he suffered a heart attack. During the illness which followed he convinced himself that he was losing a stone a day after being weighed at a chemist's shop (16st. 8lbs.) and then checking his weight the following day on a public weighing machine on Brighton Pier (15st.6lbs.) The possibility that the scale might be inaccurate simply did not occur to him. Nor did his survival beyond the next fortnight reassure him!

From Brighton he moved to Clapham, in February, *'the air thick with fog and the Common covered in snow.'* Influenza and double pneumonia followed. In the summer he moved to Pevensey where, in search of good health he cycled, played cricket and bathed in the sea. He became increasingly hypercondriachal and cast about for any form of medication which would counter what he perceived as an increasing array of life threatening illnesses. He discovered a book which advocated Nauheim Baths as a treatment for heart trouble. Such baths were undertaken at Hastings in the care of a local doctor. After the second bath, taken during the second week in December, 1899 he suffered a severe stomach attack and spent Christmas Day in bed enduring much pain. [45]

It was during this period of extreme discomfort that he wrote an article entitled *'The Voice of the Hooligan'* which was published in *'The Contemporary Review'* in December, 1899. In this article Buchanan attacked Rudyard Kipling who at that time was the most widely read and most generally popular writer in English throughout the English speaking world. Kipling was also stridently supportive of British action against the Boers and pleading for a national, defensive army imbued by a sense of soldierly duty and national pride as a way of harnessing the allegedly brutal and licentious masses and of giving them a place in society. As much as anything Kipling was pleading for soldiers to be well and properly treated and urging the nation to look to its future. Another virulent attack upon another major literary figure did Buchanan's waning reputation much harm and exposed the extent to which he wholly failed to understand the thrust of Kipling's pleas. This was only part of Buchanan's persistent and virulent criticism of Kipling who, whatever his faults, did touch and awaken a major part of the nation's consciousness and for a time had much of the nation marching to his tunes. All too frequently Buchanan seems to have believed himself to be the only one in step.

Despite his experiences with the Nauheim treatment he persisted with the baths into January, 1900 and his condition went into a steady decline. He returned to London to consult Dr. Stodart Walker and then moved to Deal seeking treatment under a new doctor. From Deal he moved to France settling in Cap Gris-Nez where the delicacies of his French cook Rosalie combined with short cycle rides produced some improvement. He returned at the end of a month's stay displaying an increasing hostility to things English and yearning for Rosalie. After a short sojourn in Boscombe he returned to London feeling well enough to cycle through traffic in a manner which filled his sister-in-law and constant companion with terror.

Robert Williams Buchanan died on the morning of 10th. June, 1901 in his sixtieth year after suffering for eight months following a stroke which left him virtually helpless. His last reported words were *'I should like a good spin down Regent Street.'*[45]

Robert Williams Buchanan in his later years

1860 - 1900 A.D.

CHANGING SKY AND SHIRE

During the last four decades of the 19th century the pace of change in the parish quickened.

One of the earliest changes was the pollution of the atmosphere by the belching bottle ovens of Longton. When a westerly wind pushed its way over Park Hall Hills and tumbled in moist freshness down across Caverswall it carried with it the unmistakable, acrid, dry taste of bottle oven smoke. On bad days when the same winds had prevailed for longer than a few hours the dirty, grey smoke pall of the city would lour over the parish scattering a layer of fine soots over the good wife's washing.

The Square circa 1908. This picture gives an excellent impression of the condition of the road surfaces in the days of horse drawn traffic. Note also the size of the two glacial erratics

As the years flowed by and more men sought employment in the towns the farmers looked to the new fangled steam-powered machines to speed and ease the burdens of threshing and winnowing. However the influence of the city had continued to shape the life of its adjacent areas and increasingly the farms had switched to the production of those commodities which had a ready sale, milk, dairy produce, meat and eggs. The period between about 1850 and 1870 was characterised by a tendency to warm and dry conditions, offering good harvests and encouraging the growth of lush pasture so ushering in a period of rural prosperity. The prices which farm produce could command tended to rise helped by the bad harvest of 1860 and the outbreak of rinderpest which destroyed a number of beasts in 1865. Wars abroad, railway building at home, the continued growth of the large towns and cities and the expansion of industrial enterprise all served to provide a ready and increasing demand for the produce of the land. Between 1870 and 1890 the weather became colder and wetter bringing with it an ebb tide of agricultural depression. Indeed until the turn of the century things were not easy for the farmers of Caverswall.

Bleak springs, followed by cool, rainy summers produced poor crop yields, caused mildew in wheat, blight, disease in cattle, foot-rot in sheep, 'thrush' in horses and a general deterioration in the quality of both arable and pasture land. In this respect 1879 was a black year for Caverswall. Winter seemed to go on and on, spring was little better than a fleeting interlude between a raw, damp, bitter winter and a sunless, rain drenched, icy summer. Cattle died from pneumonia, and foot and mouth disease, sheep succumbed to foot-rot and liver fluke whilst the low-lying lands along the Blithe were almost constantly under water. The Square at Caverswall was a morass throughout the year. To add to the burdens of the farmer men began to talk of imports of grain and meat from America and Canada. There was even talk of crops being cultivated in great glass houses designed to keep off the worst extremes of the weather. Hope shone briefly when it was heard that a Commission of Inquiry was to investigate the problems facing farmers but faded in the face of the continuing decline. Parish farmers quietly thanked God for the proximity of the Longton markets and got on with the task of making the best of a bad job. It was this period of bad weather which finally completed the switch from arable to pasture farming in the parish although it is fair to say that, from 1850 onwards, the parish had been increasingly dependent upon the urban market and had shaped its life accordingly.

Further changes in the appearance of the landscape took place during the last four decades of the 19th. century. The purchase of Caverswall Castle by Sir Joseph Percival Radcliffe brought a strong Catholic influence back to the village. Almost immediately plans were put in hand for the erection of a proper focal point for Catholic worship in the parish, the appearance of the Catholic Church of St. Filumena designed by the architect Gilbert Blount extended the ecclesiastical geography of the parish.

It was the Radcliffes who drained the moat during those cold wet summers of the early 1870s and transformed the great empty ditch into charming gardens which existed until a future owner introduced a lake where the Italian Gardens had been.

That ill-luck which seems to have stalked so many of the owners of the Castle with its almost uncanny bias against male heirs struck also at the Radcliffes. Both Bernard, born 12th December 1869 and Roger, born 3rd April 1872 died young adding two more graves to the tiny Benedictine cemetery in the Castle grounds. Both died from the effects of the chill damp airs associated with the moat.

In 1865 a toll ford existed at the point where the Weston Coyney to Cellarhead road crossed the marshy, meandering River Blithe. The ford was owned by an absentee clergyman named Martin who had somehow acquired possession of the old Malthouse Mill. In 1868 with the mill in decay and its mill pond silting up Reverend Martin removed the toll gates and granted free passage to the public. The Caverswall Parish Council thereupon determined to erect a bridge across what could be an extremely wet and muddy crossing. Tenders were invited and assessed at a meeting held in the 'Coyney Arms' better known as 'The Candlestick' at Hulme. That bridge served until the road was improved during the early 1960s although its shape in relation to the road, it lay in the centre of an elongated 'S' bend, had made it a hazard to traffic long before that date.

In 1870 the Approved School, later the Detention Centre and more recently the Home Office Young Offenders' Centre was opened.

The school in Salters Lane was built in 1878 so displacing the scatter of small private schools which had sprung up to meet the needs of the locality. The school gloried in the full title of the 'Caverswall, Hulme and Werrington County Primary School' and was the creation of the old Caverswall School Board. It fulfilled a need which had been met at the southern end of the parish in 1825 and at Meir in 1877. The Meir school was also a creation of the Caverswall School Board under its Chairman the Reverend Dr. Arnold.

The Log Book for the Meir School records the following note for 15th October 1877:

'Mr. Kendrick opened the Meir Board School according to instructions received from the Rev: Dr. Arnold, Chairman of the Caverswall School Board. Of the 59 children admitted, 33 had been attending a Dame School, 3 had not attended any, 22 could not form their letters and 12 could not say them.'

By 8th February, 1878, the roll had risen appreciably for it was recorded:

'Average attendance for the week, 74. A gradual improvement in the attendance has been made and it would be greater still were it not that the trades in the district are so stagnant. Children are frequently kept at home because their parents have not the school pence.'

St. Peter's Church, Caverswall. This view shows most of the stages of its development from the Early English through to the Victorian vestry and the new south porch.

A year later significant alterations including some of the most casual and insensitive reshaping imaginable were inflicted upon St. Peter's Church at Caverswall. The Faculty or Licence refers to the church being *'in great need of restoration and repair'* and goes on to talk about adding a new South Porch, to providing new floors, a new roof, new heating apparatus and vault. Indeed the whole Faculty makes interesting reading:

COPY OF THE FACULTY OR LICENCE
authorising certain alterations to the Church, 1879

To all Christian People to whom these presents shall come,
We, Robert Charles Herbert Esquire Master of Arts Vicar General of the Right Reverend
Father in God William Dalrymple by Divine permission Lord Bishop of Lichfield and
Official Principal of His Episcopal Consistory Court of Lichfield lawfully constituted and
more especially to all and singular Clerks and literate persons whomsoever and
wheresoever in and throughout the whole Diocese of Lichfield:
Greetings:
Whereas it hath been represented unto Us on the part and behalf of the Reverend
Francis Goddard, Clerk, Vicar or Incumbent of the Vicarage of the Parish Church of
Caverswall in the County of Stafford and Diocese of Lichfield and Charles John Welch
and John Robert Stirrup the churchwardens there that the parish church of Caver-
swall aforesaid being in great need of restoration and repair hath been surveyed by a
competent Architect by whom Plans have been prepared in which it is proposed (amongst
other alternatives) to put new roofs over the Nave and North and South Aisles to put
new floors to the body of the Church and Tower, to form a water table and channel
round the exterior of the Walls of the body of the Church, Chancel and Tower, to place
new glass and lead to the windows excepting those in the Chancel and the windows now
filled with stained glass, to erect a new South Porch, to provide a new heating apparatus
and vault, to reseat the body of the Church throughout, to take down and remove the
Gallery Pulpit and Font and to replace the Pulpit and Font in suitable positions, to
restore the present Chancel Screen and to substitute an Arch in lieu thereof, to erect a
Reredos at the East end of the said Chancel and generally to do all such acts matters
and things as may be necessary to be done in carrying out the alterations and improve-
ments as aforesaid And whereas the said Vicar and Churchwardens have duly peti-
tioned Us to grant our Licence or Faculty to authorize and empower them to carry out
the Restoration of the said Parish Church and Chancel in accordance with the Plans
hereunto annexed. Know ye now therefore that We being desirous to comply with the
reasonable request of the said Vicar and Churchwardens (the due forms and orders of
law in this case requisite having been first had and observed) Do commit and grant this
our Licence or Faculty to the effect and in manner herein before prayed. Provided
always that if it shall be necessary in making any of the alterations as aforesaid to
remove or disturb any vaults graves tombstones or monuments due care shall be had
thereof and any bodies or remains there may be found shall be decently re-interred
within the churchyard of the said parish and the monuments or tombstones replaced
in a suitable position. In Testimony whereof we have caused the Seal of Our Office to be
hereunto affixed this ninth day of June in the year of Our Lord one thousand eight
hundred and seventy-nine.

To find cheap flooring materials and additional stonework the restorers seem to have
utilised whatever came readily to hand thus the floor of the church and the internal walls
now contain an intriguing array of sepulchral slabs and ornamented stonework some of
which dates back to the 13th or 14th centuries.
In 1891 Holy Trinity Church, Meir, was consecrated to cater for the expanding population
of that fast growing offshoot of Caverswall which was rapidly becoming a suburb of
Longton. Four years later the Primitive Methodists finally abandoned their old chapel at
Washerwall and switched their affections to the new chapel which had been erected at
Cellarhead in 1870 on a site adjacent to the old bull-ring.

THE RADCLIFFE FAMILY

The Radcliffe family were Catholics and purchased the castle during the middle years of the fifth decade of the nineteenth century. They encouraged the use of a room at the castle for devout worship and set in train the building of St. Filumena's church.

The moat was considered to be a constant source of damp related illnesses and Sir Joseph Percival Radcliffe arranged for it to be drained and replaced by an Italian garden which, in turn was supplanted by a lake created by Mr. Brian Milner during the 1980s. His decision to drain the moat may well have been prompted by the death in infancy of his two sons. Their names were Bernard and Roger. (There is no evidence that they were drowned.)

It was said that the garden was designed in such a way that a perambulation of its paths covered one mile and that it was used by the ladies of the house for the purpose of regular exercise.

The Radcliffes who were linked to the Doughty and Tichborne families by marriage had the misfortune to lose much of their wealth in fighting off the spurious claims of Arthur Orton the Tichborne Claimant and in consequence were forced to sell the castle in 1878 to members of the Wedgwood family and move to Rudding Park in Harrogate.

The family fortunes revived somewhat and in 1915 Craig, Taylor and Co. Ltd. of Stockton launched a steel screw steamer of 5,754 gross tons named after a descendant of the old Caverswall family, Clarissa Radcliffe. The S.S. Clarissa Radcliffe survived being torpedoed and shelled in 1918 when her Captain was brother to the serving vicar of Caverswall. She was eventually sunk with all hands in 1943. The battle-scarred ensign of the S.S. Clarissa Radcliffe hung behind the pulpit for many years after her captain presented it to his brother until the ravages of time took their final toll.

The spread of building apart very little else happened to change the face of the parish during the latter half of the 19th century. Drainage works using the new types of clay land drain pipes were set in hand but had little effect on the wettest areas of the parish which over a hundred years later, are still marshy lowlands prone to flood in wet weather. Small scale craftsman led industries flourished or faded as they encountered the challenge of the towns. Mining was still important around Hulme and Adderley whilst the pottery bias of Meir could no longer be denied.

The appearance of the railway in the late 1840s and the increasing use of the stations at Meir and Blythe Bridge had done something to speed travel. On the other hand the increasingly popular bicycle had made it possible for a greater number of people to move more easily over short distances and on market days there were vociferous criticisms of the delays experienced by travellers to and from market using the Meir-Normacot roads. Caverswall became an attractive focal point for those seeking a short walk or cycle ride.

St. Filumena's Roman Catholic Church, Caverswall. Provided by Sir J.P. Radcliffe who also funded the Presbytery and St. Filumenas' School.

Personal disasters seldom come singly. Scarcely were the sons of Sir J. P. Radcliffe laid to rest than a new tragedy in the shape of costly litigation fell upon the family. Sir Joseph's wife, Lady Catherine Doughty was a member of the Tichborne family with interests in and a claim upon the family estates in Hampshire. The 10th Baronet died in 1862. His elder son, Robert Doughty-Tichborne, having died in South America, his younger son, Alfred, succeeded as the 11th Baronet. The dowager Lady Tichborne refused to believe that Robert had died and launched a world wide newspaper campaign to find him. In 1867 a man purporting to be Robert arrived in Paris and was 'acknowledged' by Lady Tichborne as the rightful heir. After a protracted legal battle lasting 188 days the impostor was unmasked as one Arthur Orton a seaman who had deserted his ship at Valparaiso in 1849. Orton was sentenced to 14 years penal servitude.

The entire resources of the Doughty-Tichborne family and its in-laws had been devoted to proving Orton false, victory left them sadly impoverished and in consequence the Radcliffes were forced to leave the Castle and seek a smaller home in Harrogate. Ownership of the castle passed to Godfrey Wedgwood.

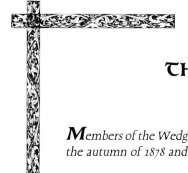

THE WEDGWOOD FAMILY

Members of the Wedgwood family were associated with the castle at Caverswall between the autumn of 1878 and the early months of 1890.

Godfrey Wedgwood and his second wife Hope, were responsible for a number of improvements to the castle. Godfrey suffered from circulatory problems and his wife from arthritis. The cold, damp and draughty castle aggravated these problems and in 1890 prompted the move to Idlerocks near Moddershall. Despite his early retirement from an active involvement in the work of the pottery on the grounds of ill-health Godfrey continued to act as a Justice of the Peace and as a director of the North Staffordshire Railway. His first wife, Mary Hawkshaw died of complications following the birth of their son, Cecil.

Their son Cecil, who regarded himself as a 'John Bull' rode to the pottery at Barlaston each day usually on his mare, Polly. He counted himself a connoisseur of horseflesh and held foreign travel in low esteem because one saw so few good horses. It was Charles Dickens who defined a 'John Bull' as one who has always made his mind up on every subject without knowing anything about it and who dealt with any critic holding a contrary opinion by the extreme measure of knocking his blessed hat off.

Cecil has been described as a tall handsome man, blue eyes and blond moustache. He was enthusiastic about the work of the Wedgwood pottery and refused an opportunity to study at Cambridge University in order to work at his trade.

In 1884 Cecil Wedgwood's coming-of-age party was held in the castle. The event was recorded in a carefully posed picture showing family and friends assembled at the foot of the staircase leading from one of the corner towers to the Italian Garden.

In the spring of 1885 Godfrey decided to leave the castle, it was costly to staff, cold, damp, draughty and in constant need of repair. The steep staircases, cold, damp rooms and long coach journeys to court or to meetings tended to aggravate his steadily increasing lameness. During 1885 the castle accommodated Godfrey and Hope, Cecil's step-mother; Mary Euphrasia, his half-sister; and Lucie Gibson Mary's governess. Lucy was an attractive Irish red-head with a fiery temper, independent mind and a strong will who had set her mind on Cecil.

On 9th. September, 1887, the day before Godfrey was due to sail to America and three days before Hope and Mary were due to travel to London to visit Hope's parents and select furnishings for the new house near Moddershall, Cecil was brought home in an ambulance having injured a leg in a fall whilst escorting a party of visitors round the works. Cecil was left at home for three weeks in the care of Lucy who, if some of the entries in her diary are read carefully, seems to have already achieved a secure expectation if not a formal understanding with Cecil. Indeed a suspicious reading of Lucy's diary prompts the suspicion that the relationship may have been well advanced by this date. During the time that Cecil was incapacitated they received only occasional visits from members of the family and Cecil's injury proved to be much less severe than was feared. The combination of a handsome invalid making a rapid recovery, a lively Irish governess and the enchanting surroundings of the castle led to romance and Cecil found himself deeply in love with a penniless beauty and enmeshed in a situation unlikely to please his father. Godfrey had hoped that Cecil would marry an heiress to strengthen the financial circumstances of the firm. Lucy thoughtfully left for a week's holiday in Ireland just before Godfrey returned from his visit to America. When she returned the dust had settled and the couple were married in Cork on 18th. July, 1888. Godfrey and Hope did not attend the wedding!

Godfrey left the castle in 1890, Cecil died aged 52 years, a Major in the Army, in France in 1915.

Cecil Wedgwood, his sister Mary Euphrasia and his favourite mare, Polly. The picture dates from 1884 .

AN EXTRACT FROM THE WEDGWOOD FAMILY TREE.
(The table refers only to those persons associated with the castle)

Godfrey (1833-1905) m   Mary Hawkshaw   m Hope (1844-1935)

Cecil (1863-1915) m Lucy Gibson (d1939)   Mary Euphrasia (1880-1952)
                                                                              m Will Mosley

Phoebe (1893-1972)   Audrey (1894-1968)

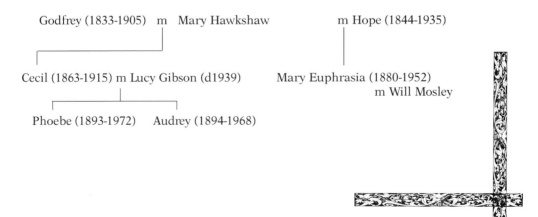

Some aspects of the life of the village during the time that the Wedgwood family occupied the castle are recorded in bound volumes of the parish magazines for 1882 and 1883 entitled 'Home Words'. They tell us that a new American organ had been installed in the church at a cost of £48-0s-0d, that a 'lending out library' had been formed in the village, that the reading room had been re-opened and that there was a widow's dole of £5-0s-0p which was distributed on Christmas day. Some 270 members of the parish belonged to one of four clothing clubs. In 1883 the parish party was held in the schoolroom on the evening of 6th. January. It opened with tea after which the vicar, Reverend Francis Goddard, read several extracts from the 'Pickwick Papers' and Mr. Beilby accompanied by Miss L. Brown played a number of pieces on the violin. The magazine also indicates that the distribution of the Good Friday dole was to be limited to 'the most deserving cases' and reports that the total salary bill for the teachers at St. Peter's school amounted to £189-3s-0d.

Village children in 1908 enjoy the delights of paddling in the River Blythe

Village children in 1980 recreate the pose of their predecessors

Blythe Bridge Road as it was at the turn of the century

Blythe Bridge Road in 1977

The ownership of the castle eventually passed to Mr. William Bowers in 1890. He spent much time, money and effort upon enlarging and improving the costly pile. A new wing was added connecting the house with the turret flanking the northern side of the gate. That it blends so neatly with the Jacobean original is a tribute to the architect, Mr. C. Lynam. The new wing provided space for a billiard room and an additional bedroom suite. The gardens and grounds were improved and a magnificent cricket ground laid out in the open fields to the south-west of the castle.

The castle as it was in the days of the Bowers family

Yet again the curse of the castle was to strike. William Eli Bowers died in 1911 aged 51. His son, William Aubrey Bowers died of wounds in 1916 leaving yet again in the castle a widow and two daughters.

THE BOWERS FAMILY

In 1890 the ownership of the castle passed to William E. Bowers who had been born at Harewood Park, Cheadle on 18th. February, 1861. He was educated at Jesus College, Cambridge and married Alice Blagg of Cheadle.

William Bowers spent a great deal of money extending and developing the castle and the adjacent cricket ground. He added a new wing connecting the house with the turret flanking the northern side of the main gate. This provided a billiard room with a bedroom suite above. Much of the oak panelling used came from Fauld Hall near Tutbury. In addition he improved the gardens, added higher parapets to the bridge and improved the lodges and the stables.

On 21st. June, 1889 pupils from the school were given a half holiday to watch the inaugural game on the newly created cricket ground.

By 1910 William Aubrey Bowers, the son of William, was captaining a successful village cricket team. Two years before he had celebrated his twenty-first birthday party at the castle. The caterers were Messrs. J. Lyons & Co. Guests regaled themselves with mock turtle soup, salmon, sweetbread cutlets, Surrey fowls, York ham and pigeon pie. He died of wounds on 2nd. July, 1916 on the first day of the Somme offensive.

Mrs. Bowers left the castle in 1932. Reminders of the family abound in the church. The metal alms plate, the carved wooden cover on the font, the choir stalls and the impressive family window at the eastern end of the church are all memorials of the Bowers family.

William Aubrey
Bowers,
a photograph
taken
to mark his
coming of age

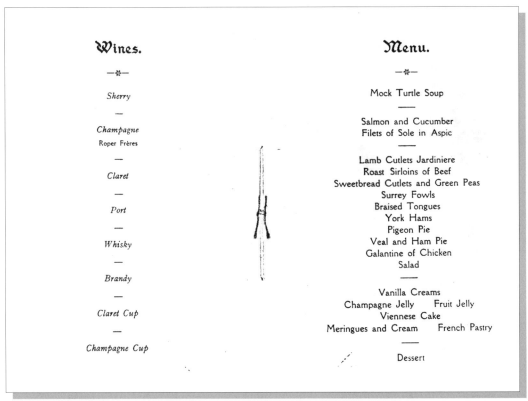

Wines.

—✽—

Sherry

—

Champagne
Roper Frères

—

Claret

—

Port

—

Whisky

—

Brandy

—

Claret Cup

—

Champagne Cup

Menu.

—✽—

Mock Turtle Soup

———

Salmon and Cucumber
Filets of Sole in Aspic

———

Lamb Cutlets Jardiniere
Roast Sirloins of Beef
Sweetbread Cutlets and Green Peas
Surrey Fowls
Braised Tongues
York Hams
Pigeon Pie
Veal and Ham Pie
Galantine of Chicken
Salad

———

Vanilla Creams
Champagne Jelly   Fruit Jelly
Viennese Cake
Meringues and Cream   French Pastry

———

Dessert

*The menu for the coming of age celebration held at the castle to mark
the maturity of William Aubrey Bowers*

**The courtyard of the castle as it was at
the time of the celebration**

William Aubrey Bowers and the village cricket team, champions in 1910

The gardeners and ground staff who worked to create one of the most attractive cricket grounds in the county. The Head Gardener is seated in the centre of the picture his status denoted by his bowler hat and blue serge apron.

Caverswall's Town Hall, described by local humorists as a building which needed a new roof every year

The castle at the turn of the century

1902 AD

GOD SAVE THE KING

The opening years of the 20th century were a strange mixture of contrasts in Caverswall. The landscape, embraced in its pattern of hedgerows moved slowly through the rhythm of the seasons almost without hindrance from extremes of weather. Winter temperatures throughout the first decade of the century averaged only some seven degrees Fahrenheit above freezing, summer temperatures hovered around 60 degrees whilst rainfall, apart from the damp year of 1902, was unexceptional. Neatly layered, bare winter hedges budded, leafed, bloomed and sprawled into the overblown gaiety of autumn before the billhook and the axe forced them back into dense, naked conformity. Ditch banks, wayside slopes and field fringes struggled from the sodden, fuscous winter soil into the first bright flush of the primrose; rose stridently to the regal carpet of bluebells and exploded into a riot of summer colour and rank luxuriance before tumbling back exhausted into a tangle of pale decay. The general appearance of the landscape was one of rural solitude. Houses clustered together at Hulme and Caverswall, straggled sparsely between the cross-roads at Washerwall and Withy Stakes, farmhouses dotted the sides of the various roads through the parish marking the true character of the place. The most impressive buildings were still the farmhouses at Hulme, Dove House and Bank House at Caverswall and the magnificent pair of semi-detached dwellings adjacent to the Auctioneer's Arms.

*The magnificent pair of semi-detached dwellings as they were in 1970 :
they are now much restored*

*Cookshill Mill originally ground corn but found the grinding of pigments
for the potteries more rewarding*

*Weston Coyney Hall as recorded in an original painting
owned by Mr. and Mrs. K. J. Slinn*

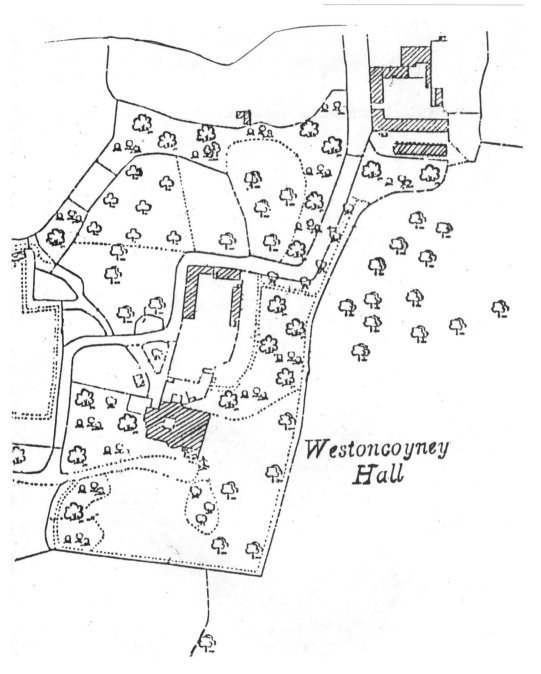

This map gives some idea of the area around Weston Coyney Hall

The four stately homes in the parish, Ash Hall, Weston Coyney Hall, Park Hall and the Castle although somewhat decayed were still indicative of a way of life far removed from the world of the ordinary village people. Many of these lived in such conditions that, when the people in the big houses 'cried' over the rapid fluctuations but steady rise in the cost of living, wondered at the accounts of the doctor or veterinarian and bewailed the increasing sullenness of the working classes, they could only weep at the impossibility of keeping body and soul together and seek to combine into unions not to better themselves undeservedly but simply to survive.

Such dourness in the face of hard lives imparted a strange tempo to the life of the parish. Work was done quickly and well, the fear of dismissal *'without a character'* and the difficulty of finding other employment were strong incentives to labour. Fun was enjoyed with a similar measure of determination, 'Carsa Wakes', the summer jubilation, was really the last and most recreational vestige of the major country fairs and patronal day festivals which had meant so much in the previous century. Its restoration as a village festival in the 1990s was a happy acknowledgement of the past. On the Sabbath the villagers who knew their place worshipped fervently in one of the appropriate buildings, their demeanour bringing a secure solemnity to the village. Yet many residents of the parish drank to excess and fought each other bitterly and bloodily in consequence. An evening's debauch tended to extend into the hours of night and end in a tumult of drunken obscenities, vomit, bloody faces and flailing fists in and around the Red House, the Auctioneer's Arms, the Red Lion, the Hope and Anchor, the Royal Oak, the Spotted Cow, the Saracen's Head and the other lesser vendors of strong waters. The excess of such bestiality overflowed into the homes of the villagers where wives and children suffered either directly in terms of physical abuse or indirectly through the dearth of money to buy life's meagre necessities. This was a particular problem for those villagers who found employment in the potteries. There the practice of paying wages at the end of the week in coin or notes of large denomination in a public house or in notes or tokens which could be redeemed only in a public house adjacent to the pottery meant that workers were under pressure to drink as they were kept waiting for either their wages or change.

Village children at the turn of the century

Sickness often struck with frightening suddenness and disastrous consequences. Tuberculosis, scarlet fever, diphtheria, pneumonia and the like still racked the tortured frames of young and old alike. Medical assistance was costly, distant and called upon only when death seemed imminent or when Reverend Fowler, Mrs. Bowers or the schoolmaster took it upon themselves to intervene. General levels of health were, however, rising steadily. Although the general physical condition of most people was still depressingly low average life expectancy had risen to forty-nine years for males and fifty-two years for females.

Against such a backdrop the glories of Empire and the Coronation Celebration held on 26th June, 1902, shone bright and glorious. Youngsters at school bred on a diet of impressive military victories against the overwhelming pagan hordes of the world's darker corners flushed with pride at the defeat of the Boers, saluted the flag, commemorated Oak Apple Day, paraded deferentially before the Vicar and the owners of the castle and recited with lusty, uneven incomprehension such stirring ballads as *The Charge of the Light Brigade', 'England and Freedom'* and *'The Pipes at Lucknow'*. For them the Celebration was an exciting and momentous occasion, for their parents a time for pride, relaxation and a brief respite from the cares of the world.

The day dawned crisp and cool with a promise of showers in the tumbled clouds. By mid-morning the immediate tasks of house and farm had been attended to and the parishioners clad in Sunday best and clutching precious coppers for fairings were beginning to flow excitedly towards the village. From Adderley Green, across Meir Hay, below Park Hall Hills and down towards the River Blithe came the people of the Adderley Green ward of the parish, across the fields and through Caverswall Wood came the people of Meir whilst somewhere between Silverdale and Caverswall the Silverdale Prize Band, specially booked for the occasion, rumbled sedately along in a horse-drawn conveyance.

By noon the service of thanksgiving in the parish church had reached the sermon; small droplets of rain raised anxious eyes to heaven as the ward processions, each a gaudy array of horse-drawn floats, fancy dresses, Sunday best and strident youth were converging on the field below the castle. Already the square, the side roads and The Dams were seemingly choked with carts and waggons whilst the exhortations of the booth holders and the shouts and laughter of the children brought an unaccustomed shrillness to the place.

At 1.30 p.m. in suitable solemnity the adults sat down to their dinner a typically English affair of roast beef, potatoes and vegetables shrouded in congealing gravy as the chilling summer wind cooled the plates and rippled the canopy of the huge marquee. Promptly at two the Silverdale Prize Band launched into the first of its selected pieces providing a distant musical background to the opening events of the children's sports. Flat Races, Human Wheelbarrow Races, Skipping Races, Potato Races, Egg and Spoon, Hopping, Tug-of-War and Vocal Solo events followed each other in a flurry of excitement as representatives of the three wards vied with each other as much for the honour of the ward as for the money prizes awarded to the victors. The programme records the nature of the events and the value of the prizes.

CHILDREN'S PROGRAMME

Commencing at Two

BOYS	Prizes		GIRLS	Prizes	
	I st	2nd		I st	2nd
1. Flat Races (60 yards)			1. Flat Races (60 yards)		
Two Races Under 9	1/-	6d	Two Races Under 9	1/-	6d
Two Races 11- 13	2/-	1/-	Two Races 11- 13	2/-	1/-
2. Human Wheelbarrow Races			2. Skipping Rope Race		
7 - 10	2/-	1/-	7 - 10	2/-	1/-
10 - 13	2/-	1/-	10 - 13	2/-	1/-
13 - 14	2/-	1/-	13 - 14	2/-	1/-
3. Sack Races			3. Skipping Rope Competition		
7 - 10	2/-	1/-	7 - 10	2/-	1/-
10 - 13	2/-	1/-	10 - 13	2/-	1/-
4. Potato Race ..	1/-	6d	4. Egg and Spoon Race	1/-	6d
5. Three-Legged Race	2/-	1/-	5. Threading Needle	1/-	6d
6 Old Tall Hat and Umbrella Race	1/-	6d	6. Polka-step Race	1/-	6d
7. Hopping Race	1/-	6d	7. Hopping Race .	1/-	6d
8. Bell Race (boys & girls)	1/-	...			
9. Tug-of-War (scholars in 3 Wards) 12-a-side		6d each			
10. Best Solo (Vocal)	2/6	1/6	10. Best Solo (Vocal)	2/6	1/6
Best Comic Dress			Prettiest Fancy Dress		
Each Ward	2/6		Each Ward	2/6	
On Field	5/-		On Field	5/-	

ADULTS' PROGRAMME

	Entry Fee	Prizes		
	Each	Ist.	2nd	3rd
I . Pony Race (Starts at 4 p.m.)	2/6	£1	10/-	2/6
2. Football Contest (6-a-side)	6d	Football Medals		
3. Flat Races				
(a) 14-16(100yards)	3d	5/-	2/6	1/-
(b) 16 - 21 (120yards)	1/-	15/-	7/6	5/-
(c) Open (120yards)	1/-	15/-	7/6	5/-
4. High Jump	6d	7/-	3/6	
5. Bicycle Obstacle Race	1/-	10/-	5/-	2/6
5a. Flat Race (Obstacle)	-	4/-	2/-	
6. Sack race	-	5/-	2/6	

7. Donkey Race	1/-	10/-	5/-	
8. Three-Legged Race	-	3/-	2/-	1/-
9. Hurdle Race	3d	5/-	2/6	
10. Skipping Rope Race (Females)	-	5/-	2/6	1/-
11. Human Wheelbarrow Race (14 - 16)	-	3/-	2/-	1/-
11a Skipping Rope Competition (Females)	-	5/-	2/6	1/-
12. Threading the Needle(Females)	-	3/6	1/6	
13. Egg and Spoon Race (Females)	-	4/-	2/-	1/-
14. Potato Race (Females)	-	4/-	2/-	1/-
15. Running Backwards	-	3/-	1/6	
16. Greasy Pig Hunt	-	Pig		
17. Climbing Greasy Pole	-	Leg of Mutton		
18. Roll and Treacle Competition	-	4/-	3/-	2/-
19. Singing Competition for Men over 55	-	5/-	2/6	
20. Singing Competition for Women over 55		5/-	2/6	
21. Tug-of-War (8-a-side)	-	Medals		

By late afternoon the children's events had been completed and competitor and specta-tor alike had been regaled in the same marquee which had earlier housed their parents. Subsequently their attention had been drawn towards the strenuous efforts of the adults as they ran, jumped, skipped, threaded needles, ran backwards and grovelled in specially prepared mud for an elusive, frightened and very slippery pig.

As the chill of a grey summer evening began to creep across the fields the marquee became a dance hall and tavern. A bonfire poured its smoke into a darkening sky and

The village school's (sic) and its pupils during the early years of the headship of H. Barton Land

fireworks brought noise and spectacle to the closing proceedings, their riot of sound and colour giving clear warning to those who lived farthest away that a brisk walk home through darkened lanes lay ahead. Within and around the Square the gaiety and exuberance heightened by alcohol continued until darkness and the prospect of work accompanied by an aching head drew a gentle shroud over the proceedings.

*The village school in 1977. Some of its pupils recreate the poses
adopted by their predecessors*

In 1901 the total population of the parish numbered some 6,880, by 1911 it had risen to some 7,500 and by 1921 had attained a total figure of rather more than 10,000 of which some 2,780 were resident at Meir. Apart from a slow and gradual expansion of housing development around the borders of the parish very little else changed. Weston Coyney was still a pleasing little farming village[44] which it was to remain until the 1950s. Werrington remained a scatter of dwellings until the 1930s saw the upsurge of ribbon development along the sides of the main road although the building of Werrington Church which commenced in 1906, the disappearance of the Red Lion Public House in 1905 and the closure of the brickworks and marl hole at the site now covered by the playing fields of Moorside High School in 1904 all brought minor changes to the landscape. Similar movements in the location of the coal workings also brought an air of change to the fringes of Wetley Moor whilst retaining the overall sense of continuity. The appearance of derricks and drilling gear in the vicinity of Dead Man's Grave during the years 1918 and 1919 marked the abortive attempts of American engineers to find oil within the parish. Adderley Green became slowly absorbed into the expanding landscape of Longton as its colliery and the Mossfield pit prospered and attracted colliers to the area.

Hulme, just over the hill from Adderley Green slowly fell away as its people drifted into the towns in search of a life easier and more generous than that which had traditionally been the lot of the people of Hulme.

The Caverswall Mens' Society entering church possibly prior to a Beating the Bounds Ceremony

The Mens' Society on duty during 'Carsa Wakes'

The Mens' Society taken some time before 1915 because both the Rev. Fowler (seated centre) and H. Barton Land, Headmaster, (standing beneath the banner) left the village in that year

1914 AD

THE MIRTH DIES

The village and parish of 1914 were not too different from their predecessors in structure, population and purpose. Change had come slowly and worked gradually upon the lives of the people. The Bowers family still influenced and dominated the village as they had done from their arrival in 1890. Reverend Fowler was replaced by Reverend Horspool in 1915 after 14 years of a ministry dedicated to the people and parish he loved so well. Men marched away proudly resolved to *give the Kaiser fits'* and some, those whose engraved names bear proud witness to their last and greatest sacrifice, failed to return.

The knitting circle, a group of ladies who knitted socks, gloves, scarves and Balaclava helmets for the troops in the trenches. Rev. Barton Horspool, brother of the captain of the S.S. Clarissa Radcliffe is seated centre.

By one of those strange quirks of historical accident which occur not infrequently the parish was reminded of one of the past owners of the Castle, Sir Joseph Percival Radcliffe, who had lost much of his fortune in the early 1880s and been forced to seek more modest accommodation in the north-east of England.

The family fortunes had been retrieved to some extent by dint of hard work and in 1915 Messrs. Craig, Taylor and Co. Ltd. of Stockton launched a steel screw steamer of 5,754 gross tonnage, the S.S. Clarissa Radcliffe, named after a descendant of the old Caverswall family,. Throughout the war years the S.S. Clarissa Radcliffe crossed and recrossed the Atlantic usually carrying cargoes of steel or coal destined for war work, from the United States to England.

On 12th March 1918 she was travelling to Newport News in ballast when, five miles offshore, she was attacked by a German submarine, shelled and torpedoed. Although badly damaged the ship was coaxed to shore and repaired in Portland Harbour before resuming her patient work. Subsequently her battle scarred ensign was presented to St. Peter's Church by her Captain who, almost unbelievably, was the brother of Reverend Frederick Barton Horspool. The ensign hung behind the pulpit until the early 1950s when its remnants were burned, the ravages of time having completed the destruction begun by German shells. The Clarissa Radcliffe continued voyaging until 1943 when she was again torpedoed by a German submarine whilst on a voyage, in convoy, from New York to Barrow. She sank with the loss of all hands.

Within the parish the strains of war were beginning to show in many ways but perhaps the most telling comment on the spirit of the people of Caverswall and the relief which surged through the village at the news of the Armistice is to be found in the log book of St. Peter's.

For 4th November 1918 there appears an entry recording the fact that the pupils had been granted a holiday to celebrate the fact that *'the 46th North Midland Division achieved a brilliant feat of arms on the Western Front on September 30th'*.

The writing is characteristic of that which precedes it throughout the period of the war, small, neat, precise and careful.

For 11th November the entry reads: *'Armistice signed by Germany. News received at 11.45 a.m. In the afternoon a Flag Demonstration was held.'*

The writing is large, sprawling and uneven, its irregularities betraying the bounding heart and shaking nerves of Headmaster Brindley in a way that no other form of expression could.

YOUR KING AND COUNTRY THANK YOU.
Christmas Greetings from St. Peter's, Caverswall.

A typically patriotic Christmas card of a type widely issued in a form which allowed the name of the parish church to be added

1920 AD   TO THE PRESENT DAY

WHEEL ME GENTLY INTO THE GARAGE

From 1920 onwards the motor car became an increasingly prevalent feature of village life. Slowly at first and then with increasing rapidity it altered the pace and style of life within the village community. Ten years earlier the motor vehicle had been a novel feature of the rural scene and press reports of a head-on crash between two cars at Meir cross-roads in 1911 had attracted much wonder and head shaking throughout the parish. Throughout the 1920s accidents became increasingly common and pedestrians marvelled at the speeds of 25 or 30 miles per hour being attained by motor buses.

The period following the Second World War saw the formation and growth of three significant local transport companies known locally as Shirley's, Ratcliffe's and Berresford's. Each was the result of individual energy, vision and tenacity. Together the three companies provided a framework around which the life and work of the local area prospered. Harold Ratcliffe provided a general haulage service for local industry at a time when the ravages and shortages of the war years were being overcome and the network of small men that was taking shape needed cheap, reliable and immediate transport. James "Jimmy" Berresford provided a coach and omnibus service which facilitated travel in those days before the family car became ubiquitous and deserved the well earned reputation for keeping going long after the others had returned to their garages when bad weather forced vehicles off the road. James "Jim" Shirley chose to specialise in bulk liquid transport and developed a flourishing family business which, at the end of the century, had a strong European connection. By complementing each other those three entrepreneurs made an important contribution to the life, prosperity and growth of the Caverswall area from 1945 onwards. Local builders made good use of this infra-structure and two of them Oswald Coupe and James "Jim" Horton played an important role in the expansion of Weston Coyney during the late 1940s and early 1950s. Both are commemorated in street names. Jim Horton played an important role in the social life of the community, he and his family were instrumental in creating and establishing the Weston Coyney Village Hall. Other local builders whose names are perpetuated in street names were Percy Axon (Axon Crescent) and Hughie Haynes (Hayner Grove)

The great red brick rash that was the Meir spread rapidly over the southern part of the parish during the 19 years between 1920 and the outbreak of war in 1939. In 1921 the population of Meir totalled 2,780, by 1939 it had risen to a figure slightly in excess of 14,000 housed in some 3,000 new homes of which 2,000 were council provided. These families brought new problems, pressures and challenges to the parish although by far the greater portion of the task of ministering to the needs of the newly created community fell upon the church of Holy Trinity, a daughter church of St. Peter's, Caverswall, which had been consecrated in 1891 to minister to the needs of the growing community. One of the principal players in the task of funding and encouraging the new church was Mrs. Bowers of Caverswall Castle whose name was inscribed on one of the foundation stones. The first organist at Holy Trinity was Havergal Brian one of the twentieth century's most prolific composers.

HAVERGAL BRIAN

Havergal Brian was born on 29th. January, 1876, in Dresden. He showed a considerable aptitude for music in his youth and became deputy organist of St. James' Church in Uttoxeter Road, Longton at the age of twelve. The principal organist at that time seemed to have been uncomfortable with the young prodigy and eventually Brian moved to the new church, Holy Trinity at the Meir. Coming from a family which believed in the virtue of having a trade in one's hands young Havergal was dissuaded from pursuing the prospect of an organ scholarship at Cambridge and he was apprenticed as a joiner.

However his love of music persisted and by the first decade of the 20th. century he had begun to receive recognition as a talented composer. His success with a setting of Shakespeare's sonnet 'Shall I compare thee to a Summer's day?' at the Three Choirs Festival in Worcester earned him the friendship of Edward Elgar. His first symphony, 'The Gothic' was not well received, some critics described it as unperformable, although its first public performance was kindly received. His work enjoyed something of a revival in the 1950's when it was championed by a number of professional musicians. He died in 1972 aged almost 97 years and left behind a total of seven operas, 32 symphonies, 15 major vocal/orchestral pieces and a vast number of lesser compositions.

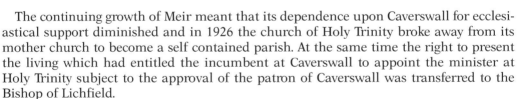

The continuing growth of Meir meant that its dependence upon Caverswall for ecclesiastical support diminished and in 1926 the church of Holy Trinity broke away from its mother church to become a self contained parish. At the same time the right to present the living which had entitled the incumbent at Caverswall to appoint the minister at Holy Trinity subject to the approval of the patron of Caverswall was transferred to the Bishop of Lichfield.

Once again the menace of war began to loom over the village. Old soldiers with memories of the 1914 - 18 war spoke pessimistically of 'the next one'. Young men thrilled to the prospect of military adventures and speculated upon affairs beyond their ken. The menace and the horror of war moved suddenly very close to the village when, in 1938, the Vicar of Caverswall, Rev: Vincent Gower Jones who had, with forethought and vision, organised a Caverswall and Weston Coyney branch of the Air Raid Protection (A.R.P) service, found himself faced with the formidable task of fitting and distributing some 2,000 gas masks. Aided by members of the Church of England Mens' Society the task was completed in just three evenings with people queuing patiently to receive their masks from distribution points set up at the Red House, the Church School and the Weston Coyney Institute. The Vicarage was identified as an A.R.P. post and so the Vicar was able to have installed the first telephone in the village.

Caverswall's Civil Defence teams at the outbreak of war

Among the myriad strains, stresses and sounds which the war years brought to the parish came the echo of strange, near alien voices. The arrival of one group is recorded by two entries in the school log book for 1939 which, in addition, are not without humour for those who enjoy bureaucratic disasters.

On 3rd August 1939 the head of St. Peter's recorded in the Log Book the news that, after much prolonged unrest and debate about the size and capacity of the school, official confirmation had been received that the buildings could not accommodate more than 100 pupils.

On 5th September 1939 the Log Book records the arrival of an additional 120 pupils from the Crowcroft Park School, Manchester. A week later the school went onto a shift system whilst the playground echoed to the strains of Mancunian voices raised in those playground singing games typical of urban schools but less well known in rural areas.

The American airmen based on the Meir Aerodrome brought yet another sound to the parish. The transatlantic twang completing such a mixture of tongues as the parish had not known since the days of William de Caveswell when Anglo-Saxon, Norman/French and Latin had been heard in daily use.

Victory in World War Two produced a more restrained response from the headmaster John Brindley, perhaps because it had been apparent for some time before the war ended that victory was certain. Nevertheless there is little doubt that the school and the village enjoyed a great sense of relief when the war ended and the task of rebuilding the village community could begin.

Until the early 1950s very little happened to change the landscape of the parish although the motor vehicle became an increasingly regular feature of daily life and a bowser was established at Sproston's Corner. Small scale sporadic building curbed by governmental restrictions, a need for licences and local authority sanctions; did little to alter the face of the land or the character of the place. Indeed a visiting writer in 1960 was able to describe Weston Coyney as a *'genuine farming village inside the City boundary '*[44]. Although the latter part of his statement was incorrect until the boundary changes of the mid '60s it is true to say that, until the great explosion of housing development during the 1960s and 1970s, Weston Coyney did retain its gentle, rural character. The establishment of the Coalville housing estate on land overlooking Billy Nuns marked the beginning of a more extensive phase of development. The use of Cornish Unit houses brought a new style of building into the parish creating a social landscape which differed markedly from the traditional stone built houses and the later brick built properties.

At the time that Weston Coyney and Werrington were expanding a similar rash of development began to nibble into Caverswall. The old vicarage, a bulky, rather damp building was demolished and a new housing development based on Vicarage Crescent established. The heart of the village remains protected by a conservation order which should preserve for ever the gentle reminders of earlier days which abound in this most interesting of villages. Sadly, however, the growth in car ownership has seen a significant change in the character of the village particularly in relation to the intensity of vehicular traffic in School Lane. A commuting population together with those who use School Lane as an alternative route has led to a steady and massive increase in traffic through the village. A traffic survey carried out by pupils from St. Peter's in 1974 revealed that on average, one vehicle passed the school every twelve seconds. In 1992 a repeat survey revealed an average of 32 vehicles a minute passing the school. The introduction of traffic calming measures has done something to divert some of this traffic to other routes and has left , as a mark on the landscape, the so called sleeping policemen or speed humps.

The castle remained in the possession of the Bowers family until 1932. The male heir to the property, William Aubrey Bowers, had died of wounds in 1916, his father had died five years earlier and once again the castle passed into female ownership. By 1932 the size of the building, the cost of its upkeep and the sad memories it contained proved too much for Mrs. W. E. Bowers who moved out and in 1933 sold the property to a group of Missionary Sisters, Servants of the Holy Ghost.

Memorials to the Bowers family abound. The metal alms plate incorporates in its inscription the 'grateful memory of Alice Bowers.' The carved wooden cover of the baptismal font has incised into it the statement that :-

'This font cover was given by his sisters for the glory of God in loving memory of William Aubrey Bowers. Born Jan: 22nd 1887 died of wounds July 2nd 1916.'

In the South Aisle the most easterly of the south facing windows was given
'To the glory of God and in loving memory of William Bowers of Caverswall Castle who was born Anno Domini 1861 and who died AD 1911; this window is erected by his widow and his son and daughters.'

William Bowers made a number of significant alterations to the fabric of the castle, building Lodges at the eastern and western points of entry, building stables and improving the gardens. Perhaps most important of all from the standpoint of the community, he laid out a cricket ground which was to become known as one of the most beautiful in Staffordshire sited as it was below the tree lined bulk of The Dams and south-west of the castle with impressively open views to the south.

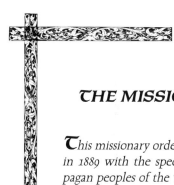

THE MISSIONARY SISTERS OF THE HOLY GHOST

This missionary order was founded in Holland by a Dutch priest, Father Arnold Janssen, in 1889 with the specific aim of converting and bringing salvation to the heathen and pagan peoples of the world.

At its peak the order had missions world wide but political upheaval in China and the First World War saw it withdraw, with reluctance, from China, Togo and Mozambique. The first sisters of the order arrived in England in 1930.

In 1933 Caverswall castle was chosen as a suitable base for a training institution which could produce English speaking sisters with a view to extending the work of the order in the countries of the Commonwealth. The first English postulants were received in 1934, the castle was also developed as a base from which sisters who wished to teach could gain an English Teachers' Certificate.

To meet the requirements of the order some structural changes were made among which was the conversion of the billiard room into a chapel.

Among the carvings on the principal staircase is one of a unicorn, a fabulous beast which, according to legend, could only captured by a maiden of unblemished virtue. Perhaps the legend of the White Lady of Caverswall and the garland of chastity is not unconnected with the folklore surrounding this carving.

Through the late 1940s and early 50s the castle grounds were thrown open on one day in the year for a garden fete in which all village communities joined. Between 1940 and 1965 the Sisters made a significant contribution to the education of Catholic pupils in the area by taking over and running St. Filumena's school. The contribution made by Sister Eloise (H.E. Waldorf) as Headmistress was an important one and gave the school a much needed period of stability.

The Missionary Sisters were the third religious order to reside at the castle. Between 1811 and 1853 it was the home to a community of Benedictine Nuns who had fled from Belgium to escape the troubles of the Napoleonic Wars. Before that, at some date around 1515 to 1540 it seems to have been a 'Priory Channons'; a priory of canons; for Leland refers to it in his Itinerary as 'late a Priory Channons, sumtyme belonging to the Montgomerikes now to the Giffards'. A modern translation suggests however that this may be a misreading of two references compounded by confused writing since the contemporary version reads . . . . . a castle or attractive fortress at Caverswall four miles from Stone. At Stone there was a priory of canons, which once belonged to the Montgomery family and now to the Giffards.

By 1930 the order had established missionary bases among pagan and heathen peoples throughout the world and financed itself, in part at least, by undertaking a variety of forms of social work in the centres of civilisation. Their first English house was established in 1930 and by 1933 the Order had grown to the point at which it felt itself to be in need of a convent, the Castle was purchased for that purpose.

The first Sisters arrived on 27th June 1933 and began the task of developing the convent in accordance with the principles of the Order.

These Sisters occupied the castle until 1966 when it passed to an allied order calling itself Daughters of the Heart of Mary who ran the castle essentially as a guest home for elderly ladies. Although the need for the services of the Order did not diminish, recruitment to it did and by 1977 the castle had become surplus to the requirements of the order.

In June 1978 the castle was sold to a group of families named respectively Milner, Bellamy, Bunn, Sherlock, Ham, Mallett and Lucas for a sum reputed to be slightly in excess of £100,000.

Part of the castle changed hands again in 1993 when Brian Milner left for health reasons and Mr. Sargent purchased his portion of the castle. Part of the main building and the corner towers were converted into unique and unusual bed and breakfast accommodation bringing a new lease of life to this attractive and fascinating castle.

Park Hall shortly before its demolition

Park Hall was allowed to decay after an inglorious period as a 'club' until it was finally gutted by fire and demolished. A housing development took over the bulk of the site but local residents fought a stern and vigilant battle to preserve the lake which remains an attractive reminder of a stately past.

On the opposite side of the road the skyline of the Park Hall Hills was saved from the attentions of both building developers and gravel extractors to remain, enriched on the City side, by the development of a country park based on the quarry created by the working of the sand and gravel. On the Caverswall side the area was planted with trees to conceal the industrial scars and bring a sylvan aspect to what had been a rather unattractive sky line. This development has brought a much valued leisure and recreational facility to the area.

As part of the 1980 Festival a troupe of Morris Dancers performed in the square. The area had to be closed to traffic on that day

Adderley Green is now closely identified with Longton, the Mossfield Colliery to which it owed much of its growth is gone and has been replaced by a more gentle but less evocative veneer of light industrial development.

Werrington has grown out of all recognition. Development has flowed over the landscape in such a torrent that of the many traces of earlier activity, almost all have been eradicated. A new parish has been formed to minister to the needs of the area and increasingly the two main elements of the former unit Caverswall and Werrington are developing their own discrete characteristics and interests. The development of the St. Andrew's Centre at Weston Coyney has added a new dimension to worship within the parish but has put at risk the church at Caverswall. The restructuring of small rural churches within the diocese saw Caverswall united with Dilhorne.

Hulme remains almost untouched, a pleasant and quiet oasis as yet free from the all engulfing tide of brickwork which has done so much since 1950 to change the appearance and the spirit of the place.

In 1999 a committee of local people working to raise money for a village hall and community centre received a grant from the National Lottery. The grant was of a sufficient size to ensure the success of the project. A site was earmarked near the Red House, on the playing field which itself occupies the site of the former village mill pond. The provision of a substantial car park on the site indicates yet again how the dominant social influence at the end of the millennium was the motor vehicle. This theme was reinforced by the opening of an improved road, using a tunnel to carry through traffic below the area known as Meir, along the line of the former Roman road at the southern end of the parish.

The original school building in 1975. The section which was added in 1906 can be identified by the change on colour of the roof tiles to the right of the building

Over the post-war years a steady stream of pupils flowed through St. Peter's school and moved on to lives and careers markedly different from those available to their predecessors. William de Kaveriswelle had his cart load of silver pennies, those who now occupy his village use plastic credit cards. The people of Kaveswelle relied upon the itinerant minstrel or the passing pedlar for news of the outside world, present day Caverswallians have access to satellite television and world news at the touch of a switch. William de Kaverswelle's right of way for two or four wheeled carts across The Dams and through the village has become a road system which carries a steady flow of motor vehicles necessitating the introduction of traffic calming measures. The mysterious potions of the wise woman have become the benefits of conception to cremation health care and average life expectancy has risen to seventy-six years. Perhaps those persons who appear in the following pageant of St. Peter's School might like to reflect on the changes they have seen and rejoice that, each in his or her own way, has had an opportunity to take something from and to give something back to the village they can be proud to call home.

A selection of photographs showing staff and pupils across the decades.

A NOTE ON RUM-TUM-TARDY-UM

The precise origins of 'Rum-Tum-Tardy-Um' are uncertain. The tune itself bears that rhythmic lilt which is typical of English country music and may well be of some antiquity.

There is evidence to suggest that it served as the marching song of the Caverswall Moorland Volunteers, a local defence unit formed by Reverend Sir George Bowles during the Napoleonic Wars. Those worthies may well have marched to the tune singing words not too much different from these:

'From Cookshill Green and Carsa come Staunch true men against Napoleon But he's too afeared, he darena' come That scurvey French knave Napoleon.'

However rural humour being what it is and Reverend Bowles being noted for one particular unclerical failing the volunteers rapidly amended the words to reflect their own views of the situation. When the threat of invasion diminished after 1805 the group became a social and charitable club whose early proclivities gave a fair indication of the problem facing 'feythur'.

With the passage of time the Mens' Friendly Society became respected in the village and earned high esteem by the quality of its work.

A group of young Caverswallians pay their own tribute to Rum-Tum-Tardy-Um during Carsa Wakes possibly during the early 1930s

A BRIEF NOTE ON THE HISTORY OF St. PETER'S C.E. (AIDED) PRIMARY SCHOOL CAVERSWALL

The earliest record of education of village children is to be found in the reply to the Bishop of Lichfields survey prepared by Joseph Saunders in 1773. the survey had been distributed in April, 1772 but the incumbent at that time was too ill to respond. it was left to his successor to provide the necessary information. In the survey it is reported that :-

The honourable lord Viscount Vane voluntarily gives to Mr. Heal fifteen pounds a year for teaching twenty eight children either boys or girls, to read, write and understand the first four rules of vulgar Arithmetic........

In 1825 William Bradbury occupied the site upon which stood '*the school house which hath lately been erected by public subscription.*' As William Bradbury was the licensee of the Red House it is probable that the site was used either for grazing stock or, perhaps more probably, given its size, as a vegetable garden. The move to purchase the site of that house and the surrounding area for £10 of lawful money from Thomas Hawe Parker secured for the village the site upon which the school still stands. It was not until 1861 that work began on the buildings which even today provide the main part of the school.

Accurate records date from 9th. March, 1863 when the first entry was made in the school log book. The duty of keeping of a log book or diary was imposed on all schools in the Revised Code of Regulations issued in May, 1862. The first entries for St. Peter's refer to heavy snow which kept many pupils away from school and parental complaints about under achieving pupils

A group of pupils from the early years of the school. The Headmaster is H. Barton Land, the lady front left is Mrs. Stone whose husband died of typhoid fever in November 1893. This picture was taken on the 8th. July 1910.

It is possible to detect a measure of cynical bitterness in the headteacher's observation that Elizabeth Simcock and her brother Albert would make better progress if they actually attended school. Elizabeth managed 187 attendances out of a possible 773 whilst her brother had attended on only 21 days in two years.

On 7th. January, 1864 the log book notes:-

Cold very severe, ink frozen. Thermometer in school-room, thirty four [Fahrenheit]

The River Blithe is a misfit stream. It occupies a valley created by glacial floodwaters not by river erosion. The broad, shallow valley flooded readily after heavy rain often cutting-off Caverswall from its neighbours and preventing pupils from reaching school.

Heavy snowfalls or rain which caused the River Blythe to flood and isolate the village for several hours at a time regularly affected attendance. Local auction sales, a meet of the Moorland beagles, special events in neighbouring villages or Carsa Wakes also caused pupils to absent themselves. Occasionally the school was granted a half-holiday as happened in 1889 when the school went to watch the inaugural match on the new village cricket pitch. In 1869 James Finch recorded that the school had been closed for a fortnight at the end of August to allow pupils to assist with the corn harvest. By 1871 that break had become a four week long harvest holiday. Occasionally the register was not marked because the pupils were enjoying a treat, gathering blackberries! In 1918 that particular treat had extended into a school closure from the 18th to the 24th. of September.

Another form of treat resulted from the provision by benefactors of substantial teas for forty of the youngest pupils which had to be eaten before the school. What the rest of the school thought of such a practice is not recorded.

The log book also records the injuries suffered by staff tumbling over sun dried mud on rutted roads or slipping on frozen cart tracks. In a calm manner it records sudden deaths like that of Mary Brassington who became ill during a writing lesson on 13th. November, 1884 and died on the following day and that of Mary E. Burgess who died of burns when her clothes caught fire after she had been left alone at home.

Even the staff suffered. In 1884 Henry Stone and his wife Jane became Master and Mistress of the school. Their son, Herbert, died on 17th. May ,1888 and a daughter was buried on 15th. June, 1892 when the log book records:-

There was no school this afternoon. The Master's infant daughter was buried.

On 7th. November, 1893 it was recorded that :-

the Master left school during the afternoon as he felt to (sic) unwell to remain.

The log book later records :-

Henry Robert Stone the late master of this school died of typhoid fever this morning. Aged 42 years.

He was buried on the 24th. November, 1893.

The finger of suspicion points firmly towards an inadequate system of sewage disposal coupled with a polluted water supply. The log book entry for the 27th. November, reads :-

Mr. Inskip the sanitary inspector and Doctor Webb of Cheadle inspected the school premises during the day for the purpose of ascertaining, if possible, the cause of the fever.

Henry Stone's successor was Benjamin Collett who left abruptly on 31st. August, 1901. During his headship the school received steadily improving reports from Her Majesty's Inspectors (HMI). In 1891 the inspector observed that:-

The children are quiet and well behaved but are rather wanting in spirit and brightness. The instruction in Elementary Subjects varies a good deal in the different classes but is as a whole fairly good. Reading is poor. . . The infants class is well and carefully taught..... the teacher seems to have too much to do . . . the room is overcrowded . . . there are no desks for the infants and the floor is bad and some windows are broken

The problem of infant desks was of long standing. It had first been commented on 1878. The new desks arrived in February, 1896.

In 1892, desks apart, the report observed that :-

The results in all classes are as good and in some instances decidedly better than those of last year...I have no hesitation in classing the school as Good

Despite all his efforts Benjamin Collett's headship marked a time of falling rolls, declining income and a lively interest in the school's arrangements for sanitation and the provision of drinking water. Collett left abruptly in circumstances which prompted an investigation by HMI and suggested some form of dispute with the incumbent.

Punishments were savage. On 19th. August, 1863, three boys named Bullock, Walters and Richardson were punished for playing truant by having to hold a brick for the whole of the morning session. In addition they were required to learn twenty-six lines of poetry and were kept in school during the lunch hour and were so deprived of their lunch. The cane was used with some frequency; one boy was caned for bringing into school a ball which was confiscated by the Headmaster, presumably because he feared for the school windows. The same boy was then caned a second time for organising *'the shouting in the yard.'*

Good deeds were recorded with equal candour. On 3rd. May, 1918 the log book records how the Vicar called in to congratulate four boys on stopping a runaway horse.

The first of a sequence of long serving Heads arrived in 1901 when H. Barton Land took up the post. He served until 1916, ran a school which *'is very well conducted and where the educative value of the work is high,'* generous praise indeed from HMI. Mr. Barton Land was much concerned about conditions inside the classrooms particularly during the winter months and especially during January, 1912. The zeal with which he pursued the then Chief Education Officer, Mr. (later Sir) Graham Balfour resulted in the installation of a new heating system. In 1916 he won promotion and moved to a larger school in Cheadle. As a mark of their appreciation the staff and parents presented him with a pipe and silver ash bowl.

H. Barton Land-Headteacher 1901-1916

John Brindley was Head from 1916 to 1945. His great passion for all things rural ensured that pupils acquired a useful skill and developed a secure understanding of their local area. Through their efforts the school could always boast an attractive and colourful display of flowers around the school house. It was John who, perhaps following the healthy eating initiative launched two years earlier, took the pupils out of school during the late summer/early autumn to gather blackberries. The fact that some pupils chose to hand in baskets stuffed with moss beneath a layer of luscious fruit suggests that, perhaps, not every pupil appreciated the point of the exercise. Possibly the comment from one of the pupils involved, *'Well we never saw any of the jam'* explains everything. John also had to cope with the problems of overcrowding and part-time working in shared premises when, at the outbreak of the Second World War, 120 pupils from Crowcroft Park School in Manchester were housed in the village. For a school already overcrowded and with an officially confirmed capacity of 100 pupils, the arrival of the Crowcroft youngsters posed problems which could only be resolved by the adoption of a split-shift system in which the staff and pupils changed over at lunchtime.

A group of pupils together with their Headteacher Mr. J Brindley

The top class together with their teacher Mr. John Brindley

John Brindley and staff shortly after his appointment as Head

In 1945 John Brindley was promoted to the headship of a residential school for boys with behavioural problems and was replaced by William 'Bill' Ricketts. For ten years Bill wrestled with rising numbers in restricted accommodation. During this period two young teachers passed through the school before going on to headships in local schools. Harry Lovatt eventually became head of The Beeches at Blythe Bridge and Ron. Scholes became head at Werrington, Saltway. The opening of a new school at Weston Coyney hit St. Peter's hard and numbers dropped to a point at which, when Bill retired there were just 78 pupils in the school. Allied to this fall in numbers was a desperate teacher shortage which saw schools all over the country competing for a limited supply of qualified staff. With its poor accommodation St. Peter's found it hard to retain staff to such a point that, when yet another vacancy was reported to them, the governors expressed the hope that *'someone more reliable could be appointed.'*

The provision of an extension in 1957 gave the school much needed indoor toilets. Prior to this improvement the log book had recorded a number of head-on collisions between pupils rushing to and from the toilets in the rain!

*Above: The village school as it was during the
headship of Mr. Ricketts
(From a painting by Mrs. C.A. Worrall)*

*Right: The teaching staff in the early 1950's.
Harry Lovatt (on left) went on to become Deputy
Head at the newly opened Weston Coyney Junior
School and later Head of the Beeches Junior
School at Blythe Bridge,
Chris. Tranter (front left) became a Headteacher
at Northwood in Stoke-on-Trent,
Bill Ricketts died just before moving into a
retirement home,
the other teacher is
Miss Webster.*

Above: As numbers rose the teaching staff expanded to keep pace with the needs of the pupils and Miss Layland joined the teaching staff

Right: Mr. Bill Ricketts and staff, Bill was Headteacher from 1945- 1973.
The teacher standing to the left of the back row returned to St. Peter's as deputy head towards the end of the 1970s as numbers rose

The staff shortly before the retirement of Mr. Ricketts in 1973. The lady seated centre is the long serving school secretary, Mrs. Constance Porter.

In 1973 Mrs. Kathleen Rogers became Headteacher, the first headmistress in the 200 year long history of Anglican education in Caverswall. In the September of that year the school opened with Mrs. Rogers and three newly trained, probationary teachers all holding permanent appointments. One of those teachers was a village girl, Hillary Brassington, who went on to become a Headteacher in her own right. This arrangement put the school on a stable footing for the first time since 1945.

The school in 1973. It was this team Barbara Machin, Hillary Brassington, Paul Adams, Constance Porter (Secretary), Rev. Jim Carr and Mrs. Rogers who laid the foundations upon which the school grew and flourished. The other man was Mr Millan, a post-graduate student teacher

In May, 1974 , the school participated in a ceremony to mark the opening of an extension which gave it a hall and a kitchen, the long awaited fruits of Mr. Rickett's labours. Prior to that event meals had been served in a temporary Horsa unit which was demolished when its decaying fabric became a danger to pupils.

With the confidence which comes from adequate accommodation and a core of settled and able teachers the school moved from strength to strength. The log book records a sequence of successes including several invitations to display its work in the County Council tent at the Staffordshire County Show, the organisation of a lively, parish wide pageant depicting almost 900 years of village history (actively encouraged and led by the Vicar, Rev. Jim Carr whose initial idea and enthusiasm proved infectious), Easter Bonnet Competitions, a variety of fund raising activities with a strong charitable theme, a variety of entertainments in which all pupils were able to participate, the display of work on the County Council narrow boat at the opening of the Stoke on Trent Garden Festival and in 1987 success in a nationally organised 'Wonderful World of Nature' competition. The prize for that triumph was a visit to the school by Doctor David Bellamy a television pundit and international personality in the battle to conserve the natural assets and resources of the planet. Doctor Bellamy arrived by helicopter and presented the school with a cheque for £1,000 and the gift of a week's holiday spent on narrow boats travelling down the River Thames, an experience enjoyed by every member of the year group.

A group of pupils dressed in the manner of their Victorian forebears who participated in the 1980 Festival

These years were not without their problems and staff changes but the hardest blow fell in September, 1979 when an electrical fault in the chair store of the recently added hall caused a fire which did extensive damage to the hall and covered every part of the school with an oily, black film the smell of which lingered for almost a year after the damage had been made good.

Dr. David Bellamy, Mrs. Rogers and the victorious team on the occasion of Dr. Bellamy's visit to the school.

The staff of St. Peters in 1990. They are (back row) Mrs. Rita Wood, Mrs. Janet Percival, Mrs. Pam. Lightfoot, Mrs. Joy Roberts, Mrs Sue. Plant. (front row) Mrs. F. Tams (Deputy Head), Mrs. Barbara Machin, Mrs. Kathleen Rogers (Headteacher), Mr. Paul Adams, Mrs. Brenda Worsdale (Secretary)

Silver Jubilee Celebrations, an open air party in 1977

Silver Jubilee Celebrations, a fancy dress parade (1977)

Throughout the 1980s the number of pupils attending the school rose steadily until it became necessary to provide additional accommodation. The provision of two more class-rooms and a redesigned main entrance was not without its problems. Barely had work begun when the digger exposed the remains of an old air raid shelter, erected in 1940, demolished in 1957 and forgotten until its vestiges were exposed in 1984.

Mrs. Rogers retired in 1994 and was replaced by Mr. David Beardmore. He had the doubtful pleasure of leading the school through its first formal inspection under the Ofsted (Office for Standards in Education) regulations and the more pleasant task of opening an additional teaching area and library built into the roof space of the original 1861 building. An improvement which had been urged and worked for by his predecessor.

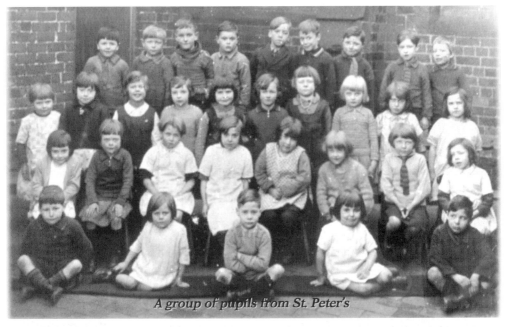

A group of pupils from St. Peter's

Despite the difficult times experienced during the 1930s these pupils seem happy

Dress and general well being show a steady improvement

A group of post-war pupils

The top class!

The school of the future, an artist's impression of St. Peter's when the trees have matured. From a painting by Tom Hinks owned by the school

HEADTEACHERS AT ST. PETERS C.E.A PRIMARY SCHOOL CAVERSWALL

1825 - 1850	No clear record.
1851 - ?	Mr. Thomas Rothwell
1863 - 1867	Mr. Edward Chinn.
1867 - 1870	Mr. James Finch
1870 - 1884	Mr. Joseph Sladen.
1884 - 1893	Mr. Henry Stone.
1894 - 1901	Mr. Benjamin Collett
1901 - 1916	Mr. H. Barton Land.
1916 - 1945	Mr. John Brindley.
1945 - 1973	Mr. William Ricketts.
1973 - 1994	Mrs. Kathleen Rogers.
1994 -	Mr. David Beardmore.

It is perhaps worth adding that :-

Joseph Sladen appeared to have an inexhaustible supply of sisters upon whom he could call to act as teachers. One of these, Sarah Jane, was examined by H.M.I. when it was found that she could not spell and was deficient in ... *Grammar, Arithmetic and Geography. She must improve generally.*

The widow of Henry Stone who died of typhoid fever in November 1893 continued to teach at the school until July, 1922. She died in February 1940.

In 1915 Mr. Barton Land worked as an orderly at the North Staffordshire Hospital between 6-30 p.m. and 4-30 a.m. assisting with war wounded before returning to school for his day job. In 1912 during the miners' strike he organised a soup dinner and tea for pupils suffering privations induced by the strike.

St. Peter's C.E.'A' Primary School the staff at the end of the century

A NOTE ON THE SCHOOL BUILDING

A plan of the original building has survived. Dated 1861 it shows how the school was designed and expected to function.

The creation of separate yards, or playgrounds, for boys and girls with their separate toilet facilities was considered inadequate by HMI who, in the report for 1878 required the two areas to be made quite separate by the creation of a dividing wall.

The location of the desks in the Mixed School and for the use of infant pupils in the gallery shows that the architect was thinking in terms of the monitorial approach. This system was devised by Andrew Bell who overcame a shortage of teachers by setting the older or more able pupils to teach the younger pupils. The system was not well received at first but was popularised by Joseph Lancaster and Robert Owen both of whom opened schools based on the monitorial system. The desks appear to have consisted of two planks, a higher and a lower, just over ten feet in length which allowed an indefinite number of pupils to be squeezed in. Pupils sat on one plank and rested their slates on the higher one in front of them.

The building incorporated a two storey Master's Residence with its own yard and outside water closet. The scullery was serviced by a water pump sunk into a well which drew its water from the spring line formed by the junction of two differing geological formations, the Keuper Sandstone and the Keuper Marl. The location of the outside toilets was intended to allow the liquor to drain away into the mill field. Solid waste was removed by the night soil cart or used as manure in the vegetable garden. Since the general fall of the ground was roughly along the line marked by the northern boundary of the site and slightly from top to bottom on the plan it is easy to understand the risk of contamination which was the prime cause of the typhoid fever which killed Mary Brassington, Henry Stone, Master and two of his children between 1884 and 1893. The poet spoke truly when he wrote *'My well and my privy drain into each other .... fevers and fluxes are wasting my mother'.*

St. Peter's School as it was in 1973. From an original painting by Tom.Hinks owned by Mrs. Rogers

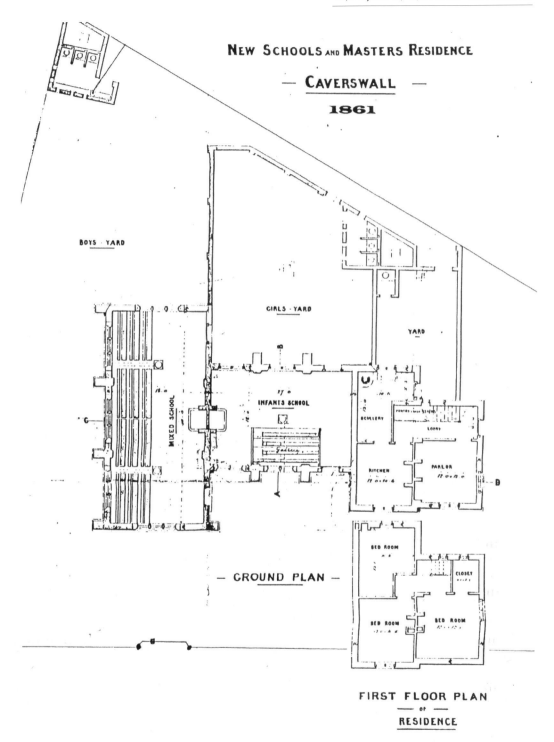

NEW SCHOOLS AND MASTERS RESIDENCE

— CAVERSWALL —

1861

BOYS · YARD

GIRLS · YARD

YARD

MIXED SCHOOL

INFANTS SCHOOL

SCULLERY

PANTRY

KITCHEN

PARLOR

BED ROOM

CLOSET

BED ROOM

BED ROOM

— GROUND PLAN —

FIRST FLOOR PLAN
— OF —
RESIDENCE

The original plan of the building - St. Peter's C. E. 'A' Primary School

The picture shows the original school building to the right of the new entrance and the modern hall. The Master's house lies to the extreme right of the building pointing towards the apex of the triangle. It was sold and turned into a private residence during the time that Rev. Patrick Youell was vicar (1966-72) largely on the grounds that pupil numbers were falling and the space was unlikely to be needed!

An aerial view depicts the school in 1990. It shows the triangular nature of the site, the original building with the Masters House to the right, the main teaching block with its 1906 extension carrying the school building to the edge of the footpath, the Hall and kitchen facility opened in 1974 and the additional teaching block opened in 1985.

A NOTE ON THE EDUCATION OF ROMAN CATHOLIC CHILDREN IN CAVERSWALL

In 1772 the Anglican Bishop of Lichfield conducted a survey of his diocese. The second question of that survey asked :-

Are there any papifts in you Parifh, and how many, and of what rank? Have any perfons been lately perverted to Popery, and by whom and by what means and how many and who are they? Is there any place in your parifh in which they affemble for worship and where is it? Doth any Popifh Prieft refide in your your Parifh, or refort in it; and by what name doth he go? is there any Popifh School kep in your Parifh? Hath any Conformation or Vifitation been lately held in your Parifh by any Popifh Bifhop; and by whom, and when; and how often is that done?

The newly arrived Anglican priest, Joseph Saunders must have been relieved to be able to respond in simple terms :-

I have not heard, neither do I know of any of thefe Matters

From 1811 to 1853 a community of Benedictine Nuns numbering fifteen in all, together with their confessor, lived in the castle. They worked assiduously among the village people trying to convert them to Catholicism. At the same time they ran a boarding school for Catholic girls drawn from the wealthier Catholic families in the Midlands. The school earned a good reputation and was soon oversubscribed. The school advertised its ability to offer :-

...the English and French languages, writing, arithmetic, history, geography, the use of globes and plain and ornamental works... all for thirty guineas per annum, to be paid half-yearly and one guinea entrance money. Tea, sugar, washing and books were extras.

St. Filumena's church designed by Sir Gilbert Blount and financed by Sir Joseph Percival Radcliffe

In 1853 for various reasons the community moved to Oulton near Stone. The castle was owned by or possibly leased for a time to a Mr Holmes. His successor and new resident of the castle was a Catholic, Sir Joseph Percival Radcliffe Bart: who built on the foundations laid by the nuns by establishing a Catholic church, St. Filumena's; a Presbytery and a school.

*St. Filumena's
Presbytery built
as part of
Sir J.P. Radcliffe's
move to establish
an effective
Roman Catholic
presence in
the village*

The log book for St. Peter's C.E. Primary School records that on 14th. May, 1866, the school admitted two pupils from Mrs. Ratcliffe's school which they had attended for five years. They were considered to be backward by the Master, Mr. Edward Chinn. Assuming that Ratcliffe is an incorrect spelling of Radcliffe this entry would seem to suggest that a Catholic school was operating in 1861. As the log book for St. Filumena's refers to holidays prior to the keeping of formal records there can be little doubt that the school predates its formal records.

During the early years of its existence the school met in a small building which subsequently became a barn. Life in those days was, to put it kindly, interesting. On 8th. January, 1868, Miss Elizabeth Looney was appointed Mistress. She worked hard and although, initially, she noted that *'the children are rather troublesome'* by November, 1868 a member of Her Majesty's Inspectorate was able to observe that it was *'a very well conducted school.'*

Throughout the following decades low levels of attendance were a frequent problem. The demands of harvest and the joys of blackberrying were additional challenges to those posed by heavy rain and deep snow. In 1869 having been warned of an impending visit by HMI the pupils were granted a holiday in order that the school might be cleaned. In May, 1871 it was recorded that smallpox was raging in the neighbourhood.

The original school building which was subsequently used as a barn. Only in the newer brickwork above the new door, the two lower windows and the two doors in the hayloft is there any indication of where windows might have been when this was a school.

The door into the original school room, now bricked up. The absence of any evidence that there were on the side shown, windows which have been filled in gives some indication of how gloomy the original school room must have been

In 1873 St. Filumena's was having structural problems, the existing building was deemed to be unsuitable. Its brick floor was uneven and damp and the premises generally were considered to be prejudicial to the children's health. The battle for better accommodation continued until 31st., May, 1878 when the pupils were given a holiday to allow the furniture to be transferred to the new building.

The present school was erected in 1878 and over the years since then has experienced much alteration and improvement

Even so things did not always run smoothly. The log book records problems with nails projecting from the floor boards and on several occasions refers to the need to close the school for cleaning before a visit from H M I. There was concern over 'the offices' because the boys and girls shared the same entrance. In 1899 HMI described the boys' urinal as 'almost unapproachable.'

St. Filumena's R.C. Aided Primary School, the building as erected in 1878. Later extensions are shown to the left and rear right of the original building.

Apart from a more intense emphasis on religious teaching with special preparation for the taking of the First Communion and for Confirmation, both of which were taught by the parish priest in school time, the curriculum followed very closely that on offer at the Anglican school.

The recruitment and retention of Mistresses was a problem. Between 1868 and 1918 the school had no fewer than twenty four Headteachers or Mistresses. the reasons for this turnover are many and various. Accommodation was a real problem even after the new building was provided. The salary for a lady teacher was low, prospects were limited, the pupils were not wholly enthusiastic about attending school, wet weather meant that pupils stayed at home or had to be dried out on arrival whilst heavy snowfalls caused problems which were compounded by the failure of the caretaker to light the fire in good time in cold weather. Temperatures as low as 30 F were recorded in the classroom during the coldest days of winter. In 1893 one of Her Majesty's Inspectors noted that *'the school is not light throughout.'* This absence of adequate natural light caused lessons to be suspended on one recorded occasion, 27th. February, 1906, because *'the morning was so dark that the children could not see to write in their books.'*

For much of the school's history during these early years the Mistress was expected to cope single-handed with up to seventy plus pupils supported only by monitors or unqualified staff. In 1887 HMI noted that . . . *'the numbers are too high for one teacher'.* In 1888 HMI remarked that the . . . *'staff should at once be strengthened'* . . . . The one assistant teacher who did survive had many short periods of absence citing a range of medical, health and domestic problems. The exasperation of the Mistress shows through a log book entry which records that *'Miss. . . . returned today after an absence of two days on the alleged excuse of the illness of her nephew'*. The catalogue of her previous excuses suggests that she had only nephews and nieces left!

From 1915 things improved steadily. The LEA became more active, the school received more professional support and guidance and central government began to play a more positive role. From this point onwards the log book records a steadily expanding level of activity by both the local and the national authority. The curriculum became tighter and more imaginative and positive action to improve children's health became a feature of school life. On 21st. September, 1931 the school received one portable Columbia Gramophone, four ten inch Columbia records and one twelve inch HMV record. By 1953 it had a wireless with an extension speaker for use in the Infants room. In February, 1955 the school gained voluntary aided status and on the 20th. June, 1958 the telephone was installed.

The most telling commentary on the history of St. Filumena's school is to be found in the reports written by HMI. The real story lies in the commitment and effort which saw the school move from *'. . . . . the children . . . are rather wanting in brightness... the Infants are backward in every respect... the instruction of the Infants must improve in every respect'* in 1882 to *'the education provided by the school is sound and in many areas of the curriculum is good'*: the opening remarks of the school's first report from the Office for Standards in Education (OFSTED). Hidden behind those reports is a record of over one hundred and thirty years of honest and sincere effort on behalf of Catholic pupils in Caverswall.

The Staff of St. Filumena's in 1998

The Recent Past - staff and pupils from St. Filumena's R. C. 'A' Primary School, Caverswall

THE HEADTEACHERS OF
ST. FILUMENA'S SCHOOL CAVERSWALL.

1868 - 1870	Elizabeth Looney.	? - 1902	Sarah Allen.
1871 - 1871	Ellen Graham.	1902 - 1902	Gertrude Walsh.
1871 - 1871	Kate Welsby.	1902 - 1903	Elizabeth Morris.
1871 - 1872	Elizabeth Stych.	1903 - 1903	Ellen Lumsden.
1872 - 1873	Mary Wilson.	1903 - 1903	Alice Winberry.
1874 - ?	Rose Anne White.	1904 - 1908	Catherine Francess
1876 -1876	Fanny Wood.		Tompkinson.
1877 - 1879	Ellem Mullins.	1908 - 1911	Mary McGowan.
!879 - 1881	Sarah Anderton.	1911 - 1912	Hilda G Doran.
1881 - 1881	Catherine Hammersley.	1913 - 1915	Magdalen A. Doran.
1882 - 1882	Fanny Hood.	1915 - 1915	Mrs. Greaves.
1882 - 1883	Margaret Anne Robinson.	1915 - 1918	Martha M. Owens.
1883 - 1887	Margaret Anne Eadeforth.	1919 - 1925	Grace Draper.
1887 - 1889	Mary Jane Fitzpatrick.	1925 - 1938	Josephine Hickson.
1889 - 1892	Sarah Allen.	1938 - 1940	Katherine Freeth.
1892 - ?	Margaret Connolly.	1940 - 1965	Sister Eloise (H.E.Waldorf).
		1965 - 1989	James Flynn.
		1990 -	Michael Wheatley.

St. PETER'S CHURCH CAVERSWALL
A LIST OF INCUMBENTS

A list of Incumbents based upon Landor, 'Staffordshire Incumbents' and Parish Records (1530 - 1680) and Hutchinson, 'The Archdeaconry of Stoke-on-Trent'.

Rectors

1230 R. . . persona de Kaveriswalle (possibly Robert) [The use of persona indicates the origin of the word parson. The persona was one who could sue or be sued on behalf of the parish]

1284 William de Fenton

Vicars

1307 Richard de Caverswell

1320 John de Smallys

1381 William Alcock (who was present in 1398)

1418 John Careswelle

1533 Nicholas Bolyvant

1535 Gregory Scarlett

1538 John Wildeblod

1554 Richard Walker

1563 Richard Hunter

1566 Richard Harrys

Curates

1568 John Bolt

1569 Thomas Bolt

1571 John Perkin

1573 William Reade

Vlcars

1590 George (Edwin) Borghe

1603 Ralph Turner

1612 Richard Barrow

1618 Alexander Howe

1630 Richard Bentley (Curate)

1637 Robert Marchenton (Curate)

1649 William Bott

1649 George Reeve

1662 John Burtinshaw

1660 James Corbet

1710 Robert Curnock (Curate)

1714 Thomas Margey

1715 John Perkes

1763 Samuel Willott

1773 Joseph Saunders

1792 Benhamin Woolfe

1795 St. George Bowles

1805 William Eddowes

1824 Ralph Sneyd

1826 Frederick Hodges

1829 Alexander Goode

1858 Henry Barnwell Greenwood

1865 Benjamin North Arnold

1878 Francis Aspinall Goddard

1889 John Gordon Addenbroke

1901 Harold Metcalfe Fowler

1915 Frederick Barton Horspool

1922 James Ransome Macnamara

1935 Vincent Gower Jones

1953 Victor Arthur Yates

1966 Patrick Youell

1972 James Arthur Carr

1985 Neil Jefferyes

The High Street in 1908

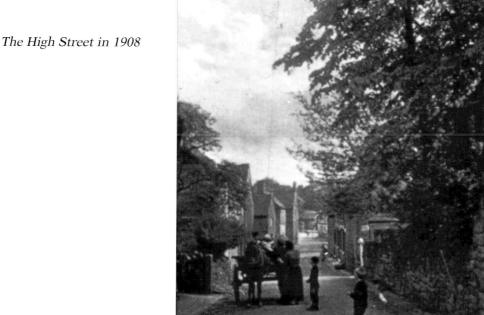

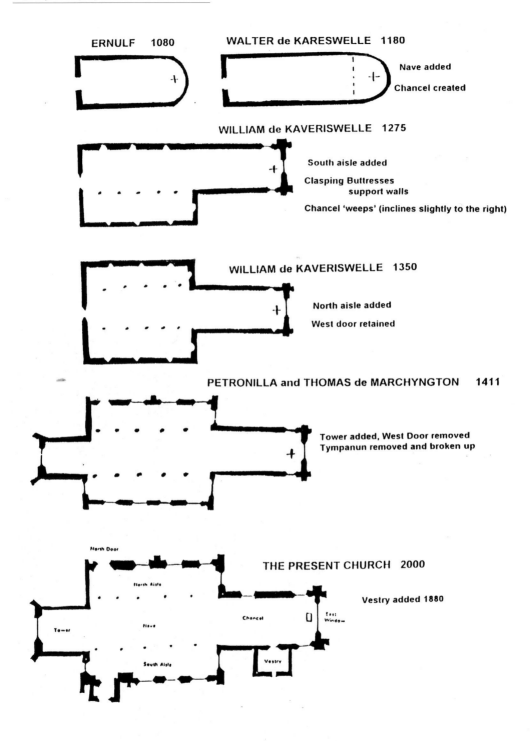

A plan of ages and stages in the evolution of St. Peter's Church, Caverswall

A Note on the Possible Evolution of St. Peter's Church, Caverswall

In the absence of clear documentary evidence when a church has been as grievously mauled during the processes of improvement and restoration as has St. Peter's attempts at dating the stages in its development must be undertaken with caution. Nevertheless it is possible to trace a probable sequence of development by measuring what documentary evidence does exist against a careful study of the fabric of the existing church as long as that task is discharged in the knowledge that some of the windows may be copies of earlier styles and that a measure of guess work is involved.

The first church erected in Caverswall was almost certainly a tiny wooden structure which would have been replaced by a slightly larger stone church, probably with the characteristically rounded, Romanesque east end, in the years before the Norman Conquest or possibly shortly after the arrival of Ernulf. It is probable that the church to which Domesday Book alludes was of this type and size.

For the Normans, who tended to believe that God's house should be the finest building in the village, the extension of the tiny Saxon building must have been a matter of some importance. The traditional way of effecting such an extension was to add a nave to the original building which became the chancel. During the three decades after 1150 AD this extension seems to have been the main concern of Walter de Kaverswelle. It may well have been his masons who fashioned the capital with nail-head carving which can be found at the respond of the first arcade on the north aisle. Equally they may well have fashioned the two massive corbel heads in the south aisle which are clearly much older than the other types found therein.

A clasping buttress, two of these were made necessary when the rounded Romanesque end was removed and the East window was added

The addition of the two aisles seems to have been carried out during the late 13th and early 14th centuries. The windows of the south aisle are of the early Decorated style which dates them at some period after about 1280 AD thus suggesting a date for the whole aisle. Two of the windows in the north aisle are of a type usually associated with the later phase of the Decorated era, 1350 AD or thereabouts, whilst the window at the east end of the north aisle is Perpendicular (1380 or thereafter) in style. On these grounds the north aisle is held to be later than the south. Equally it must be acknowledged that neither aisle may have been built and completed in one go. They may have been built in sections over an extended period of time or may have been extended outwards at some time.

With the exception of the Early English capital already mentioned the other capitals on the piers in the nave are all of the type described by the term scroll moulding which dates them somewhere round about 1300 AD a fact confirmed by the Decorated character of the bases of all of the piers save the first in the north aisle. Here the base is of Early English character matching the capital at the respond in the opposite side of the arcade; were they originally one and separated subsequently?

It seems probable that it was during this period of alteration that the east end of the chancel was squared off to produce the con-gle lancet window on the north side of the formation which exists to this day. The sin-chancel dates from about 1250 AD.

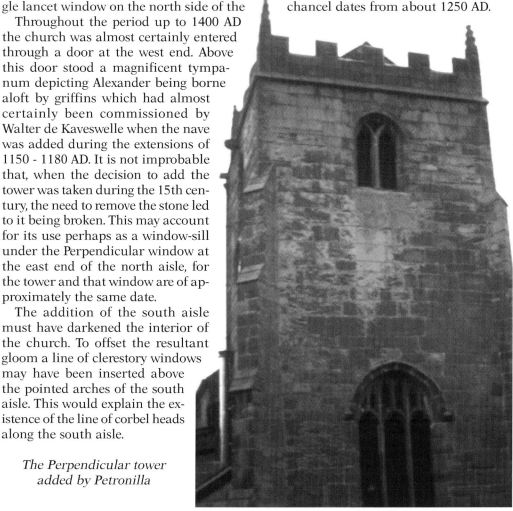

Throughout the period up to 1400 AD the church was almost certainly entered through a door at the west end. Above this door stood a magnificent tympa-num depicting Alexander being borne aloft by griffins which had almost certainly been commissioned by Walter de Kaveswelle when the nave was added during the extensions of 1150 - 1180 AD. It is not improbable that, when the decision to add the tower was taken during the 15th cen-tury, the need to remove the stone led to it being broken. This may account for its use perhaps as a window-sill under the Perpendicular window at the east end of the north aisle, for the tower and that window are of ap-proximately the same date.

The addition of the south aisle must have darkened the interior of the church. To offset the resultant gloom a line of clerestory windows may have been inserted above the pointed arches of the south aisle. This would explain the ex-istence of the line of corbel heads along the south aisle.

*The Perpendicular tower
added by Petronilla*

During the time that Petronilla was the lady of the manor (1410 -1450 approximately) the Perpendicular tower was added and the west window was installed. It seems possible that, the original entrance having been lost, a new doorway possibly on the north side was installed. This is pure speculation however because both doorways appear to owe much to the work instigated by Mathew Cradock in the 1630s. The south doorway seems to be of early English date but may be a copy. If it were of this age why was the tympanum not left in situ?

The woodwork of both doors appears to be typical of the mid 17th century although the hinges suggest that they might be older than that.

Only one of the traditional gargoyle style water spouts installed to drain the roof of the tower remains, it may be seen on the north side of the tower.

An extensive alteration of the fabric took place under Mathew Cradock during the third decade of the 17th century. The original pointed arches were pulled down and new round ones built using the original bases and capitals of the piers (was it at this stage that the Early English base and capital were carelessly separated?). Above the new arches were installed the clerestory windows which now light the interior of the church whilst the east window and both doorways were either added or significantly improved. In general though the ground plan remained unaltered.

In 1777 there was a gallery on the north side of the nave arcade which presumably accommodated the musicians. There was also a small gallery or pew on the south side of the nave which do not survive. These were removed at some point after 1879.

In 1879 a Faculty was granted giving permission for certain alterations to be made. The vestry was added, the chancel screen was removed and the arch rebuilt, the decaying porch over the south door was renewed, the musicians gallery and its staircase was removed from in front of the tower, a new floor was laid and the aisles and nave were re-roofed. At the same time the old family pews and box pews were removed and the present pattern of seating installed. This work included the provision of a chancel arch with double plain chamfers and stiff leaf capitals which is in the Decorated style and dates from about 1880.

Those features of the church which may be readily identified or to which reference has been made in the text have been summarised on the sketch plan included on the opposite page.

In his *'Buildings of England - Staffordshire'* Pevsner states *"By Kempe of 1880 the glass in the clerestory and more"*. The Kempe Society disputes this statement on the grounds that there is no record of the work in Kempe's papers. Kempe was working with the Wedgwoods during the time that the family lived in the castle so the possibility remains that Kempe produced the stained glass during that time.

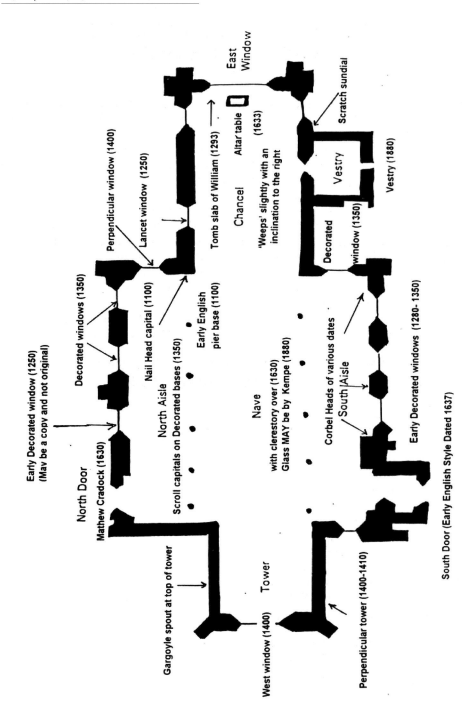

A plan of ages and stages in the evolution of St. Peter's Church, Caverswall

A BRIEF NOTE ON THE HISTORY OF
St. FILUMENA'S CHURCH

The following notes are taken largely from the Official Catholic Directory of the Province of Birmingham. The list of Catholic priests was provided by The Reverend Dr. John Sharp, Diocesan Archivist, to whom I am indebted.

Before 1811 the spiritual wants of the Catholics in Caverswall were supplied by itinerant missionaries. In 1811 the Benedictine Dames of Ghent settled at Caverswall Castle and opened a school. The nuns' chaplain attended to the district, and the public were admitted to the Convent chapel. On 26th. January 1813, a choir for the nuns was opened with a chapel adjoining for the congregation. After the appointment of a resident priest at Lane End (Longton) in 1820, the congregation in the vicinity of Caverswall was attached to the Lane End mission. In 1853 the Dames moved to Oulton, the small chapel which had been erected was demolished to prevent its use for secular purposes. Shortly after Caverswall Castle came into the hands of Sir Percival Radcliffe, Bart. The present Gothic church, school and presbytery were built by the Radcliffe family. the church was opened 28th. January 1864. It was designed by Sir Gilbert Blount.

It is believed that the church and its school were named after Filumena, one of the Radcliffe daughters, who in turn was named after a minor Catholic saint.

A LIST OF ROMAN CATHOLIC PRIESTS WHO HAVE MINISTERED TO THE CATHOLICS OF THE CAVERSWALL AREA

1811 - 1819	Robert Richmond
1819 - 1830	Richard W. Hubbard
1830 - 1853	William Jones
1853 - 1859	Vacant
1859 - 1866	(served from Longton)
1866 - 1867	Thomas Barry
1867 - 1868	Joseph J. Daly
1868 - 1873	John Stringfellow
1873 - 1882	Charles Meynell
1882 - 1884	Joseph Verres
1884 - 1889	John Rahilly Donworth
1889 - 1902	Edward H. Moore
1902 - 1903	Isidore Green O.S.B.
1903 - 1908	Nathaniel Higginson
1908 - 1917	George A. Brabazon
1917 - 1931	William ODoherty
1932 - 1934	John Joseph Hanrahan
1934 - 1940	Patrick William Noonan
1941 - 1942	Michael J. Fox
1942 - 1951	Hugh Francis Marron
1951 - 1958	Basil Frederick Wrighton
1958 - 1960	Thomas Rohan
1960 - 1967	Edward Cotter
1967 - 1990	Bryan Halton
1990 -	Seamus Edward McInerney

SOURCES AND BIBLIOGRAPHY

The materials used during the preparation of this text have been amassed over some 40 years. Originally collected for the purposes of personal enjoyment and interest I committed the unpardonable sin of failing to keep a careful note of all sources from which extracts were gleaned.

As far as possible I have attempted to record herein the sources of all material used in the text, however it is impossible to record accurately the gleanings of almost 40 years of avid reading and zealous but unscholarly note-taking.

To any who may feel offended by that casual approach and its inevitable consequence I offer a humble apology.

Particular mention must be made of the two booklets of the late J. D. Johnstone:

> *Werrington, Some notes on its history, 1946*
> *and*
> *St. Peter's Church, Caverswall, Some notes on its history, 1948.*

These texts were my first acquaintance with the history of the area and it is a tribute to the thoroughness and scholarship of their author that time has not significantly affected the content of those works.

My thanks must also go to Mr. Brian Milner of the Castle for allowing me to have sight of an unpublished text written by a member of the Order which until recently occupied the Castle, it proved a most interesting document albeit slightly unbalanced in emphasis and interpretation .

My thanks to the two Headteachers, Mr. David Beardmore and Mr. Michael Wheatley for granting me access to the school log books and other material.

Among the original documents cited at length are the following items which were originally issued to St. Peter's School, Caverswall, in the mid 1960's, by the County Record Office as part of its early efforts to develop an interest in the study of historical evidence.

For the permission to quote from these and the other documents held in the County Record Office I am most grateful.

Enclosure Acts and Awards which refer to Caverswall.
Plan of the Manor of Caverswall dated 1840.
Part of a letter dated 3rd December 1745 and signed J. Comyn.
Public Health Act (11 & 12 Vict. c 63).
The Bishop of Lichfield's enquiry into the State of his diocese.
A copy of his questionnaire and the replies from Caverswall and Dilhorne.
The Muster Roll for 1539.
White's Director of 1851 .
The Subsidy Roll for 1327.
The Hearth Tax Return of 1666.
The Church Terrier for 1766.

BIBLIOGRAPHY

Anglo-Saxon Chronicle, The, Everyman Edition, 1955.

Annals of the English Benedictines of Ghent, (Unpublished).

Archdeaconry of Stoke-on-Trent, The, Hutchinson.

Black Death, The, Ziegler, Pelican, 1975.

Borough of Stoke-on-Trent, The, Ward, S. R. Publishers, 1843 - 1969.

Buchanan, Robert Jay 1903

Calendar of Patent Rolls, The, William Salt Library.

Calendar of County Customs, A. Whitlock, Batsford, 1978.

Carver M O H North Staffs Journal of Field Studies 20 (1980) 1-8

Compleat Gentleman, The, Gailhard.

Complete Peerage, The, Hylton George.

Cradock Family, The, (Author Unknown), William Salt Library.

Court of Common Pleas, The, Hastings.

Definitive Edition of Rudyard Kipling's Verse, Hodder and Stoughton, 1973.

Diary of Samuel Pepys, The, Everyman, 1958.

Domesday Book and Beyond, Fontana, Maitland, 1969.

Domesday Geography of Midland England, The, Cambridge, Darby and Terrett, 1971.

English Castle, The, Braun, Batsford, 1936.

English Farming, Past and Present, Ernle, Heinemann, 1968.

English, Wayfaring Life in the Middle Ages, Jusserand.

Farming Techniques from Prehistoric to Modern Times, Fussell, Pergamon, 1966.

Food and Feast in Tudor England, Sim Sutton, 1997

Historical Geography of England Before 1800, Darby, Cambridge, 1963.

History of Cheadle. A, Plant, 1881.

History of Staffordshire, A, Greenslade and Stuart, Darwen Finlayson, 1965.

History of Staffordshire, A, Nightingale, 1723.

Itinerary, Travels In Tudor England John Leland Sutton 1993

Jolliffes of Staffordshire, The, Hylton George.

Life on the English Manor, Bennett, Cambridge, 1960.

Life in Shakespeare's England, Wilson, Pelican, 1954.

Local History in England, Hoskins, Longman, 1968.

London Life of Yesterday, A, Compton-Rickett.

Man at Play, Armitage, Warne, 1977.

Mediaeval Village, The, G. G. Coulton.

Medieval Woman, Baer O"Hara, 1986

Memorials of Old Staffordshire, Beresford.

Memorials of Old Staffordshire, Wedgwood.

Natural History of Staffordshire, The, Plot, Oxford, 1686.

North Staffs: Field Club Transactions, Blizzard, 1937/8.

Notes on Staffordshire Place-names, Duignan.

Oxford Dictionary of English Place-names, The Concise, Ekwall, Oxford,1960.

Old Cookery Books and Ancient Cuisine, W. Carew Hoglitt.

Paston Letters, The, Everyman.

Personality of Britain, The, Fox, National Museum of Wales.

Property Transactions, William Salt Library.

Property Inquisition of William Vane, William Salt Library.

Rise and Fall of Merrie England , The, Hutton, Oxford 1984

Romance of Staffordshire Wedgwood.

Staffs: Historical Collections A vast, rich and useful selection of transcripts, William Salt Library.

Selected Poems of John Clare, Reeves (Ed.), Heinemann, 1969.

Shepherd's Calendar, The, Clare, Oxford, 1973.

Sheriff, The, Gladwin, MacCartney, 1984

Stowe's Chronicle, 1615.

Survey of Staffordshire, Sampson Erdeswick.

The Wedgwood Circle 1730-1897,Barbara and Hensleigh Wedgwood , Studio Vista 1980

Topographical History of Staffordshire, A, William Pitt.

Topographical, Ecclesiastical and Natural History of Staffordshire, A, Thomas Cox.

Time, Taste and Furniture, Gloag, 1925.

Tudor Housewife The, Sim Sutton, 1996

Victoria History of the County of Staffordshire, Oxford.

Villeinage in England, Vinogradoff.

Wealth of England 1496 - 1760, The, Clarke, Oxford, 1954.

Witches and Neighbours, Briggs, Harper Collins 1996

In conclusion reference must be made to the benefits derived from a study of:

(a) The Parish Registers of St. Peter's Church, Caverswall.

(b) The wall monuments in St. Peter's Church.

(c) The features of the parish landscape.

(d) The school log books of both village schools

REFERENCES AND ACKNOWLEDGEMENTS

My thanks go to the publishers of the text listed below and the County Archivist's Office for permission to reproduce the items listed hereunder.

I. Quoted in 'An Historical Geography of England Before 1800', Edited H . C. Darby, C.U.P. 1963.

2. The Anglo-Saxon Chronicle, Everyman, Volume 624.

3. Victoria County History, Volume IV.

4. Historical Collections, Volume 11, The Staffs. Chartulary Series 11, No. XV.

5. Staffordshire Historical Collections, Volume Xll, The Chartulary of St. Thomas.

6. Staffordshire Historical Collections, French Roll, 21 E 111, 1347.

7. A transcription appears in Staffordshire Historical Collections.

8. The Canterbury Tales, Chaucer, Penguin Classics, 1956.

9. The Black Death, Ziegler, Pelican, 1969.

10. The Paston Letters, Edited, Warrington, Everyman's Library, 1956.

11. Staffordshire Historical Collections, Volume XV, Extracts from the Plea Rolls Assize Roll, I - 33 H IV.

12. Staffordshire Historical Collections, Volume XVII, De Banco, Easter 4 H Vl.

13. Staffordshire Historical Collections, Volume Vll, Richard 11 to Henry Vll, Bundle 73.

14. Staffordshire Historical Collections, Volume Vl, New Series, De Banco, Mich: (20 E IV).

15. Staffordshire Historical Collections, Volume X, New Series, Part I (Volume Vl fol: 187/91).

16. Staffordshire Historical Collections, Volume X, New Series, The Court of Star Chamber .

17. Staffordshire Historical Collections, Muster Roll Staffordshire, AD 1539.

18. Trans. North Staffs. Field Club, Volume LXXII, 1937/8, Caverswall Castle, Mrs. M. E. Blizzard.

19. An Historical Geography of England Before 1800, Edited Darby, Chapter IX, Leland's England, E. G. R. Taylor.

20. Life in Shakespeare's England, John Dover Wilson, Pelican, 1954.

21. Staffordshire Historical Collections, Fines of Mixed Countries, 33 H Vial.

22. Staffordshire Historical Collections, Final Concords Octave of St. Hillary 7 Eliz:

23. Staffordshire Historical Collections.

24. Staffordshire Historical Collections, Parliamentary History, Volume 11.

25. Magna Britannia et Hibernia, box 5, 1728.

26. Staffordshire Historical Collections, Volume 1, 4th Series, The Order Book.

27. Staffordshire Historical Collections, Volume 11, 4th Series, The Gentry of Staffordshire .

28. The Jolliffes of Staffordshire and their Descendants, Hylton George H. Jolliffe, 1892.

29. Legacie Hartlib, 1651, Quoted in English Farming Past and Present, Lord Ernle, 1961.

30. The Hearth Tax Return for 1666, Stafford

31. The Natural History of Staffordshire, Plot, 1686.

32. Old Cookery Books and Ancient Cuisine, W. Carew Hoglitt.

33.   Peerage Memoranda, Earl of Oxford.

34.   Memoirs of a Lady of Quality.

35.   Patrick Guthrie to James Gibbs, 10th August 1736, Pastlands Ms, Volume VI, Historical Ms. Com.

36.   The Diary of the Earl of Egmont.

37.   Property Transactions, William Salt Library, Stafford.

38.   Extract from a letter held in the County Record Office.

39.   Copies of letters held in the County Record Office.

40.   A Topographical History of Staffordshire, William Pitt, 1817.

41.   Property Inquisition of William Vane, Document held in the William Salt Library, Stafford .

42.   Property Transactions, William Salt Library, Stafford.

43.   White's Directory for 1851, County Record Office, Stafford.

44.   Potbank, Mervyn Jones, Secker and Warburg, 1961.

45.   Robert Buchanan, Harriet Jay, 1903

The superscriptions at the head of each section are based on or drawn from the historical poems of Rudyard Kipling (op cit).

My thanks go also to those people of the parish who have assisted me in so many ways with the task of preparing this account. To those older citizens who allowed me to interview them and to all who have loaned pictures and material for inclusion and are too numerous to mention individually, I record my thanks.